GW00393962

Nice Girls DO Travel

Kathy Cuddihy

Nice Girls DO Travel

Cover Design: Mike Rahr

For Sean

CHAPTER 1

Sometimes the place you are used to
is not the place you belong.
From the film The Queen of Katwe

All those unending questions made me crazy! *What are you going to be? Have you decided what you'll do with your life? Have you chosen a university?* It was bad enough when I was in the third year of high school; it became intense by the fourth and final year when soon-to-be graduates were expected to have mapped out their future. In the 1960s, with no internet search engines to assist, this wasn't an easy task for those of us who lacked a vocation.

When pushed to consider traditional studies, I leaned towards law or psychiatry but my heart longed to do something totally untraditional: to travel and have adventures. This passion, nurtured since earliest childhood, couldn't be easily abandoned or put on hold. Now that I was on the cusp of independence, I yearned to go somewhere exciting, unknown. Somewhere far away. After all, none of the gripping stories I read took place in Montreal, where I lived. They happened in the jungles of Asia, on the rivers of Africa, across the deserts of Arabia. While classmates decided career paths, I planned odysseys, sometimes with the help of a patient Filipina travel agent who showed me interesting routes to places I never had heard of but knew I had to visit.

As the closing date for university applications approached, tension grew. I still hadn't made a commitment. As much as I loved learning, I remained indecisive about any alternatives to my romantic notions of setting off to explore the world.

Into the breach of this ambivalence stepped my paternal grandmother, the indomitable Grannie Daley. Everything Grannie did was finely calibrated to fall well within conservative parameters. Her attachment to propriety conflicted with my inclination to follow dreams rather than customs.

"You need to get on track: go to university and make a good marriage," she insisted

"Travel will educate me, give me new experiences," I argued.

"The experiences are precisely what I'm worried about," Grannie said with a sniff. "Nice girls don't travel. At least, not by themselves they don't."

Grannie's concern had merit. Globetrotting wasn't a common or inexpensive undertaking from Canada in the 1960s. The gap year hadn't become the norm and there wasn't yet a vigorous demand for intercontinental flights. It was rare for young women to go abroad alone on a one-way ticket when they didn't know anyone at the other end. Despite my best efforts to nudge her towards my point of view, Grannie remained rigid in her disapproval of my desire. Then she surprised me.

"In the spirit of compromise, I'm willing to help you travel and get a proper education at the same time."

This would be perfect. I already had hatched a plan for when I left high school: summer school in Florence, Italy and then university in France. Would Grannie buy into my nascent scheme? I stopped fidgeting and gave her my full attention.

"I'll pay for you to go to any Ivy League university."

"What's the difference between going to school in the States and studying abroad?" I asked, disappointed with the geographic limitation of the offer.

"In the States you'll be close to home. And," she paused for emphasis, "you won't be under the influence of a bunch of foreigners."

Aha. The crux of the matter. And the death knell for any hope of reaching a middle ground. 'A bunch of foreigners' was exactly the type of people I wanted to encounter.

I took a moment to mull over the offer. There was no denying its generosity and the opportunity it presented. But I sought different opportunities. I yearned for the challenge of adapting to unfamiliar cultures, learning languages, seeing exotic sights. Acceptance of

Grannie's offer, I felt, would be a betrayal of these ambitions.

"I'm going to travel," I stated with renewed resolve, "and it won't be close to home. I'm going to travel around the world. Before I'm twenty-one," I added for good measure.

Suddenly this persistent longing had form and had become audible. My brain froze with the magnitude of my words. How could I have allowed myself to say such a thing? I hadn't actually made a promise, so there would be no disgrace in climbing down from this rash statement. I wavered, tempted to return to the safer ground of manageable objectives. No, Grannie would see my retreat as a victory.

"You're setting yourself up for disappointment." She shook an arthritically-deformed finger at me. "Is that what you want, to be a failure? To live a life of regret?"

Her words gave me pause. Failure was a distinct possibility. A probability, in fact. With no source of income and no marketable skills, how would I be able to circumnavigate the globe within the next four years? But wouldn't it also be a kind of failure not to try?

"I'm sorry, Grannie, but I want to travel. I need to travel. A life of regret would be to follow someone else's dream instead of my own."

Grannie pursed her lips and brushed imaginary crumbs off her silk skirt.

"Well, Missy, I can see there's nothing more to be said on the matter. I've done my best. You're on your own."

She gave a final disapproving glare and left the room.

I was alone with the impact of my decision. Grannie had become an unintended catalyst. If she hadn't pushed me to make such an impulsive declaration, no doubt I would have followed tradition and gone to university. Now fate had set me on a different path, one I felt honour-bound to try to see through.

Grannie disappeared back to her home in Toronto. My parents didn't discuss her attempt to get me 'on track'. Apart from pointing out the advantages of a university education, they neither overtly deterred nor supported my travel desires. Why, I wondered, didn't they encourage me to do what I loved?

Evidently I would have to figure out a way forward on my own. This wouldn't be the first time. At the age of thirteen, I wangled an invitation from a former school friend who lived in Ottawa. After diligently saving every penny from weekly allowances, birthday money and anything extra I could earn, I finally had enough to pay for the trip. As soon as the summer holidays started, I was off. The train whistle shrieked its announcement of departure. Eagerly, I waved goodbye to my parents and settled into the two-hour journey feeling wonderfully grown up.

A week later, I *flew* home. This was my first commercial flight and the whole point of the exercise. At last I was on an airplane. Goodness knows I had spent enough time watching them pass overhead, wishing I could be winging my way to far-flung lands and unimaginable exploits. The forty-five minute Ottawa-Montreal flight was too short and too local to satisfy my wanderlust but it was a good first step.

The success of this trip made me realise that resolve and careful budgeting could transform dreams into reality.

If I wanted to pursue my goal sooner rather than later, I needed a travel-related job that offered training. Then it came to me: I could work for an airline! I shared the idea with my mother.

"Stewardesses are nothing more than glorified waitresses," she stated categorically.

Nevertheless, I went for an interview at Air Canada. They politely rejected me on the basis that I was too short. I suspected this was tactful corporate-speak for 'you're not glamorous', a prerequisite in those early days of commercial flights.

In the end, my father determined my immediate future.

"Whatever you choose to do," he announced after yet another inconclusive career discussion, "your plans have to include nursing or secretarial training. With either of those professions you'll always be able to get a job."

Neither alternative appealed to me. Nursing required an aptitude for science, a willingness to work with sick people and at least two years of study. I opted for the one-year secretarial route.

In the meantime, I continued to dream and to plan. I had no

fixed itinerary and therefore no hint of how much an excursion over a prolonged period would cost. Clearly it would be expensive. It didn't occur to me to ask my parents to help out financially, nor did they offer. Perhaps they hoped that the absence of a handout would diminish my determination to pursue this unorthodox path. I suspect, however, they had the wisdom and courage to let me grow. They had brought me up to be self-sufficient and to accept responsibility for my decisions. If I achieved my pledged goal, the sense of accomplishment would be greater for having done it on my own.

CHAPTER 2

*There are moments which mark your life. Moments when
you realise that nothing will ever be the same and time is
divided into two parts: before this and after this.*
Anonymous

Notre Dame Secretarial School, or The Motherhouse as it was commonly called, was Montreal's best business school. Anyone who made it through the tough course run by military-minded nuns came out on the other side with top skills. Studies included the usual shorthand and typing as well as economics, accounting, business law and, for a bit of culture, French literature—in French. It was a stressful, demanding curriculum that I regularly considered abandoning during the first couple of months. The only thing that kept me going was the fact that this was a vital first step toward my ultimate goal.

After getting past my initial resistance, I adapted to the rigorous routine and began to enjoy Motherhouse life. The nuns, it turned out, weren't as austere as they pretended to be. As we got to know each other, they came to tolerate my pranks and occasional defiance with good grace. The nine-month gestation period passed quickly.

In May, job offers were doled out to the freshly-minted secretaries. The nuns felt I would be a suitable candidate for a position at McGill University's Faculty of Law. McGill had an international reputation for excellence, especially in the field of medicine. I now learned that the law faculty, officially created in 1848, was the oldest in Canada.

On the appointed day, at the appointed hour, I made my way up Peel Street. The given address brought me to a limestone mansion complete with two turrets and a tower. The structure looked more like a small French château than a law faculty. Not that I knew what a law faculty was supposed to look like.

Jeanne Hale, the no-nonsense administrator greeted me with a crisp "good morning" when I presented myself. She looked me over as though she were buying a new car and then brusquely laid out the terms of employment. Finally she arrived at what was, for me, the most important part of the conversation: salary.

"We're offering two hundred and seventy dollars a month to start," Jeanne said.

"That's lower than what I had in mind. I can't work for less than three hundred dollars."

Jeanne gave me an incredulous stare but I didn't know if it was because of what I said or that I had dared to say anything at all.

"I'm sorry, that's just not possible. We have established guidelines and we don't make exceptions," Jeanne announced with finality.

Jeanne offered the going rate for Motherhouse-trained novice secretaries in 1968 but I had calculated how much I needed to earn in order to save enough to travel abroad within the next two years. 'Established guidelines' were an unexpected complication. As I considered thanking Jeanne for her time and leaving, her next sentence caught my attention.

"You'll be meeting with Professor HR Hahlo who is visiting us for a year from South Africa. He's the Dean of the Faculty of Law at Witwatersrand University in Johannesburg," Jeanne explained. "Professor Hahlo is well respected as a foremost authority in the field of family law." She fixed her gaze on me and added, "Be sure you make a good impression."

Africa! Suddenly this job had something going for it. A potentially interesting boss was a good selling point.

Graduating at the top of my class gave me confidence about my secretarial abilities but I walked into Professor Hahlo's office with a bad case of nerves. This was my first job interview. All the drills at school aimed for the ideal combination of speed and accuracy but what if one came at the expense of the other? I couldn't recall receiving any instructions on how to handle interview stagefright. Was it permitted to erase typing mistakes? Was it even permitted to make mistakes? The nuns expected their students to strive for perfection but perfection didn't always come to the fore when needed.

The professor's dumpy, balding figure stood to greet me. He was only about five inches taller than my five feet three inches. I reminded myself that traits such as personality and intelligence weren't measured with a ruler.

Professor Hahlo observed me through heavily hooded eyes as Jeanne made introductions. He shook my hand and then invited me to sit down.

"I will dictate a letter to you and you will type it. Is this all right?" he asked.

His heavy German accent took me by surprise. My uncertainty about the ground rules was bad enough without coping with comprehension difficulties. I could do only my best. I gave Professor Hahlo a nod.

I made several typing errors but didn't fix them, reasoning that a correct but smudged page would be less acceptable than a clean but incorrect page. Mistake. *Big* mistake.

Professor Hahlo kindly made the excuse that perhaps his accent had confused me. Jeanne Hale was less forgiving. She looked at the page, frowned and said, "Thank you. That will be all." She uttered the words with a finality that left me in no doubt about my failure.

It therefore astonished me when Jeanne called the next day.

"You fell short of the required standards," Jeanne announced without preamble. "Despite this glaring reality, you've got the job. We strongly advised Professor Hahlo to interview other candidates but he wants to hire you. We have no choice but to accede to his wishes." After a pregnant pause, she added, "He also insists that we pay you the salary you request. This is entirely irregular." Jeanne exhaled audibly. "You'll have a one-month probationary period."

I felt dizzy with disbelief—and relief. In light of the disappointing interview performance, my demand for a higher salary had made me look foolish. Yet my probably unreasonable demand had been met.

"Thank you. I won't let you down."

"I hope you won't," Jean said primly. "We'd like you to start tomorrow, if that's agreeable. At nine o'clock. Sharp. I expect your punctuality to be better than your typing."

"I'll be there."

It was a precarious start but it was a start.

**

What made Professor Hahlo decide to hire me? And at a salary that exceeded 'established guidelines'? I'm sure the Faculty of Law administrators asked the same questions but I soon exceeded 'required standards'. Once I had got past the stress of the interview test, my skills reemerged.

Much of my work involved typing Professor Hahlo's manuscripts. We discovered I had a knack for editing. Because of an affinity with grammar and vocabulary and a good memory for what I'd read on previous pages, I could draw Professor Hahlo's attention to repetitious words and phrases, complicated explanations and the rare error or omission. I had earned his respect.

"You're coping well, Kathy. Congratulations." Jeanne said. The first month had passed successfully; I was now a permanent member of staff. "We'd like you also to work for a young assistant professor, if you don't mind. His name is Stephen Scott. He probably won't have a lot for you to do."

"That's fine," I agreed, "but Professor Hahlo will still be my main boss, right?" I felt a loyalty to this man who had showed such blind faith in me.

"Of course," Jeanne assured me. "He'll have first call on your time."

The contrast between the two men could not have been greater. My new boss was an altogether more casual individual. He introduced himself with an amiable, "Hi. Just call me Stephen," accompanied by a happy grin and a firm handshake.

An exaggerated clearing of her throat indicated that Jeanne didn't approve of such informality.

Stephen had floppy black hair and a maladroit manner but his spontaneity gave him a boyish charm. I liked him immediately. He quickly revealed an impudent nature that appealed to my own leanings in that direction.

Taking dictation from Stephen was never boring. He used language creatively and often mischievously, such as when he finished a letter to an engineer with the sentence, *May you have many successful erections.*

First thing one morning, Jeanne called me into her office. Her face wasn't in stern mode, so I assumed she wasn't going to issue a reprimand. We had developed a comfortable relationship but she sometimes had to caution me to curb my enthusiasm for fun.

"Stephen needs someone to type his doctoral thesis," she announced, coming directly to the point. "He's offering to pay you extra for this work, even if you do it during office hours." Jeanne gave a sigh of resignation. By now she had accepted that rule-breaking came as part and parcel of having me around. "Professor Hahlo has no objection if you'd like to take on the project. Needless to say, Stephen's thesis cannot interfere with your regular responsibilities."

"How much is he paying?" I asked immediately.

Jeanne put on her disapproving face. "A dollar per page."

I gasped. *Please, God, let him have a very long thesis.*

Jeanne absently shuffled a few papers on her desk before expanding on her response. "The going rate for this type of thing is ten to fifteen cents a page. In exceptional cases, twenty-five cents." She then said abruptly, "You're extremely lucky that Stephen has more dollars than sense."

Sanctioned moonlighting at an indulgent rate? How could I refuse? Stephen's generous contribution would ensure that my travel plans kept on target—and might even allow for an early departure.

***

Douglas Duncan was the Managing Director of Professor Hahlo's Cape Town publisher Juta and Company. Correspondence between the two was frequent. Since the letters always began with the words 'Dear Douglas', I came to call him Dear Douglas; eventually even Professor Hahlo used the reference, not just with me but with Dear Douglas himself.

I developed a fondness for this distant stranger. Through his eloquent letters he revealed himself to be an attentive and gracious gentleman. Dear Douglas eventually introduced himself into my life by adding greetings and personal notes. I felt I had acquired a pen pal. He soon would become much more.

Less than a year after starting to work for Professor Hahlo, he called me into his office. I had a sharpened pencil and steno pad at the ready. Today, though, I wouldn't be taking dictation.

"As you know, at the end of the academic year in May I will return to Johannesburg," Professor Hahlo said.

When I had been given this information at the time of my hiring, it meant nothing to me because Professor Hahlo meant nothing. In the meantime, though, he had become more than a boss. We were an unlikely pairing—he was like an old tortoise and I was more like a young hare—but we had formed a bond. Now that bond would be severed. I was so dismayed about losing contact with Professor Hahlo that I temporarily tuned out of the conversation.

"Kathy? Did you hear what I said?"

"Sorry. I missed that. Can you please repeat it?" I mumbled.

"How would you like to go to South Africa?" he asked solemnly.

My head snapped up as my brain tried to process the words. Uncharacteristically, I was speechless.

"You wouldn't be able to work for me because I already have a secretary at the university. Dear Douglas can offer you a job in Johannesburg with a respected medical doctor who is also a well-known writer, editor and publisher. I've discussed the situation with my wife and you could live with us until you get settled. What do you think?"

The astonishing proposal made me barely capable of thought. What an opportunity. What a terrifying opportunity. Africa was still referred to as The Dark Continent, a far-away place of ominous mystery. In my wildest dreams I had never considered starting my great adventure with such a giant leap into the unknown.

Professor Hahlo chuckled as he observed my reaction and then gave another prompt.

"All the pieces are in place. You just need to get there."

"I'm overwhelmed," I said. "This is so unexpected ... and scary."

"Do you ever wonder why I hired you?" Professor Hahlo asked as he observed me from across his paper-piled desk. "It was partly because I could see intelligence in your eyes but mostly because you had spirit. It is not such a common quality, you know. I was curious to see what kind of person you were. You haven't disappointed me." He smiled. "I know my offer is sudden and perhaps a little frightening but once you get used to the idea, I suspect you will embrace it."

How long had Professor Hahlo been planning this with Dear Douglas? What even made him come up with the idea in the first place? Asking your secretary to join you halfway around the world sounded unconventional, even by my liberal yardstick.

"I don't know anything about South Africa except that it's at the other end of the world," I admitted. "How different is it from here? Do they celebrate Christian customs like Easter?"

Professor Hahlo gave a hearty laugh. "It might be at the other end of the world but it is still part of the world! They celebrate Easter and Christmas and birthdays. One thing you will learn if you travel is that, despite their differences, people everywhere have a lot in common. I think you will love the country and the people. And the winters are much warmer than in Canada."

I could feel a pounding in my chest. Did I have the courage to put my conviction to travel the world into practice? I swallowed, trying to get rid of the lump of fear that had lodged in my throat. Then, without waiting for my head to outvote my heart, I made a decision.

"I'd love to go, Professor Hahlo. At least, the deeply buried brave part of me would love to go. Once it's had a chance to surface, I'm sure I'll be more excited. Thank you so much." I thought about the glaring practicalities for a moment. "I need to find out how much the trip will cost but thanks to Stephen I've been able to save faster than expected. I probably can afford to leave within a couple of months of your own departure."

"Very good. I'll tell Dear Douglas. I know he'll be pleased to meet you."

"I'm looking forward to meeting him, too."

I hoped the flesh-and-blood man would match up to the image he had created through his correspondence.

"If you never have been on a ship, sailing from England to Cape Town would be a good introduction. It's a lovely voyage. The journey would give you a chance to meet South Africans and learn more about the country."

This suggestion sounded utterly romantic. With flying starting to become popular, long sea voyages were being relegated to the pages of the past. When the idea took hold, I knew this would be a perfect beginning to the many exciting experiences I fantasised awaited me. I returned to my desk and immediately phoned my long-suffering travel agent friend, happy to be able to offer her some concrete business.

I decided it would be best to wait until dinner to reveal to my family this unanticipated turn of events. Instinct told me they might not share my enthusiasm, so face-to-face would be the preferred approach. Unlike Grannie Daley, my parents never overtly had discouraged my travel zeal. They knew from experience that to tell me I couldn't do something only made me more obstinate. That didn't mean they applauded my ambition.

My breathless announcement mid-meal was met with stunned silence. Liz, my fifteen-year-old sister, stopped chewing, parking her food into a cheek. Her large green eyes stared unbelievingly at me and then shifted nervously to my mother and then to my father.

"South Africa has a harsh political environment for anyone who isn't white," my mother said, apropos of nothing.

Mom was known for her swathes of knowledge, some trivial some not, on topics ranging from the arcane to the inane. This unelaborated, incongruous sentence was the equivalent of her being thunderstruck.

"That's an awfully long way to go on a one-way ticket. What if something goes wrong?" my father quizzed. "And how do we know this Professor Hahlo doesn't have ulterior motives?" he asked with the suspicious mind of a concerned parent.

My hackles raised at such a suggestion. I argued in Professor Hahlo's defence but my father held fast to his misgivings.

"I'd like to meet this man and make my own judgments," he insisted. "Give me his phone number. I'll invite him to lunch at the club."

My cheeks burned with embarrassment as I imagined the encounter. Would Professor Hahlo withdraw his invitation if my sometimes irreverent father became offensive in his vetting process? The thought was unbearable but I knew I wouldn't be going anywhere until Dad got his way.

Neither my father nor Professor Hahlo discussed the lunch with me but my father must have been convinced of Professor Hahlo's honourable intentions and Professor Hahlo evidently tolerated the interrogation. The trip was on.

CHAPTER 3

If you talk about it, it's a dream, if you envision it,
it's possible, if you schedule it, it's real.
Tony Robbins

After years of talking about travelling, my announcement of an actual departure date to a destination far off the beaten track received shocked reactions. No one was more surprised than Marilyn Hawkins, my best friend. We had been inseparable for the nine years we had known each other. I called her right after the news-breaking dinner with my family.

"You're kidding, right?" she said after a brief silence. "Please tell me you're kidding!"

"You know I've been saving to travel," I said weakly. I could feel Marilyn's unhappiness through the phone lines.

"Saving is one thing. Suddenly taking off to deepest, darkest Africa is quite another. Without a return ticket," she sputtered. "By yourself!"

Marilyn's reference to deepest, darkest Africa came from probably inaccurate Hollywood movies and probably exaggerated adventure novels. She pleaded with me to abandon this seemingly reckless course of action. I wasn't sure if she was concerned about the inevitable pause in our close friendship or about some unknown danger she feared might be lying in wait for me.

"I know it sounds crazy, Mar, even to me, but it's something I've got to do. Otherwise I'll always regret turning my back on such a rare opportunity. Not knowing whether or not I could have done it would eat away at me. Better to have tried and failed than never to have tried at all," I said, misquoting Tennyson.

"I understand you need to do the follow-the-dream thing but why can't you dream about places closer to home? Why does it have to be so remote, so ... foreign? Are we even going to be able to communicate with each other?"

"Of course we will," I said with feigned conviction. "I'll write every week."

But would the letters be delivered? How reliable was the postal service in 'deepest, darkest Africa'?

"It's all too uncertain, too mysterious. I'm afraid for you."

"It'll be fine. Really," I assured her. "As soon as I've got this out of my system, I'll come home and we can pick up where we left off."

"Promise?"

"Promise."

I didn't want to contemplate any other option.

The attitudes of friends and their parents indicated that they presumed I would come to my senses before it was too late. My own family probably held out this hope, although no one said anything to deter me. Except, of course, Grannie Daley. She didn't miss an opportunity to make known her disapproval of my 'perverse plan'. Her intolerance, inflexibility and lack of faith in me only made me more resolute.

My widowed maternal grandmother Grannie Scott lived with us and was my only unreserved source of support.

"Part of me worries about the potential dangers of this adventure of yours but another part knows this will be one of the best times of your life, not to mention a comprehensive street education. You've always been a plucky lass; that will serve you well." Her Scottish brogue sounded particularly comforting with these words.

"Not a day goes by when I don't think about staying home, Grannie," I confessed. No one else would hear such an admission from me.

"It's leaving that's the hard part, dear. Once you're on your way, you'll come into your own. I've always felt you were a caged bird. Now you'll have a chance to fly."

Grannie went over to her bookshelf and removed a favourite photo album. She flipped the worn pages to a younger version of my grandfather and her with a small child standing in front of a towering, white ocean liner. I could tell by the hint of a smile that she reminisced about her own adventure long ago.

"Your grandfather and I were afraid when we left Scotland to come here. We were going to a distant land with no job, home or family. Your mother was only three years old. Leaving the familiarity and security of our country and kin was probably the most difficult thing we ever did. That experience taught us that anticipation of the leap is more daunting than the leap itself. You overcome your fear by knowing the unknown."

I wanted to believe Grannie because I loved her dearly. I *needed* to believe her so doubts wouldn't overwhelm determination.

The final weeks passed in a blaze of preparations. This included getting numerous vaccinations for the trip. I now was protected against diseases I never had heard of and certainly wouldn't want to contract. I checked and rechecked the validity of my passport, reconfirmed that no visas were required and made sure—yet again—all the pre-board paperwork for the voyage was in order. Nervous energy made me pack and unpack my new, orange Samsonite suitcase on a regular basis. I didn't want to forget an item that might be unobtainable at the other end of the world.

Most important of all, I finalised my itinerary. Since I was paying for a trans-Atlantic flight, I wanted to get my money's worth and see as much a possible. It cost little to add a couple of layovers en route. Ireland would be my first stop. This was the land of Grandpa Daley's birth and the setting for numerous tales told during my childhood. A week later I would fly to Glasgow to visit Scottish relatives. The final flight would be to London. From there I would go to the port of Southampton to board the SA *Vaal* to Cape Town.

The SA *Vaal*, my travel agent told me, was a one-class passenger mailboat. Mailboat, a new word in my vocabulary, seemed self-explanatory: I imagined that South Africa was so far away and hard to reach that the post office waited until they had sufficient bags of letters and parcels to fill a ship's hold.

At last—or too soon, depending on the swing of my mixed

emotions—the day of my departure arrived. When it was time to go, I gave Grannie Scott's frail frame a crushing hug and made her promise to write often. My sister Liz already looked lost.

"I can't believe you're really leaving," she said. It was almost an accusation.

"It's not forever," was the only solace I could offer.

Dad put my suitcase and guitar in the trunk of the car while Mom quietly took her place in the front seat. I suspected her silence was cautionary: if she spoke, she might try to persuade me to stay home. She loved me enough to let me go.

We drove a few yards down the road to Marilyn's house for a final farewell. This was the hardest part of leaving. What would I do without this cherished companion with whom I exchanged confidences every day? I saw the tear build-up in Marilyn's eyes as we released each other from a fierce hold. I quickly turned to her mother before I lost control. Mrs Hawkins wrapped me in her arms. I stored her strength and love for the journey ahead. Then I felt my father's hand on my shoulder.

"We need to get going if you don't want to miss your plane," he said quietly.

Mrs Hawkins let me go, simply saying, "Look after yourself, sweetie."

I forced myself to put one foot in front of the other and got into the back seat of the car. Never in my life had I felt more afraid. I desperately wanted to say, "Let's go home," but pride eclipsed fear. The imagined shame of *not* carrying through my commitment was worse than all the uncertainty that lay ahead.

At the airport, my parents stood to the side as I checked in for the flight and received a boarding pass. This was my last opportunity to change my mind. I remained mute.

In an unusually sentimental gesture, my father pinned a small, enamel Canadian flag on my jacket.

"This is so you don't forget where you're from," he said. "And where we'd like you to return. We'll be waiting for you whenever you're ready to come home."

Then there was nothing for them to do but to say their goodbyes and leave me alone to step into an unfamiliar world. A quotation by André Gide popped into my head: *Man cannot discover new oceans unless he has the courage to lose sight of the shore.* It was time to leave the shore.

***

I retreated to the ladies' washroom until boarding time, just in case my inclination to throw up became a physical reality. I'm not sure how long I perched on the toilet, elbows on knees, head in hands, indulging in frightened self-pity. Then an announcement on the public address system caught my attention: final boarding for the flight to Shannon! How had I missed the previous calls? I ran through the airport and down a passage that led to the gate.

"I'm sorry," the attendant said, "you're too late. The flight is closed."

I stared at her in astonishment. *This can't be happening.* I fought the panic that threatened to take hold. For a guilty moment I wondered if I accidentally had willed a stay-home excuse to materialise. I summoned all my willpower to reverse the situation. *Give me a break*, I prayed.

"She has a boarding pass." A second attendant had noticed the strip of card clutched in my sweaty palm.

"All right, go through. You'll have to hurry. They've already removed the back boarding ramp."

I sprinted across the tarmac and up the front steps leading into the shiny red and white Air Canada plane. A tall, glamorous stewardess welcomed me on board as I gasped my way into the cabin.

"Follow me, please," she said after checking my seat number.

We walked through the luxury of first class into the bowels of economy.

"Hmm," she muttered, seeing my seat was occupied. The passenger's boarding pass was in order. "We have a slight problem."

We returned to the front of the plane where another late-comer waited at the entrance. The head steward was in the process of asking a stand-by passenger in first class to disembark.

"We have only one seat available. One of you will have to take another flight," he said.

Neither of us volunteered. At the risk of being thought of as greedy for miracles, I prayed for another lucky break. The tension was palpable. I prayed harder, mentally shouting my request. It worked! The steward gave me a nod and showed me to the vacated seat. I nearly wet myself with relief. I was on my way. In style. Surely this had to be a good omen for the rest of the trip.

I buckled my seat belt and, for the first time in weeks, felt utterly calm and confident I was doing the right thing. I now knew what Grannie Scott meant when she said *if you can gather the courage to take the first step, the rest are relatively easy.* This important lesson would stay with me for the rest of my life.

It was pure indulgence in first class. Even before the plane took off, a stewardess brought glasses of champagne to the privileged occupants of the forward cabin. I seldom drank alcohol but I couldn't resist the temptation to celebrate my good fortune. Nor did I forego the adult indulgence of a pre-dinner drink. Or wines with an outrageously delicious dinner. And a delightful digestif after dinner. I leaned back in my seat, satisfied. The feeling of light-headedness, I presumed, came from the thrill of travelling first class.

Before going to sleep, I got up to go to the toilet. As I washed my hands in the tiny basin, I casually glanced in the mirror, did a double-take and then stared in amazement. *What on earth?* My face, neck and chest were covered in a creeping red rash. Surely when I landed in Shannon the authorities would despatch me to a quarantine facility. This was not good. Nervously I cracked open the toilet door and signalled the steward.

"I don't know how this has happened," I whispered on the verge of tears, "but it looks like I've come down with measles ... or something worse. What am I going to do?"

The steward chuckled.

"My diagnosis is too much of too many drinks. Get a couple of hours of sleep. I'm sure your disease will be gone in the morning."

I returned to my seat and, until breakfast, hid under a blanket. The next time I checked the mirror, a rash-free reflection stared back at me. The experience taught me another important lesson: it's best not to mix drinks.

Soon the famous green fields of Ireland passed under the plane's belly. The sun wasn't shining but inclement weather didn't dull my excitement.

"Welcome to Shannon," the pilot announced as the plane taxied toward the terminal.

I couldn't erase the smile from my face. This was the first day of my Great Adventure.

CHAPTER 4

The journey of a thousand miles begins with one step.
Lao Tzu

E xcept for bloodshot eyes, I was pretty sure there were no signs of overindulgence that might cause a health alert. Nevertheless, I approached the immigration desk with a degree of unease. The officer gave me only a passing glance before stamping my passport. A murmured thanks was a shadow of my immense relief. I collected my bags, entered the arrivals hall and headed to the tourist information desk in search of accommodation.

"There's a nice B&B on the main road. It's close to the city centre. Will I call and ask if they have a room?"

A moment later the young woman confirmed the reservation. "You can catch the bus outside the terminal. There's a stop right in front of the B&B. Enjoy Limerick," she added in her pleasant Irish lilt.

My Irish experience began with the novelty of a double-decker bus. Unlike Canadian buses, where passengers entered and paid at the front, double-deckers allowed no access to the driver who sat in a glassed-off area and focused on driving. A conductor collected fares, answered questions, kept order and made sure everyone got on and off safely. The conductor nodded when I gave him the name of the B&B.

The guest house sat in a row of colourfully-painted, three-storey houses with tiny but well-tended front gardens. I opened the black wrought-iron gate and made my way along the concrete path to the imposing front door. Pushing a nipple-like button protruding from a metallic breast resulted in the shrill ring of the bell. A moment later, a stout woman with tightly-permed brown hair answered.

Only after giving me a critical once-over did she invite me in.

"Travelling by yerself?" she asked as she handed me a pen to fill in the guest registration.

"Yes," I answered proudly.

"You seem young to be galavantin' so far from home on yer own. Do yer parents approve?"

I became alert to the reproachful tone of voice.

"I'll be visiting relatives," I replied.

I didn't add that the relatives were in another country. Judging by her noncommittal grunt and the fact she reached for a room key, the answer satisfied her. She led the way up the double flight of steep stairs to the top floor.

"The bathroom's down the hall but there's a sink in yer room," my hostess said, subtly trying to regulate her breathing after the ascent. "We lock the front door at 10:00 pm." She gave me a hard stare, as though one side of her fought with the other about imparting additional information. "I'll give you a house key," she said finally. "If you return late, be sure not to make any noise. Or bring any … guests. This is a respectable place." Her lecture complete, she returned to lower altitudes.

I studied my surroundings. A discordant medley of flower print fabrics made the room seem small. It got points for cleanliness but went into arrears with the soft mattress and hard pillows.

Eager to explore Limerick, I freshened up and went across the street to wait for the next bus.

"Hop on," the conductor responded when I asked if he was going into town.

His frayed collar and cuffs disturbed me. Did Irish transport companies have a slack uniform policy or were poor wages to blame?

I debated whether to go upstairs but decided that the advantage of a quick exit outweighed unobstructed but relatively uninteresting urban views of terraced houses. Minutes later the conductor pulled the bell chord to let the driver know a passenger would be getting off. This was my stop.

"Head up that way," he said pointing straight ahead, "That's where the tourists go. You'll be sure to find something to interest you."

I stepped off the platform. While I looked around to get my bearings, the noisy old bus rattled off, leaving a wake of smelly exhaust.

My first order of business was to find an Irish-knit sweater, something special that would be my main souvenir of this visit. As I wandered through the city centre checking out each and every gift shop, it became apparent there was little to tempt a tourist in 1960s Ireland unless they were in the market for Irish sweaters, Donegal tweed, Waterford crystal, linen, Belleek china or endless armies of made-in-China leprechauns in a variety of sizes and poses.

A small shop caught my attention. Its window displayed the usual variety of woollen products but randomly scattered balls of wool, knitting needles, a spinning wheel and sheep skins showed imagination. I went inside.

As I carefully examined numerous stacks of cardigans and pull-overs, a voice startled me.

"Are y'all right?"

I turned to see an older lady in a tweed skirt and flower-print blouse. It seemed clashing patterns weren't restricted to home dec-orating. Her question confused me. Did I not look all right?

"Can I help you find something?" she clarified.

"Oh. Thank you. I'm not sure yet what I'm looking for."

The woman nodded. She no doubt had heard the same answer countless times before.

"Work away, so. Give us a shout if you need anything."

After trying on a number of styles—actually, all the styles—I selected a cream-coloured crew neck pullover.

"Originally these sweaters were knitted for the fishermen on the Aran islands, off the west coast," the saleslady explained as she wrote the details of the sale in a ledger.

"Don't they do that anymore?"

"Oh, they do. But the fishing trade isn't what it used to be, so now it's the tourists they're hoping to hook," she said with a smile.

"I love the designs," I said running my fingers over the detailed work.

"Each family had a unique pattern so they could identify fishermen if they drowned. The cable stitching is meant to represent fishermen's ropes but it also wishes a safe return. The additional diamond pattern in the jumper you've chosen symbolises wealth and success."

"That clinches the deal," I said, nominating the sweater as my good-luck charm.

She folded the bulky item and placed it in a paper shopping bag.

"Don't be thinkin' of drycleanin' it," she said sternly.

"Absolutely not," I assured her. "My grandmother taught me how to hand wash wool."

"That's good. Proper care and you'll have this for many years. Don't use soap or you'll wash out the natural lanolin. This makes the sweaters water-resistant and warmer."

I cashed the required number of traveller's cheques and took proud possession of my purchase.

Shopping complete, I checked out what the city had to offer. I was disappointed. The low feeling inspired by the down-at-heel bus conductor now transferred to Limerick itself. Not even the tourists looked happy to be here. The damp, grey weather exaggerated the city's dreary atmosphere. Many buildings hadn't seen a fresh coat of paint in years. Baskets of summer flowers would have brightened the streets but these were noticeably absent.

After a filling but flavourless supper of three types of potatoes and overcooked meat and vegetables, I headed back to the B&B.

"Would you mind if I store my guitar and suitcase for a few days while I tour?"

"Let me see how much luggage you have," the host replied. His wife had left him in charge during the quiet evening hours.

Together we climbed the stairs to my room.

"Sure, that won't be any bother at all. I'll put them away safely until you come back," the man said as he removed the cases.

I thanked him, confirmed when I would return to collect the

bags, and said good night.

***

The early morning bus from Limerick delivered me to the centre of Cork, Ireland's largest city after Dublin. The pleasant geography of hills, winding streets and a river provided visual interest.

My guidebook told me Cork had begun as a monastic settlement in the 6th century and became a Viking trading port about four hundred years later. In more recent times, the city gained fame as a rebel stronghold and a centre for anti-treaty forces during Ireland's civil war. Was it the history of defiance that attracted me or was it the buzz, so noticeably absent in Limerick? People here seemed happier, funnier, friendlier, more outgoing. The bright sunshine and warm weather might have influenced my impression.

My main purpose in going to Cork was to kiss the Blarney stone. Legend has it that this act grants the ability to talk with wit and fluency about anything and everything to anyone and everyone. No trip to Ireland would be complete without accomplishing this mission.

A local bus took me to the quaint village of Blarney, five miles from Cork city. The *raison d'être* of the few pretty houses, shops and cafés built around a large central garden square was the woollen mill and the Blarney estate. Tourism allowed the village to thrive.

I followed the pilgrimage of mostly American visitors down the road and through the castle gardens. Guidebooks failed to mention the requisite climb up narrow, irregular steps of a five-hundred-year-old, eight-storey ruined keep that had no barriers to protect against a sheer drop. Not an exercise recommended for anyone suffering from vertigo!

After reaching the top without mishap, I followed the snaking line towards an opposite wall. There stood a portly Irish gentleman whose trilby, waistcoat and neatly trimmed beard gave him the appearance of a magnified leprechaun. His job was to supervise and assist. It worried me that, in order to perform the ritual, each person lay face up on the stone floor at the edge of an opening in the stonework.

"The stone's on the outer wall of the castle," the guide explained when it was my turn. "I'll hold yer legs and ease ya down the hole so ya can give it a kiss. Hold on to them bars for support."

What? I looked down at my mini skirt and knew I wouldn't be able to make the stretch in any way Grannie Daley would approve of. I stood aside to consider my options. Tourist after tourist passed me by.

A lull in the line left me alone with the man in charge. He tactfully made no remarks about my prolonged occupation of the battlements. Instead, demonstrating his own gift of the gab, he offered to tell me more about the origins of the Blarney legend.

"One version of the story started in the time of the first Queen Elizabeth." He lit his stubby pipe before continuing. "The English queen wanted a pledge of loyalty from our Cormac McCarthy, the Lord of Blarney. Wily old Cormac put her off with eloquent diplomacy. A lot of nice talk with no substance, y'understand. The queen was captivated. From that time forward, whenever anyone tried to use charm to pull the wool over her eyes, she accused them of having the gift of Blarney. Believe it or not," he said with a smile and a puff on his pipe.

"What does that have to do with the stone?" I asked.

"Absolutely nothing," the guide said, unbothered by the lack of a link. "That was about how Blarney got to be associated with fine rhetoric."

"Is there a story about the stone?"

"Of course there is. 'Tis said our Cormac had a lawsuit brought against him. Worried about losing, he appealed to the goddess Clíodhna. *Kiss the first stone you see on your way to court,* she says to him. He followed instructions."

"And won?" I asked.

"And won with bells on," the guide confirmed. "He was so eloquent, the judge had no option but to find in his favour. That's when Cormac decided to embed the stone in the castle."

"But why is it in such an awkward place?" I asked, worried that I might have to leave with nothing more than a couple of good anecdotes.

"I don't rightly know," he admitted. "Someone musta wanted to keep it secure, make it more difficult to steal. Some legends say it was the Prophet Jacob's pillow or the stone Moses struck with his staff to produce water for the Israelites. There's also a tale that Scotland's Robert the Bruce gave the stone to McCarthy in recognition of his support in the Battle of Bannockburn. Mind you," he said in a conspiratorial whisper, "the stone is supposed to have come here in 1314, eighteen years before the battle!" He chuckled. "Who knows what the true story may be? 'Tis the end result that's the important thing."

Finally, the castle was about to close. Soft rain underlined the fact that I had to make a decision.

"Don't worry, pet. I have something to put across you." He pulled an old blanket from a box that lay off to the side of the rampart.

Well, why didn't he say that in the first place? I could have been on my way a couple of hours ago. I succumbed to the curious ritual and prayed the wet conditions wouldn't cause him to lose his grip as he eased me over the parapet. Before I knew it, I was sitting upright once again, infused, I hoped, with the hard-won gift of blarney.

***

Surrounding lakes and mountains make the lively town of Killarney one of Ireland's most popular tourist destinations but getting there isn't for anyone in a hurry. Narrow roads, mountain passes, slow traffic and fat sheep grazing on the verges caused the fifty-five-mile drive from Cork to Killarney to take nearly three hours.

The town was choking on B&Bs. I chose The Copper Kettle because of its name and colourful signboard. The jolly welcome of the owner convinced me I had made the right decision.

"We have a delicious Irish breakfast," she said as I filled in the registration form. "It'll be enough to keep you going all day."

This is the sort of information a budget-conscious traveller likes to hear.

That evening at the guest house I met a fellow Canadian named Margaret. She and her American friend Barbara were teachers on summer break.

"There's live traditional music at a local hotel bar tonight," Margaret announced. "Would you like to come with us for a bite to eat before going to the session?"

At first, I was relieved to connect with women from my own culture, people who shared the same vocabulary and, presumably, similar outlooks, despite the age difference. Then I became less comfortable with this easy choice. What was the point of international travel if I hung around with Canadians and Americans? On the other hand, this was an opportunity to socialise. I accepted.

After a tasty dinner of Irish stew, we walked down the busy street to the large, crowded, smoke-filled hotel bar. No sooner had we bought drinks and found seats than a motley trio of male musicians and their flame-haired female singer appeared on the raised platform that served as a stage. A flute, fiddle and drum-like instrument I learned was called a *bodhrán* provided a stirring accompaniment to one of the clearest, most beautiful voices I ever had heard. I could imagine such haunting music entertaining ancient Celtic kings.

The next day, my new friends and I joined forces to visit Ross Castle, the famous lakes of Killarney and the Muckross estate. Instead of a bus tour, we opted for Killarney's quintessential mode of transport, the jaunting car. These two-wheeled, horse-drawn carts could be seen jogging along local roads or parked in groups waiting for passengers. Originally they were used extensively throughout Ireland. Now they pretty much were restricted to Killarney and its environs for the pleasure of tourists.

We negotiated a price with a young jarvey, or jaunting car driver, who assured us his story-telling abilities were second to none. This, we had been told, was one of the main reasons visitors loved the jaunting cars: for the bonus of folklore and humour that comes with the ride.

As we drove along, I watched to see how the jarvey managed his horse.

"Could I take the reins?" I asked eventually.

"No, Miss, it's not safe," he replied, showing surprise at my request.

"Don't worry, I drive a horse and cart at home," I lied.

The young lad digested this qualification, shrugged and handed me the thick leather straps.

I tempered the pace at first but then upped the speed as my confidence grew. A sudden sharp curve on the muddy path tamped my adrenalin rush. Thankful to have manoeuvred it without mishap, I brought the cart to a gentle halt and returned the reins. The old horse shook his head and snorted.

That night the teachers and I repeated our dinner and music practice. Like the previous evening, I was awed by the haunting and distinctive melodies. Part of the magic of Ireland, I realised, was its music.

The following day, Margaret and Barbara left for Galway. I stayed in Killarney to tour part of the famous Ring of Kerry, a route that goes from Killarney, around the Iveragh peninsula to Kenmare and back to Killarney, a total journey of one hundred eleven miles. I chose the abbreviated excursion that excluded Kenmare. Nevertheless, the tour bus left early in the morning and didn't return until the evening. I had learned that even short distances in Ireland require a generous amount of time.

In some places the road looked barely wide enough for our vehicle. At times we could see and hear the wild fuchsia hedges kissing the sides of the bus. There was plenty of land. Why, I wondered, didn't they simply make wider roads?

"What happens if we meet a bus coming in the other direction?" I asked our guide.

"Sure, we've that taken care of," he assured me. "All the coaches travel counter-clockwise. Cars that travel clockwise don't usually have a problem squeezing past."

The tour was a picture postcard of Ireland. I saw patchwork fields like those mentioned in the song *Forty Shades of Green*. Flocks of sheep dotted the hills and reclined by the mountain roadsides, observing the human traffic with disinterest while they chewed the lush grass. Here, the sea left the shore, as so many Irish have done over the centuries. Our guide entertained us with history, literature and myth. We learned about ancient forts, megalithic ogham stones carved with Ireland's earliest form of writing, standing stones that marked important pagan sites and beehive-shaped cells that were relics of ancient monastic life. Religious orders had contributed to Ireland's early reputation as the Island of Saints and Scholars. The enchanting journey was a major deposit to my memory bank.

The following day I returned to the Limerick B&B where I had left my suitcase and guitar. The landlady greeted me with a frown and pursed lips.

"You said you were coming back last night," she said. "I saved a room for you."

"No," I replied, regretful the misunderstanding had resulted in lost revenue, "it was always today. And I didn't book a room. I just left my bags here. Your husband told me that would be OK."

Her eyes squinted at this piece of information.

"And when, may I ask, did you talk to my husband?"

"He came to my room the night before I left to ..." I didn't have a chance to finish my sentence.

"HARLOT!" she spat out. "This is a respectable guest house. I won't have young girls carrying on under this roof, especially with my husband!"

The undeserved outburst—and the choice of vocabulary—staggered me. 'Harlot' belonged in the Bible or a Harlequin romance!

Guests exiting the dining room and new arrivals coming in the front door froze in place. Hastily I tried to explain the situation.

"He just came to ..." I sputtered.

"Don't you tell me what he came to do. I know what men get up to."

At this point, her husband appeared on the scene. He must have heard the commotion and anticipated the outcome because he had retrieved my belongings.

"For goodness sake, Nuala, stop it will ya. I was just storin' her bags."

The wife's angry glare silenced further clarification.

"You may think it's proper to go to a young girl's room," she said, turning her fury on the poor man, "but I don't. Nor would any other decent person."

Suddenly the paranoid landlady lashed out at me again.

"Get out, and never return."

No fear of that, witch. I picked up my cases, slinked out the door and headed for Dublin.

***

It took much of the four-hour bus journey to recover from the trauma of the harridan's hurtful and unwarranted accusations. Although I tried to put the incident out of my mind, I couldn't help stewing over the injustice. Eventually, common sense prevailed. I heard my mother's voice offering her usual good advice: *the woman is more to be pitied than persecuted.*

Now I focused on finding accommodation in Dublin. A fellow traveller suggested staying at the YWCA, a hostel with plenty of people my own age. I paid in advance for two nights in one of their clean and comfortable dormitories.

In this capital of culture, where did I head first? Why, the smelly old Guinness brewery, of course. Like kissing the Blarney stone, this was an essential ingredient in the Irish experience. I wasn't a beer drinker but the black-brown stout with the thick, creamy head was too famous not to sample.

"Guinness is healthy, full of iron and other marvels," the enthusiastic guide told the tour group. "Race horses and hospital patients get a dose of Guinness every day. What better endorsement could that be? The rest of us drink the stuff regularly just to make sure we never fall into either of those two categories," he added mischievously.

In later years, legal objections would be raised against Guinness's bold promotion that *Guinness is good for you.* With advertising mastery, the company simply changed the wording to *Guinnless is bad for you.*

As each of us was handed a complimentary pint at the end of

the tour, our guide added to our growing Guinness knowledge.

"Never sip Guinness. Otherwise you get a bitter taste from the gases in the froth. Take a good gulp and enjoy the full flavour." He supervised our sampling and then continued. "With a well-pulled pint, you can write your initials in the head and they'll still be discernible when you get to the bottom of the glass."

We dipped fingers into glasses, scoring the thick foam. When the last sips were taken we knew Guinness was as good at pulling pints as making stout.

Now that I had the brewery experience under my belt, I focused on the city itself. I learned that Dublin had been founded as a Viking settlement in the 9th century. A glorious tangle of narrow streets and wide avenues was occupied by terraced houses, dark, smokey pubs and clusters of shops and eateries. Church spires were the tallest architectural feature in this city dissected by the River Liffey and two canals.

That evening, after a light supper, I attended a play at the Abbey, Ireland's most famous theatre. This was only the second time I had seen a live performance. The feeling of creative intimacy the theatre offered was the start of my lifelong love of the stage.

The next day I browsed the main shopping areas. Some of the window displays made me feel I'd been caught in a time warp: much of the furniture and clothing looked like it had been transported from the 1920s. Other shopfronts were so charmingly old-fashioned that I had to enter. Bewley's Café, on Grafton Street, with its Egyptian-influenced façade and beautiful interior stained glass windows was a coffee and tea emporium *par excellence*. It, too, harked from the 1920s but reflected the best of the period. I treated myself to coffee and a piece of cake before continuing my walking tour.

Architecture fascinated me. As I stood in front of the august Shelbourne Hotel on St. Stephen's Green, I admired a row of elegant townhouses to the left of the twenty-two acre Victorian park.

"Those are some of Dublin's famous Georgian doors," a voice said.

I turned to see the hotel's doorman, a tall, top-hatted, middle-aged man with a friendly face and easy smile.

"What's so different about the doors?" I asked.

"It's what's around the doors that makes them special. Look at the door-cases and fanlights, the features beside and above the doors."

How could I have missed such detail? I particularly loved the semi-circle of glass above each door that became transformed into art as a result of the creative placement of wood, lead or wrought-iron glazing bars. The creative glasswork allowed light into dark hallways but also provided pleasure to passers by.

By the time I returned to the Y, my dorm mates were getting ready to go out.

"Join us," prompted Maire, one of the two Irish girls I had met. "We're going to the Embankment. The Dubliners are playing."

"What's the Embankment?" I asked. "And who are the Dubliners?"

"The Embankment's a popular pub. They have some of the best music," Maeve, the other girl said. "The Dubliners are a local legend. They're brill."

"What kind of music do they play?"

"Folk mostly, but some of their songs can be a bit raunchy."

"And some are politically provocative," Maeve said, interrupting Maire.

"They're hugely popular with the people," Maire continued, "but stuffy old RTE, our national broadcaster, unofficially banned their music for a few years."

This information intrigued me. I played folk music myself—but didn't have any raunchy or provocative songs in my repertoire. I accepted their invitation.

The event was held in a room above the pub. There was no admission charge. Evidently the pub recouped expenditures through ample sales of alcohol. From what I had seen so far in Ireland, this wasn't an unrealistic expectation.

Maire, Maeve and I were lucky enough to get a standing spot in the front row. As promised, irreverent and sometimes controversial compositions were sprinkled amongst more traditional Irish folk songs and ballads. A combination of complex instrumentals and gravelly voices provided great entertainment for the appreciative audience. I became a Dubliners fan.

During the break, I literally bumped into a man I recognised as one of the lead singers.

"Sorry, luv," he said in a distracted manner.

"That was Luke Kelly," Maire told me as we watched him continue upstairs unsteadily.

"His shockingly red nose goes well with his shock of red hair," I remarked.

"Music is his forte," she laughed, "not sobriety."

The next day, my last in Dublin and in Ireland, I visited museums, absorbing information on the country's history and culture.

An early morning flight to Glasgow persuaded me to save both time and money and sleep at Dublin airport. Hoping to remain inconspicuous, I passed the time window shopping in the departure area.

"Wudya be plannin' t'spend the night here?"

I turned to see an airport security guard. Disappointed at being discovered so quickly, I nodded and waited to be evicted.

"Follow me," he said. I was surprised not to hear a sterner voice. "Here, let me help ya with them bags."

At least he wasn't going to make a spectacle.

Instead of leading me onto the street, he took me into a large, dimly lit room with rows of bench seating. The space was unoccupied except for another girl about my age.

"We won't be usin' this lounge 'til the mornin'. Ye'll be safe here."

He arranged the cushions comfortably and tucked my coat around my shoulders.

"Pleasant dreams," he said kindly.

Before the night was out, eighteen of us had been made comfortable by this good soul.

As I drifted off to sleep, I reviewed the experiences of my first week. I hadn't got lost, robbed or assaulted—unless I counted the verbal abuse in Limerick. There had been no time for loneliness and no need to feel fearful. Every day, I had seen, learned and met something and someone new. My expanded horizons gave me confidence and an immense sense of satisfaction. This, I knew, was what I was meant to be doing. Then my internal critic intruded. So far, I hadn't deviated from an established tourist trail. Soon I would venture off-piste. I snuggled deeper under my coat. One step at a time, I reminded myself firmly. One step at a time.

CHAPTER 5

Strength doesn't come from doing something you can do.
It comes from doing something you thought you couldn't do.
Autumn Calabrese

As the plane flew over the Irish sea, I watched for a sighting of Scotland, excitedly anticipating a reunion with Scottish relatives I had met two years previously when I went with Grannie Scott to Britain for two months. Grannie was reunited with kin she hadn't seen in forty years and I was introduced to international travel and the Scottish branch of my mother's family.

I would be staying with George and Mary Crawford on this one-week stopover. The last time I visited, they lived outside London. Recently they had moved back to Glasgow.

I joined the surge of emerging passengers and quickly spotted George elbowing his way towards me. He gave me a powerful hug. George's arm strength compensated for his height deficit.

"Oot the way, brute." Mary pushed him aside and gave me her own strong embrace.

I loved George for his humour and Mary for her energetic approach to everything she did. Unlike my less demonstrative parents, these people didn't just feel emotion, they expressed it verbally and physically, at full speed and high volume. I was a willing recipient of their affections.

"Come on, lass," Mary said as she took control of the luggage trolly, "let's get you home."

"We have a full schedule to keep you busy. You're going to have such a good time you won't want to leave," George predicted, putting his arm around my shoulders and guiding me to the exit.

We drove to the village of Rosneath in a car filled with animated chatter and no small number of jokes sourced from George's limitless stock. Soon we pulled into the driveway of a two-storey house in a tidy neighbourhood of similar homes. Mary gave me a quick tour, showed me to my bedroom and left me to unpack.

When I went down to the kitchen a short while later, she had the table set with a plate of homemade shortbread and a pot of tea. Grannie made shortbread only at Christmas, so this was a special treat. George and Mary enjoyed watching me enjoy.

As soon as we finished, we were off to see Kate and Tom, Grannie Scott's sister and brother-in-law and Mary's parents. Kate was a taller, sturdier version of Grannie. Tom justifiably had the nickname Big Tom, or 'Tam' as the Scots pronounce it. He reminded me of a St. Bernard: massive hands and feet and a large body but a gentle nature. They lived nearby in something called a caravan park. I never had heard of or seen such a thing. Caravans were vehicles I associated more with gypsies than with elderly relatives. I didn't know what to expect.

"It's beautiful," I exclaimed after Kate had taken me around their home. "It's cosy but you have plenty of space. It seems perfect for the two of you."

"Yes," she agreed, "it's what's called a double-width. That's two caravans put together. It's plenty big for the likes o' us."

To add to the charm of the place, an impressive show of colourful flowers and bushes surrounded the caravan. I was old enough to appreciate the time and effort that went into such a production but not at the stage where I wanted to do anything more than admire results.

"That's mostly Tam's handiwork," Kate said as she set the table for lunch. "It keeps him out o' mischief."

Tom gave a goodnatured grunt in the background.

Afternoon seamlessly rolled into evening. Laughter frequently interrupted the lively conversation. It was the type of environment I loved.

Finally Mary announced it was time to go.

"Ye'll be here all night if someone doesn'y'a make a move," she said as she marshalled George and me out the door.

At home, George offered a nightcap.

"Och, leave her, George," Mary reprimanded. "She can barely keep her eyes open."

My spirit was willing but my body couldn't go the distance. I excused myself, thanked them for a wonderful day and then fell into bed, exhausted but content.

The rest of the week was as busy as George had promised. The pinnacle of the social whirl was a trip to the highland games in Inverary, about half an hour north of Rosneath. George was a champion drum major. He always had his rubber-padded block of wood and a set of drumsticks handy to beat out the complex rhythms that danced in his head.

While George played his role in the festivities, Mary and I followed the rousing pipe bands through the streets and cheered on the muscular contestants in ancient games such as tossing the caber and the shot put.

"Is it true," I asked Mary as the two of us made our way to the Scottish dancing competition, "that men don't wear anything under their kilts?" My curiosity was piqued by this salacious piece of information.

"That's the tradition," Mary confirmed while scanning the gathering crowd for a gap that would allow us a good view. Suddenly she tugged my arm and steered me to a narrow spot near the front. "Now, if you'd asked George that question," she continued, "he would'y come back wi' the cheeky explanation that the way to tell if a man is wearin' anything under his kilt is to look for dandruff on his shoes."

Mary chortled, I blushed. Forever after, I couldn't stop myself from glancing down at kilted men's shoes.

During the course of the week, the conversation periodically came around to my upcoming trip to South Africa. Mary and George dismissed my anxieties.

"Leaving home is the hard part," Mary insisted as we enjoyed one of her delicious meals. "You've got past the worst of it."

"It doesn't feel like that. Every day there's a new challenge. Sometimes I miss a predictable life."

"No you don't," George argued. "Predictability is too tame for you. If life didn't throw challenges at you, you'd go looking for them."

I thought about that for a moment. There might be truth in the statement but that didn't make things easier.

"I could have flown directly to Johannesburg but Professor Hahlo recommended sailing. I hope I've made the right decision. What if I don't like the other passengers?"

"No need to worry about the voyage, darlin'," Mary assured me. "You'll find lots of people to like and lots of people will like you. I bet you'll be sittin' at the captain's table in no time."

"What's the captain's table?" I asked, intrigued.

I debated briefly whether or not to help myself to another Yorkshire pudding and then gave in to temptation.

"Well, each night at dinner the captain chooses certain guests to join him. Usually it's famous, distinguished or rich passengers who get invited. But there's always exceptions for exceptional people such as yourself."

"Thanks for your vote of confidence but I'm inclined to fly under the radar for the time being."

I still suffered twinges of angst from the episode in Limerick.

"That's only because you're still testin' your wings," George said as he put another slice of roast beef on my plate. "You don't have an under-the-radar personality. You're destined to make your mark. Just give it time."

How did some adults have such a clear view of my future? To me, it was a fog I stumbled through, one unsure day at a time. It was welcome, however, to have George and Mary's unconditional support for my unorthodox path.

Too soon, it was time to say goodbye. Again, I was in a car with people I loved being taken to an airport. I checked my luggage, got my boarding pass and claimed precious hugs and kisses from George and Mary. This departure was almost more difficult than leaving Montreal. After Glasgow, I would be on my own.

"Haste ye back," was all that George could say. He had tears in his eyes. I turned and hurried to the gate before they could see my own tears.

***

I saw Fred as soon as I entered the arrivals hall at Heathrow. The head of his lanky body was taller than any other in the crowd of people waiting to meet passengers. I steered myself in the direction of his self-conscious wave.

We had met during my previous visit when Fred returned from two years in Australia. His main appeal was that he was English, well travelled and a mature ten years older than I. We enjoyed an innocent, month-long friendship that had undertones of intimacy but faltered at affection. After I returned to Canada, we kept in touch by letter. A stopover in London was an opportunity to fan the embers of the relationship. I didn't want to think about the potential implications of a rekindled romance but it would be interesting to see how the reunion panned out.

"Kathy, you look fantastic." Fred set aside his British reserve and swept me into his arms. "It's good to see you. I've missed you."

"It's great to see you, too, Fred," I replied.

Something made me hold back from saying I had missed him. Perhaps it was the realisation that, in fact, I hadn't missed him, at least not in a lovesick way. Evidently this hadn't been one of those situations where absence makes the heart grow fonder.

"Would you like me to take you to your hotel and then dinner or do you want to go straight for a meal?" Fred asked as we walked to the parking garage.

The mention of going to my hotel triggered warning signals. Probably groundless, I admitted, but potentially awkward nevertheless. What if A Situation arose? Fred always had been a gentleman but what if he had changed, become more ... amorous?

"Can we eat now? I should have an early night. My cousin thinks I may have to be on the boat tomorrow instead of Friday when it sails."

"Not a problem," Fred said agreeably.

We began catching up in the car but only in the restaurant could we give each other undivided attention.

"Well done for achieving your travel goal. You certainly chose an offbeat destination," Fred said after we had placed our orders.

"The destination kind of chose me. If it had been up to me, I probably would have started globetrotting in Europe."

Fred nodded.

"It's as though distance adds to the imagined perils. I remember my nervousness before setting off for Australia. The unknown is overwhelming at first but once you're on your way, you wonder what all the fuss was about."

"I'm well on my way but I haven't got past the overwhelming stage," I confessed.

"Once you've taken the big step of getting on the boat, I suspect you'll feel less unsure. By then, you'll well and truly be on your way."

It was at dessert when Fred changed the direction of the conversation.

"You haven't changed a bit."

The register of his voice became deeper, more personal. He punctuated the words by leaning towards me and placing his hand over mine.

"I'm not sure that's a good thing," I said. "It's been two years, after all."

"I don't mean physically. I can see your lovely blond hair is shorter, that sort of thing. I mean you. Your personality. You're still the optimistic, spirited innocent who so captivated me."

I felt a blush warming my cheeks. As I wrestled with the dilemma of whether or not it would be polite to remove my hand, the waiter arrived. Fred retreated to his side of the table.

"You seem to have changed, though, Fred. You seem ... settled," I said when the waiter left.

And therein lay the problem. Instead of the world traveller who once dazzled me, I now saw an ordinary man who appeared older than his years, worn down by the humdrum he had allowed to become his life. The removal of my rose-tinted spectacles squelched any possibility of romance. Fortunately he, too, realised that the tenuous candle of intimacy had extinguished itself. We parted as we had begun: affectionate friends.

I felt relief to start this new chapter of my life with no emotional encumbrances. It would be easier to move forward if I wasn't yearning for someone I had left behind.

**

First thing the next morning, I made my way to the shipping office of the Union-Castle Line, the parent company of the SA *Vaal*. The agent examined my passport and booking confirmation and returned them to me.

"When is embarkation?" I asked, hoping my use of the correct terminology would make me appear less like a neophyte.

"Not until tomorrow," he replied while preparing a packet for me. "These are all your necessary documents. Your ticket is here as well as information about the ship."

He went over each item, neatly placed everything in an envelope and handed it to me.

"What happens next?"

"There's a Union-Castle office at the docks. Show them your ticket and they'll give you a boarding card."

"Where *is* the boat? And how do I get there?" I was starting to feel panicky. This was my opportunity to ask questions. What if I forgot something important?

"There's a special boat train that leaves Waterloo station tomorrow morning," he explained. "It will take you straight to the docks at Southampton."

I must have looked as unsure as I felt.

"Don't worry, luv. Everyone on the train will be going to the same place. There will be plenty of people to help you if you need a hand. You'll be fine."

I weakly returned his smile and left the office, not entirely convinced. Still, the procedure seemed straightforward. All I had to do was get on and off a train and onto a ship. Surely I could handle that! But what if I missed the train? Lost my ticket? I put the brakes on these negative thoughts.

In the meantime, I had half a day to kill. London offered a wealth of diversions. *When a man is tired of London, he is tired of life*, Samuel Johnson said. I considered visiting the National Portrait Gallery or the Victoria and Albert Museum but rejected these cultural options in favour of retail therapy. Only the diversion of shopping could calm my nerves. The marvels of the famous Carnaby Street would do the trick, I reckoned. This was the primo piece of real estate in the landscape referred to as Swinging London. Here, the new fashion movements called 'mod' and 'hippie' were on full display. High-end boutiques flourished alongside busier shops crammed with moderately-priced versions of expensive outfits and accessories. On my previous visit, I had embraced mini-skirts and returned to Montreal with a trend-setting wardrobe. But the fast-moving London scene had evolved in my two-year absence. Now, many of these new styles were more daring than I was.

Fellow pedestrians were equally interesting. Stereotypical men in bowler hats and pin-striped suits hurried past long-haired clones of rock stars. Dolly-birds in high heels and short skirts mingled with kaftan-wearing women with colourful head-gear, as well as anti-fashionistas with beads and peace-sign jewellery around their necks. I loved the energy—and the synergy.

Finally I called it a day. I grabbed a bite and returned to the hotel. Tomorrow at this time I would be *at sea*. The thought was romantic, adventuresome … terrifying. I sat on the edge of the bed and stared at my hands, hoping for an injection of courage. Nothing. No courage but, slowly, renewed resolve. It was bad enough when other people didn't have faith in me; it was foolish not to have faith in myself. *I can do this*, I whispered, *I will do this.*

CHAPTER 6

If you remain in your comfort zone, you will not go any further.
Catherine Pulsifer

I stared out the train window at the approaching port of Southampton. Cranes, sheds, shipping containers and large trucks cluttered the busy concrete waterfront.

As the train's screeching brakes brought the carriages to a halt, I gathered my two pieces of luggage, disembarked and got swept along in the crush of passengers heading towards the Union-Castle office. Everyone formed orderly queues and seemed at ease with the routine. Was I the only person with butterflies in my stomach?

"Next!" the agent said.

I approached the kiosk window and passed my ticket and passport to the agent.

"First ocean voyage?" he enquired pleasantly.

I nodded, wanting to scrub away the aura of inexperience which evidently surrounded me. The agent returned the documents and gave me a boarding pass.

"*Bon voyage*, young lady. Enjoy the journey. Next!"

This was it. This young lady was on her way. I stepped into the pale English sunlight and walked toward the embarkation area. A towering white ship gently tugged at her moorings, as though anxious to be on her way. SA *Vaal* was written in tall black letters on her side. The name sounded as foreign as the ship's distant destination. Later I learned that Vaal is the name of the largest tributary of South Africa's mighty Orange River.

I stood for a moment admiring this vessel that would be my home for the next twelve days.

"Would you like me to help you with your bags?"

I turned to see a stocky, muscular man standing at my elbow.

He didn't wear a porter's uniform, so why was he offering this service?

"My name is Dirk Caney," he said. "I'm a fellow passenger. If you give me your cabin number, I can drop these things off for you." When I didn't jump at his offer, he smiled and continued, "I promise you, you don't want to be lugging bags up gangways, down stairs and along corridors, especially when you probably don't know your way around."

My first instinct was to suspect him of ulterior motives. But what motives? The suitcase was heavy and contained nothing he would find worth stealing. And where would he go? Giving him a good look-over, I couldn't find anything obviously wrong with him. He appeared to be in his mid-thirties, was well dressed and had an honest face. Based on these superficial pluses, I decided to trust him. Besides, I loved his accent, which I presumed must be South African.

"That's kind of you, Dirk. Thank you. My name is Kathy." After politely shaking hands, I searched for my cabin number and read it out to him.

Dirk lifted my suitcase as though it was empty and then bent towards the guitar case.

"I'll keep the guitar with me. It's not heavy and I don't like to be separated from it."

No use in being reckless, I reasoned.

"The boat sails in a couple of hours," Dirk said, unfazed by my wariness. "Can I invite you for a drink when we've left port?"

"Thank you. That would be nice," I said.

Dirk waved and marched confidently up the gangway. Following him would have been the logical thing to do. Instead I lingered on the dock and breathed in the cleansing salt air. Today was a day of firsts: an ocean voyage—to Africa, of all places—and entry into the world of socialising as an adult in an outrageously unfamiliar environment. I suddenly felt I was growing up.

***

The corridors below deck were long and confusing. I took several wrong turns, despite receiving directions from helpful staff members. Eventually I arrived at my assigned quarters. My suitcase sat just inside the metal, watertight door, mocking me for doubting Dirk's good intentions.

I had anticipated that an interior cabin would be dark and cramped. Only the more expensive accommodations had port holes. Instead I walked into a well-lit, spacious room. A table and chairs and a four-drawer dresser separated two sets of bunk beds.

An array of full-length gowns was spread out on one of the lower bunks. The name card attached to that bed read *Bronwyn Montague Southey*. Name and wardrobe suited each other.

I took my name card from those remaining on the central table and staked my claim to the other lower bunk. In lieu of elegant clothing, I lay my guitar on the bed.

While unpacking, two blond sisters about my age entered the cabin. They greeted me politely but retreated into a shell of reserve when they found out I was neither South African nor an Afrikaner, a South African of Dutch descent.

Then the mysterious Bronwyn arrived. Wow! Her tall, slender good looks complemented her unusual name and smart clothes. Long, thick black hair, beautiful green eyes and a mahogany tan made me think she had had an impossibly fortuitous dip in the gene pool.

"Hello," she said, including everyone in her greeting, "I'm Bonnie."

Her three cabin mates replied with a roll call of their own names. None of us merited more attention so Bonnie devoted herself to finishing the job of unpacking. At this point, the Afrikaans girls left. I was alone with the awesome Bonnie.

"I love your dresses," I said as an ice-breaker. I figured anyone who made such a show of clothes that could have been hung straight away in the wardrobe might need a little extra attention.

"Thank you. After my year of finishing school in Switzerland I was invited to the annual Oxford-Cambridge boat race. There was a ball afterwards."

This astonishing pronouncement was made in a plummy accent

and without missing a beat in her sorting process. She really was a complete package: lifestyle matched her other advantages.

We briefly exchanged information about each other while she opened and closed her chosen drawer and laid out her perfumes and cosmetics. It seemed the only thing we had in common was our age. Nevertheless, she extended an invitation to join her friends and her for drinks when the ship sailed.

"Thanks, Bonnie, but someone already has invited me."

Bonnie turned to examine me more closely and perhaps reconsider her first impression.

"All right. Maybe another time," she said vaguely.

She excused herself and breezed out of the cabin.

I did my own more humble unpacking and went back on deck. A blast of the ship's horn signalled our imminent departure. Passengers pressed against the railings, waving to friends and family. Dockers cast off the moorings, allowing sturdy tugboats to guide the ship out of the port and into open waters.

"There's no going back now, is there?"

Once again the mysterious Dirk Caney had appeared.

"That same thought just occurred to me," I said with a sigh.

"I take it this will be your first trip to South Africa?"

"Definitely," I replied. "And my first time at sea." It was pointless to hide my inexperience.

"Well, you couldn't have picked a better ship," Dirk assured me. "This is a floating luxury hotel, first class all the way. Once you know a few people, you'll have a great time. Where are you headed?"

"Ultimately to Johannesburg. I have a secretarial job waiting for me."

"Johannesburg is South Africa's least loved city and its most dangerous," Dirk said solemnly, "but there's no doubt it has a throbbing pulse."

"Will you stay in Cape Town?"

"No. I have to get back to the east coast. I manage a large sugar cane plantation outside Durban. If you ever get to that part of the country, come and visit," he added hospitably.

Sugar cane plantation manager. Now that was an occupation I hadn't come across. I planned to learn more but for now I contented myself with watching the shoreline diminish and then disappear.

"Let's go have that drink I promised you," Dirk said, breaking the comfortable silence.

As we entered the noisy bar, Dirk noticed several people on the far side of the room waving at him to join their group. It took nearly fifteen minutes to get to where we were going because he kept meeting friends.

"Is there anyone you don't know?" I asked in astonishment when we had detached ourselves from yet another cordial couple.

"A lot of us travel back and forth on a regular basis," Dirk explained. "You get to know everyone pretty quickly. You just want to make sure to get in with a decent crowd. These are good people," he said as we finally made our objective.

Dirk's good people immediately welcomed me into their circle. Being the youngest in the group, they took me under their collective wing. My new companions were a mix of Rhodesians, South Africans and Zambians returning home from extended leaves.

"Because so many people in southern Africa have European ties, it's not unusual to take several weeks of holiday, if not every year then every two years. It's a long way for us to travel to reconnect with family and friends so we like to make the journey worthwhile."

This information came from Diane Carlstein, a pretty, young woman whose father managed a diamond mine in Kimberly, the heart of South Africa's diamond industry. In the ultimate example of product promotion, Diane wore a magnificent rectangular diamond on her finger.

As I glanced at the mélange of African nationalities, it struck me that they came in only one colour: white. There wasn't a black face to be seen, not even among the crew. I had heard about South Africa's controversial policy of apartheid. Now I was seeing a form of this forced separation of races in action. The injustice of the situation upset me. How could any government make such inhumane behaviour the law of the land? Instinct told me it would be better to know more about local politics before jumping into a conversation on this sensitive subject with uninformed opinions.

On other topics relating to South Africa, however, I had no hesitation in asking every question that popped into my head. My willing tutors uttered words I had never heard and painted compelling images of places and things I had never seen. I couldn't wait to explore the country.

The sound of a gong on the public address system interrupted our conversation.

"That's the call for the first sitting at dinner," Dirk explained.

"I'd better get a move on. That's when I'm supposed to eat," I said, removing my cardigan and handbag from the back of a chair. "Thank you, everyone. It's been lovely meeting you."

"You might want to speak to the head waiter about changing your dinner time," William suggested as he tamped down the tobacco in his pipe. William was a big game hunter based in Salisbury, Rhodesia. A deep scar down the side of his craggy face testified to the danger of his profession. "The first sitting is pretty much for families. Young families. The second sitting would probably suit you better."

"We'll be getting together after the second-sitting," Margaret said. "Do join us in the lounge."

"I will. Thank you."

The large dining room had starched linen tablecloths, attentive waiters and an extensive, four-course menu. The food was exceptional, a fact at odds with the British reputation for unappetising, over-cooked meals. It was on the SA *Vaal* that I first ate sweetbreads, a dish variously described by my table companions as bull's balls and calf's thymus, neither of which sounded like anything I wanted to ingest. My culinary bravery was rewarded with an agreeable new taste sensation. Here, too, I sampled traditional British foods such as pressed ox tongue and farmhouse brawn as well as more familiar dishes like sole, steak and roast pork.

My assigned seating on that first evening was at a child-free table. Although my companions were friendly, the background was noisy. I followed William's advice to switch to second sitting for the rest of the voyage. At this later session, everyone dressed—and behaved—more formally.

Later, I joined my new friends in the lounge and spent a happy evening listening to tales of Africa.

The next morning, a snappy, white-gloved steward approached me as I finished breakfast.

"Radio telegram for you, Miss."

"What's a radio telegram?" I enquired, removing the square white envelope from a silver tray. To me, the two words didn't belong together.

"It's a form of communication used between ships. This message came for you during the night from a passing navy vessel."

That sounded dramatic! Mystified, I thanked the steward and looked for a quiet spot on deck to discover who would contact me in such a manner. I opened the folded paper and read *Bon voyage, Livingstone. Best of luck. Goodnight* (underlined in red). *Love Michael.*

I felt my mouth form a silly grin and my heart beat a little faster. Michael was my wickedly handsome Scottish second-cousin. We met when his career in Britain's merchant navy brought him to Montreal three years previously. Since then we had kept in touch irregularly by phone and letter. Whenever we spoke, we always signed off with inane repetitions of 'good night' until one of us conceded defeat. I had had a mad crush on Michael. If asked, I might even have run away with him. At least, this was the scenario my romantic mind conjured up. I knew Michael was at sea and he knew I was sailing to South Africa; I never guessed we would be on two ships passing in the night.

***

Life aboard the SA *Vaal* was a world of comfort, fine dining and fun. There were no unpleasant demands and no unachievable expectations. Early each day, a steward wished me good morning and placed a cup of freshly brewed coffee on my bedside table. After that I could go back to sleep or get up and have a large or small breakfast and then become involved in one of the many shipboard activities that ranged from deck quoits to exercise classes to lectures and sundry pastimes in between. A delicious lunch was followed by more keep-busy options. Or I could do nothing more strenuous than hunker down in a deck chair with a good book and soak up the sun and invigorating sea air. Evenings were filled with games, socialising in several bars, cinema or specially organised parties. I barely could digest this feast of pleasure.

Bonnie and I developed a cautious friendship despite the fact we moved in different circles. Hers was a young crowd of beautiful people who partied all night. My set was more mature—in age, not necessarily behaviour. Nevertheless, our paths crossed period-ically, on occasion by design.

"Shall we go to the captain's cocktail party together?" Bonnie asked, applying mascara to her already long lashes.

We were getting ready to go out for the evening. Separate evenings, I had presumed.

Bonnie's suggestion surprised me. Every male on the ship had eyes for her. Why would she want to go to a cocktail party with me? In fact, I had planned on giving the event a miss. I looked upon the invitation as social crumbs: compensation for all the people who wouldn't be invited to sit at the captain's table. Second best didn't appeal to me.

"Sure, why not?" I heard myself replying. If the gathering was good enough for Bonnie, I should reconsider. "I've never been to a cocktail party. What's the deal?"

"It's no big deal. You dress up, get free drinks and make small talk. The unwritten rule is to keep circulating. Don't monopolise anyone for too long and don't let anyone monopolise you. Mingle." She noticed my confused look. "You'll get the hang of it soon enough. It'll probably just be stuffy old fogeys." She paused. I sus-pected she thought I might think she referred to my friends. Get-ting no reaction, she continued. "We might strike it lucky and meet someone interesting. We don't have to stay long."

Arriving at the cocktail party with Bonnie made me feel insig-nificant. The conversation slowly died when we entered the room —or, when Bonnie entered the room. I'm sure no one noticed she had someone with her. I discretely slipped into a group of people standing to my left and let Bonnie have the spotlight. I tried to follow her instructions to mingle and make small talk but neither skill came easily. I didn't want to cause offence by moving to another group, one I evidently thought might be more stimulating. Nor could I think of any topic that would interest me but qualify as superficial small talk. Evidently my newly-acquired gift of blarney didn't extend to cocktail parties.

Less than an hour later, I felt a gentle tap at my elbow.

"We can leave, if you like. There's a party in the Kiddies' Rumble Room. It'll be a lot livelier than this bunch."

I followed Bonnie out the door, feeling the stare of dozens of eyes observing our exit.

Among her peers, Bonnie became animated. It was as though still water had become effervescent. Perhaps, too, my persona altered in her eyes. The bottom line was that our friendship graduated to a new level that evening as we got to know each other better.

We were chatting together when someone shouted, "Here he is." Everyone turned to see who had arrived. In walked the most beautiful man I had seen on the ship. Or anywhere else, for that matter. He was tall, tanned and had striking blue eyes made all the bluer by his blue-black hair. His boldly striped sports jacket indicated he had a fun side. Needless to say, he made straight for Bonnie.

"Hi, doll," he said, giving her a peck on the cheek.

"Kathy, meet Dave McQuoid-Mason, one of my favourite Rhodesians," Bonnie said.

"One of?" Dave said.

Dave's good looks were surpassed only by his charm and obvious popularity. He excluded no one. His acceptance of me, and therefore the group's acceptance, made it easy to float between my crowd and Bonnie's. I had the best of both worlds.

***

Late at night, two days after leaving Southampton we dropped anchor off the Portuguese island of Madeira. According to the ship's information sheet, the volcanic island was discovered accidentally in 1419 by the Portuguese explorer Joao Gonçalves Zarco when a storm blew him off course. Bonnie had a less historical take on the island.

"Madeira's most famous for its wine."

By now I knew she was well versed in matters concerning alcohol.

"The sweet version is good with dessert," she continued.

Wine with dessert? Ice cream with dessert, yes, but wine? I obviously had a lot to learn.

Instead of passengers going ashore, traders came to the ship in an armada of small boats. Through an ingenious pulley system, baskets of hand-embroidered linens were hoisted up to eager shoppers gathered along the railings. Beautiful table cloths, napkins, hand towels and baby clothes were opened out and admired by potential buyers.

"It's an honour system," the woman beside me explained. "Each item has a price attached to it. If you want to buy something, you put the correct amount of money in the basket and send it back down to the boat."

The novel approach to commerce intrigued me but I didn't partake in the exercise.

Within a couple of hours, the SA *Vaal* was steaming south to Las Palmas, capital of the Spanish-owned Canary Islands. It was at Las Palmas in 1492 that Christopher Columbus, or Cristóbal Colón, as the Spanish call him, spent time on his first voyage to the Americas.

It didn't take much imagination to figure out Las Palmas meant 'the palms' but I couldn't see excessive numbers of them. Presumably, the once plentiful supply had been sacrificed to make way for the crowd of brightly-coloured houses that crept up the sides of domineering mountains.

The itinerary allowed passengers several hours to explore the island. The outing was my first taste of a sub-tropical location. Instead of taking an expensive excursion, I happily wandered the narrow streets, admiring old buildings and pretty shops, captivated by the vibrant displays of flowers that cascaded over walls and covered the sides of structures in riotous profusion.

An encounter with shipboard companions got me an invitation to join them for lunch. At the end of the meal, I accepted the offer of a glass of Madeira to accompany the orange and almond cake.

"Interesting," I remarked impartially.

In truth, I preferred ice cream with dessert.

***

For the next ten days, SA *Vaal* continued her journey without further stops or sightings of land. Passengers adjusted to the ship and to each other and settled into the job of enjoying the temporary escape from the routine demands of their land-based lives. Fine weather and calm seas encouraged an atmosphere where everyone was friendly, relaxed and sociable. I liked these travellers from the southern hemisphere. Even the outdoorsy, pioneer types had an air of sophistication. With the exception of the prickly issue of apartheid, we shared values and interests. Foreigners weren't as foreign as Grannie Daley believed.

Reaching the equator was an excuse for a special ceremony: King Neptune initiated those crossing the imaginary line for the first time. For me, this was a momentous occasion. I felt like an explorer headed for new lands. The southern hemisphere! The name sounded exotic. I knew the view of the constellations in the southern sky would be different from what was visible in the north. I also knew the seasons were reversed. This became obvious with the gradual drop in temperature as we travelled south. Were there other distinctions? Someone told me water went down drains counter-clockwise south of the equator but I had my doubts about this piece of trivia.

One event which got everyone involved was the costume ball. In my experience, only children dressed up and that was done at Halloween. Adults doing it in the middle of summer seemed strange.

"We're out in the ocean," I moaned to Bonnie. "How on earth are we supposed to get hold of costumes in the middle of nowhere?"

"Use your imagination," Bonnie replied. "There are plenty of bits and pieces on board to make fun costumes."

I stared in astonishment at this powerhouse of party energy. Creativity was evidently another skill in her bag of tricks.

"Can you help me?" I asked meekly. "I left my imagination on shore."

"Sure, Kath. Don't expect Hollywood costume design but I can certainly figure out something for you to wear."

Somehow Bonnie cobbled together bits of coloured paper, scraps of fabric and reshaped wire coat hangers to turn me into a fairy.

Not everyone had to forage for costume materials. Some people, familiar with the shipboard tradition, came prepared. Diane of diamond fame amazed everyone when she entered the room as Marie Antoinette, wig and all.

"How did you pack such an elaborate costume into your suit-case?" I asked in awe.

"Oh goodness, Kathy, suitcases couldn't possibly accommodate my wardrobe. I travel with steamer trunks. I knew there would be a ball so I picked up this costume in Italy."

This really was another world, a world that fascinated me.

A couple of days before we reached Cape Town, the mood among the passengers changed. For some, there was excitement, for others sadness. Shipboard friendships would fade, or at least be put on hold until future meetings. Addresses were exchanged and invitations to visit were extended. For me, the trip had been an exceptional experience. In only twelve days I had seen my self-confidence grow and my social poise develop.

On 31 July, the final morning of the voyage, the ship buzzed with activity earlier than usual. South Africa's coastline had been sighted. Many of us went on deck to witness the spectacle of land-fall and the arrival in Table Bay.

"That's Robben Island," a red-faced Afrikaans gentleman be-side me said as he looked toward a rocky lump of land on the ocean surface. "That's where we send troublemakers. People who try to disrupt our society."

From more liberal sources, I learned that Robben Island's 'troublemakers' were primarily black political prisoners who resisted South Africa's repressive apartheid policies. The government counted on the island's remoteness to make it more difficult for opposition leaders to rally support. Men like Nelson Mandela who survived the brutalities of the island regime became symbols of the power of the human spirit and the right to freedom for all.

Since the island raised negative emotions in my companion, I switched to safer ground.

"So that's Cape Town?" I asked rhetorically, pointing to the distant cityscape.

"Yes, it is," he said, smiling once again. "You see that big, flat ledge of a mountain? That's Table Mountain. It's one of the most famous backdrops in the world. You can't beat this view of it." He sighed in appreciation of the vista. "Now, young lady, you'll have to excuse me. I need to finish packing. We'll be docking soon. It's usually pretty chaotic with everyone anxious to leave and immigration being bloody officious. Don't leave things until the last minute," he warned. "Enjoy your stay in South Africa," he added with a wave.

I stood for a few more minutes absorbing the beauty of the approach. Then I returned to the cabin to collect my belongings, ready to face the next phase of the adventure.

CHAPTER 7

*Embrace uncertainty. Some of the most beautiful chapters
in our lives won't have a title until much later.*
Bob Goff

The instant my feet touched the ground, I felt a surge of energy from Africa's ancient earth. The place seemed foreign and familiar at the same time, as though I had returned to my primordial roots. While I soaked in the sensation, a man with a red boutonniere caught my attention. Our eyes locked and he immediately walked in my direction.

"Are you Kathy?" he asked.

"Yes," I smiled. "And you must be Dear Douglas."

We shook hands and discreetly studied one another. Douglas Duncan was as elegant in appearance as I had imagined. His smiling, open face immediately dispelled any concerns that he might be a 'stuffy old fogey', as Bonnie would have said. His gracious mannerisms made words like gentleman and chivalrous spring to mind.

"Let's go home," Douglas said picking up my suitcase. "Susie is dying to meet you."

After a short journey through the city and into the suburbs, the car pulled into the driveway of an expansive, one-storey, thatched-roof house in a secluded cul-de-sac.

"This is *Vredenburg*, one of the oldest remaining Cape-Dutch constructions. It dates from about 1775," Douglas said as we got out of the car.

"The place looks huge."

"Yes," Doulas admitted. "It's big and rambling."

"Don't stand out there talking," a female voice admonished as the front door swung open. "Come in and let me welcome you properly."

"Kathy," Douglas said with a chuckle and a shake of his head, "this is the indomitable Susie, or the Duchess of Vredenburg, as I like to call her. Susie, this is the lovely Kathy."

I instinctively added the word 'formidable' to Douglas's description of his wife. Despite the smile and the outstretched arms, the tall, striking woman in front of me looked like she would brook no nonsense. I reminded myself to be on my best behaviour. Then, contrary to my first impression, Susie gave me a motherly embrace and ushered me inside.

A large room served as an entrance, seating area and dining room. Bookshelves and artwork filled the walls. Antique furniture, intriguing ornaments and attractive hand-woven carpets completed the decor. An ambience of casual culture and warmth permeated the space.

"You'll be in the back wing. Our daughter Susie has a room there as well. She's a couple of years younger than you. She's out a lot but when she's at home she might be good emergency companionship in case you get tired of us old ones."

Douglas and Susie showed me to a sunlit guest room with French doors that opened onto a walled garden. Douglas placed my suitcase near a chest of drawers while Susie opened a cupboard to make sure there were enough hangers.

"Come, you can see the rest of the house," she said, satisfied that everything was in order.

The sprawl of rooms seemed endless, yet the house felt cosy.

"Our eldest son Beavan is studying printing and management in England. At least, we hope that's what he's doing. No doubt Swinging London has plenty of other distractions. Tom, who's your age, is reading law here at the University of Cape Town. He has rooms just off the *stoep*."

"What's a *stoep*?" I asked, mentally adding this new word to my growing list.

"That's what we call a verandah," Susie explained. "South African vocabulary is often a mix of English and Afrikaans. You'll pick it up soon enough."

No matter what room we entered, books formed the principal decorating feature, not surprising in the home of the managing director of a publishing company. Douglas noticed my interest.

"Help yourself to any book while you're here. They're meant to be enjoyed."

"Thank you." I brushed my hand across a row of spines, disappointed I didn't have some mechanism to suck in all the stories and knowledge, like a literary vacuum. "It'll take all my time just to read the titles."

"Shall we have a cup of tea so you can catch your breath?" Susie enquired at the end of the tour.

No sooner had the words been spoken than a buxom black woman appeared. At least, she looked black. Douglas explained later she was a Cape Coloured. This ethnic group originated from unions between early Dutch settlers and black, Malay or Indian slaves.

"This is our wonderful Isabella," Susie said fondly. "She ably manages our home and our lives. We would be lost without her."

Isabella beamed.

"Welcome, Miss Kathy. We've been looking forward to your visit."

Isabella placed the laden silver tray on the polished dining room table. She poured each of us a cup of tea and then offered an assortment of freshly baked cake and biscuits. This was my introduction to being spoiled by Isabella.

Although the Duncans did everything they could to make me feel at home, it took a couple of days to get over my shyness and to stop worrying about saying or doing the wrong thing. The dramatic ice-breaker happened when Isabella served coffee after dinner. As we sat at the table chatting, I inexplicably tipped the delicate china demitasse before it reached my mouth. In horror, I watched the hot liquid pour onto the table.

"Well that's the best dinner table entertainment I've seen for a while." Susie paused her laughter to ask Isabella to bring a cloth. "You should have seen your face. It was priceless."

Douglas and young Susie, too, were laughing. I joined the merriment, relieved that my *faux pas* had been received so graciously. From that moment forward I was totally at ease with the Duncans.

Isabella's determination to look after me overrode my weak attempts to be self-sufficient. She woke me each morning with a glass of freshly-squeezed orange juice and regularly tried to fatten me up with her delicious cooking. When a cold threatened, Isabella insisted I stay in bed. She then scurried to the kitchen to concoct a herbal paste which she deftly massaged onto my chest. Whether it was the devoted care or the magic potion, the worst of the symptoms had disappeared by the next day.

Susie senior was an inexhaustible tour guide. We drove through verdant countryside, walked along magnificent stretches of unspoiled beach, explored city streets and visited places of historic interest.

"*Groot Constantia* is the Cape's oldest wine estate," Susie said as we drove up the oak-lined avenue. "The Cape-Dutch manor house dates from the late 1600s. It's been converted into a museum but the rest of the property is still a working winery."

I never had seen a vineyard. The tour of the homestead and some of the estate gave me a new appreciation of the skill required to produce high-quality wine. *Groot Constantia's* reputation was unparalleled in South Africa.

Before we left, Susie took the opportunity to replenish the family cellar.

"It wouldn't do to run dry," she commented as she supervised the placement of several cases of wine in the back of the car.

When we got home, the elusive Tom Duncan made an appearance. The presence of a foreign female under his roof reinforced his intensely shy nature. I seldom saw him for the first few days because he hid behind the protective curtain of studies in a wing of the house far removed from my own. Unexpectedly, and no doubt at the urging of his parents, he asked me to go to a movie, or bioscope as the South Africans say. The success of the evening gave him the confidence to extend a further invitation.

"The aircraft carrier HMS *Hermes* is in port. I've been invited to a party on board. Would you like to go with me?"

Travel certainly provided unusual opportunities. I accepted eagerly.

After a tour of the ship, guests socialised in the ward room with the officers. Between Tom's shyness and my inexperience at mingling in these types of events, we pretty much had to rely on each other for conversation. We both agreed it was a pretty boring event.

"Do you know where the ladies' room is?" I asked Tom.

I needed a bit of distraction and this seemed as good as any.

"I've seen women heading off that way." Tom pointed to a grey metal doorway. "It's probably well marked since there usually isn't a need for female toilets on a navy ship."

I headed off in the suggested direction. After opening a couple of wrong doors in the narrow corridor, a toilet revealed itself. *Pretty snazzy for an aircraft carrier,* I thought. I washed my hands, re-applied lipstick and tried a door just off the bathroom, thinking it might be a shorter route back to the ward room. Instead it opened onto an intimate lounge. There, sitting at a round table playing cards, was the ship's Commanding Officer and five cronies. My intrusion surprised all of us. The CO gave a sheepish grin. He knew I knew he had been caught ducking out of his own function. He nodded at an orderly and asked him to guide me back to the party. I met up with Tom and told him what had happened.

"Evidently he knows from experience how best to spend his time," Tom remarked.

By mutual agreement, we headed home.

***

After nearly a week in Cape Town, it was time to make plans for my trip to Johannesburg. Dwindling savings reminded me I needed to get back to work.

"I had several invitations to visit people but my cabin-mate Bonnie Southey lives near a place called Norvals Pont. She told me this was on the way to Johannesburg," I said to Dear Douglas. "Maybe that's the most practical stopover."

"Give me her details and I'll check on things for you," Douglas responded.

I expected to find out nothing more than the schedule and cost of the journey but Douglas came home that evening with unexpected additional information.

"Bonnie comes from good stock," he began. "Her family has been in the country a long time. One of her ancestors was a Governor of Griqualand East in the late 1800s. Her father, Percy Southey, is a respected breeder of race horses. I think you'll be fine staying with them."

The résumé astonished me. Bonnie had referred to her family simply as farmers. What impressed me more than Bonnie's background was the fact that Dear Douglas had cared enough to vet my prospective hosts.

"The train actually stops at Norval's Pont, which is about half-way to Johannesburg. Would you like to call Bonnie to make sure your visit is convenient? Then I could make a booking for you. I recommend a sleeper compartment.

"A sleeper? How long will it take?"

"It arrives at Norvals Pont in the evening of the same day you leave. A sleeper would be more comfortable. Don't worry, the train is safe and inexpensive. Unless you're thinking of taking the famous Blue Train, which is the height of luxury."

"I'm going to have to pass on that option. Maybe when I have an income I can entertain the idea."

"Speaking of income," Douglas continued, "I've spoken with Dr Shapiro in Jo'burg. He's the medical editor you'll be working for. You can start whenever you like. I've also spoken with Bobby Hahlo. Give him a ring a day or so before you leave the Southeys and tell him when you'll arrive in Jo'burg. He wants to meet you at the station."

I nodded. "What's Dr Shapiro like?"

"He's a pleasant enough fellow. Demanding but well thought of in medical and publishing circles. If you could charm Bobby Hahlo, I'm sure you'll get on fine with Dr Shapiro."

Once arrangements had been made, it was time to be on my way. Isabella made sure all my clothes were clean, freshly ironed and neatly packed.

"You look after yourself, Miss Kathy," Isabella said, enveloping me in a generous hug. "You get sick again, you tell Master and I'll send you some remedies."

"Oh, Isabella, what am I going to do without you? Thank you for taking such good care of me."

I gave her a kiss on the cheek and then turned to formidable but loving Susie.

"We'll miss you, Kathy. Come back and see us soon."

Another strong embrace, another fond kiss, another sadness at leaving special people. Dear Douglas drove me to the train station and helped me settle in the private compartment.

"Be sure to lock the door," he cautioned. "You don't want to take unnecessary risks."

"Thank you for everything, Dear Douglas," I said, giving him an affectionate hug that I didn't want to end. "You and Susie have been so good to me."

"It was our pleasure. Be sure to keep in touch. And remember you're always welcome in our home."

The massive black engine expelled a hiss of steam, like a snort from a prehistoric beast. I was on my way. I leaned out the window, returning Douglas's wave through a billowing fog of smelly coal exhaust. When I could no longer see his diminishing shape, I put my head back inside and closed the window securely to try to keep out the dizzying odour of fuel.

As I leaned into the upholstered seat, I realised this was the first time since leaving home that I would have hours of solitude. Travelling, I had come to realise, fosters companionship—and what fine companions I had had.

CHAPTER 8

Tourists don't know where they've been,
travellers don't know where they're going.
Paul Theroux

"Next stop Norvals Pont," the conductor called as he walked from one carriage to the next. "Norvals Pont next." He repeated the announcement in Afrikaans.

In minutes the train arrived at the small country station. I looked out the window and saw that the few people waiting on the platform were male. Where was Bonnie? Had she forgotten I was arriving tonight? It hadn't occurred to me that I might be stranded! As my mind sped through possible solutions to this unexpected problem, a tall, slender man with round, horn-rimmed glasses, thinning hair and a moustache gestured to me to lower the window.

"Are you Kathy?" he asked, once I had pushed the glass down.

I nodded. How is everyone always able to identify me so easily?

"I'm Bonnie's father. Hand me your cases."

I obeyed his curious instruction, hoisting my suitcase with some difficulty to the required height and balancing it on the metal sill until he took control. As awkward as the exercise had been, it was nice to disembark luggage free.

"Welcome, Kathy. I'm Percy Southey," he said, shaking my hand. Short-sleeved shirt, long shorts, knee socks and polished brown shoes made Percy look like a character out of a novel of African exploration and adventure. The only thing missing was a pith helmet. "Bonnie's sorry she couldn't be here to meet you. She's been in bed for the past few days."

"Is it serious?" I asked with concern. Bonnie could be annoying at times but she didn't deserve to be bed-ridden.

"Nothing rest and proper care won't cure. The doctor says it's a form of malnutrition." Percy peered at me, perhaps checking to see if I suffered the same symptoms. "Apparently she didn't eat well on the boat."

My diagnosis of her problem was less kind: too many trips to the bar, not enough to the superb dining room. Sympathy for Bonnie's condition diminished.

We drove along a narrow, unlit dirt road to *Southford Stud*, the Southey farm. The main house had one of those lovely wide, covered verandahs, or *stoeps* as I now knew them to be called. At the sound of the car, the front door opened and an attractive, full-figured woman appeared. She had Bonnie's beautiful eyes, so I knew immediately who she was.

"Welcome, my girl. I'm Bonnie's mother Val. We're so happy you took the time to visit. It will mean a lot to Bon."

This piece of news surprised me. Bonnie and I had developed a cordial relationship but I wasn't aware it had reached a level where a visit from me would mean a lot to her.

Percy unloaded the cases from the car and we went inside.

When I entered Bonnie's room, she sat up in bed and greeted me with a feeble smile. Her transformation was shocking. Festering sores surrounded her mouth area and her once glowing features were now pale and drawn.

"Well look at you," I said with a grin.

If this wasn't poetic justice for Bonnie's sometimes uppity attitude, nothing was.

"I have malnutrition," she said with difficulty. She could barely move her lips. Her intense stare begged me to support this story and not to reveal any details of shipboard antics to her family.

"It must have been a lack of fruit on the ship, do you think?" I asked, maliciously enjoying my moment of power. Finally I looked better than Bonnie!

"Probably," came the muffled reply. Then I heard a strangled giggle. "Don't make me laugh," she pleaded. "It hurts too much."

I disregarded this instruction at every opportunity. Bonnie's parents were delighted she was in good spirits again and I was delighted to have the upper hand, even if it might be temporary.

Early the following morning I stepped outside to see the Karoo in daylight. The air still had a nip but already the sun was flexing its muscles. The landscape reflected the effect of chilly, mostly dry winters and hot, always dry summers. Occasional hills and outcrops broke the endless miles of otherwise flat, stoney semi-desert. A purple-blue haze cloaked the distant mountains, providing the only break in the prevalent colour scheme of grey-beige and infrequent splashes of green from sparse, low-growing vegetation and a row of shelter trees planted by the Southeys.

"The Karoo covers more than a third of South Africa. It's a part of the world that people either love or loathe. There's just no maybe," Dear Douglas had told me in Cape Town.

Now I understood the statement. At first glance, there was nothing here, no distractions, no noise, simply isolation. What a stark contrast to my own homeland of forests and lakes and fertile fields! Yet the desolate panorama spoke to me. It appeared barren only if you didn't make the effort to look closer. In my brief walk I noticed tiny flowers pushing their delicate heads out of the parched dirt. Geckoes sunbathed on rocks and a snake slithered down a hole that might have gone undetected. There was clearly more to the Karoo than a first glance revealed. I could learn to love this vast terrain.

When I returned to the house, Bonnie's dad stood on the *stoep*.

"Good morning, Kathy. Did you sleep well?"

"Like a log," I replied. "I feel so refreshed. I took the opportunity to do a little exploring."

"Did you see anything interesting?"

No doubt Percy would know by my answer whether I was a 'love' or 'loathe' person.

"More than I expected," I replied. "So much more."

Percy smiled and nodded. We quietly enjoyed the morning freshness.

"We own five farms which stretch pretty much as far as the eye can see, about fifteen thousand acres," Percy said eventually. "The Orange River is one of our borders. This is our son David's property. He's in Europe at the moment. The government expropriated the family homestead *Groenfontein* because the surveyors for the Hendrik Verwoerd Dam 'mistakenly' thought the property would be at risk with the flooding." Percy uttered these last words with a trace of bitterness. "We're fighting to get the place back but I sometimes despair of that ever happening. It's an Afrikaans government at the moment and we're British stock. Not a good formula for success."

"I'm so sorry. How terrible for you and your family," I said. "What an unimaginable loss."

"That's an understatement, my girl." After a moment's silence, he shrugged off the melancholy. "The land is so arid that properties have to be large in order to generate a decent income. Sheep farming is the main business in these parts. Karoo mutton is a delicacy. We breed racehorses as well."

"I'm used to seeing horses in grassy pastures. What would inspire anyone to have a stud farm in a semi-desert?"

"I know what you mean," Percy said with a laugh. "The land may not be green but it's rich in trace elements and calcium and the water has plenty of beneficial minerals. That plus the climate give us excellent horses. Would you like to see them?"

"Yes, please," came my enthusiastic reply. Like many females, I had a passion for horses.

We walked a short distance to the stables. A fleet of stable boys was busy grooming. The horses looked like equine versions of oiled bodybuilders.

"I don't suppose I could ride any of them?" I enquired hopefully.

"No, not these ones," Percy said firmly. "They're too highly strung. A leaf blowing across the path can make them skittish. We have stock ponies you and Bon can take out. They aren't smooth runners because the natives exercise them and they ride differently than whites. You'll get used to the gait, though."

As we headed back to the house, I asked about the windmill that lazily turned its arms in the light breeze.

"That's for water. The boreholes supply the house and the animals. In an emergency, we use it on the land," Percy explained. "We also have to produce our own electricity. It's enough for our basic needs but you'll find the lighting a bit dim. Survival is hard work in this part of the world."

Not only did Percy look like a character from an adventure book, he lived the life of one.

***

The daily routine at *Southford Stud* fascinated me. I never had lived in a house with what seemed like a platoon of full-time servants. Their black skin distinguished them from the lighter Cape Coloureds. Although everyone was respectful, they kept their emotional distance from me. I missed Isabella's open affection and spoiling attention.

"Do these people talk strangely?" I asked Val as I followed her into the kitchen one evening.

"They're Xhosa. They use clicking sounds in their language."

I listened as the women chatted among themselves in the musical dialect.

Val gave instructions for the preparation of a light supper and then walked with me into the living room. "Having all this help might look impressive but it's not easy," she explained. "Most of them need constant supervision. We look after large, extended, multi-generational families, so we try to give everyone something to do to keep them out of mischief."

Many of the girls had only one job to perform, such as cleaning the bird cages that hung on the *stoep*, or sweeping yesterday's dust.

One afternoon Val offered to have my clothes ironed. Because one of the dresses had extensive beadwork around the neck, I wanted to make sure the maid knew the trick to ironing it without causing damage. I found her working her way through a pile of laundry.

"Val, Val, come quickly," I shouted, shocked at what I saw.

Val ran in from the kitchen, wiping her hands on a dish towel.

"What's wrong?"

"What's wrong?" I repeated, surprised that she hadn't seen the problem instantly. "Look! That blackened piece of metal is going to ruin the clothes."

Val looked at the astonished maid and then at me.

"Kathy, that's an iron. She heats it on the stove." Val pointed to a fuel-burning cooker. "It won't damage anything if it's used properly. And the maid knows how to use it."

I was incredulous.

"My grandmother uses those as door stops. She told me they were antiques. It never occurred to me they're still used for their original purpose. I apologise."

Val laughed. Not all staff problems disappeared so easily.

"Because we have limited electricity, these suit the purpose perfectly. Don't worry about your clothes."

The ironing maid did a beautiful job, certainly better than anything I could have done myself, even with the fanciest steam iron. Another lesson to be absorbed: modern doesn't always trump traditional. More importantly, I had to learn not to make impulsive judgments about people and situations.

The Southeys ate their main meal at 1:00 pm and had a light supper in the evening. Lunch was virtually the same menu every day: Karoo mutton, fresh vegetables, fruit salad and homemade vanilla ice cream. Val's cooking demonstrated why Karoo mutton was so sought after.

"This is the best lamb I've ever had," I said with a sincerity prompted by my happy taste buds.

"We raise Vandon sheep," Percy explained. "Aside from being suitably hardy for this environment, they're bred with an emphasis on high-quality meat."

I uttered equally genuine praise for the desserts and came back for seconds.

"What are those seeds in the salad? They have the most amazing taste." I had singled out this mystery item as the ingredient that packed the punch.

"That's granadilla," Val answered. "You might know it as passion fruit."

"I don't know it by any name at all. This is the first time I've had it but it won't be the last. Granadilla has just become my favourite fruit."

"It grows throughout the southern hemisphere." Val asked one of the maids to bring a whole granadilla to the table. She handed me a dimpled, purple-brown fruit about the size of a billiard ball. "The inside has the seedy pulp you see in the salad. They're nutritious as well as delicious."

"This is the sort of thing you should be eating, right Bon?" A naughty smile accompanied my suggestion.

"Sounds like good advice, Sis." This support came from Geoff, one of Bonnie's two older brothers. He winked at me to show he was in on Bonnie's cover-up.

Bonnie grunted her agreement and gave each of us a steely look.

Most days Geoff joined us for lunch. He recently had returned from three years of working on stud farms in Australia and New Zealand. He owned *Montagu Stud*.

Similar facial features confirmed Bonnie and Geoff as siblings but there the physical similarity ended. Geoff was a tall, gangling redhead whose tanned skin was covered in freckles and a mat of curly reddish-blond hairs. He had that same impish spirit as Bonnie.

One day, instead of the usual fruit salad after lunch, a maid placed a plate in front of me. In the centre sat something that looked like a barbed hand grenade. A dessert knife and fork rested on either side of the plate. These were the only clues I had about how to eat this ... whatever it was.

"It's a prickly pear, Kath," Bonnie volunteered. "It's well named. Be sure not to touch the spines."

How was I supposed to eat it without touching the multitude of spines? I stared at the strange fruit, trying to figure out this culinary conundrum.

"Put your fork in the centre to secure it and then cut a slice off each end," Percy said as he demonstrated. "Slit the skin from end to end and use your knife and fork to peel it off."

Following Percy's lead, I discovered pale green flesh beneath the protective outer layer. I sampled a small piece. It tasted cool and refreshing, a perfect hot-weather food.

"I guess this is the South African equivalent of a watermelon," I said after more bites. "But a little trickier to eat."

"Prickly pears are the fruit of the cactus plant. Farmers like them because their thorns keep wildlife away from crops. Not only does this type of fencing not need repair, it feeds us," Geoff said.

Lunch wasn't the only opportunity for new eating experiences. As we sat having pre-dinner drinks one evening, Val came into the living room with a plate of small, thinly-sliced, brownish-red disks.

"Try some *biltong*," she said. "We make it ourselves."

I put a piece in my mouth. It had a pleasant spicy flavour but, my word, it took some chewing. I had expected a crunchy, easily-despatched texture, not something that involved time and effort. Everyone laughed at my predictable reaction.

"It's meant to be tough," Percy explained. "*Biltong* is a cured meat. When there used to be no means of refrigeration, meat spoiled quickly in the high temperatures. Curing was a perfect way for the early Dutch settlers to preserve meat on their long treks."

"Most rural families have their own recipes," Val continued. "We use springbok but you also can use other game, beef or ostrich. *Biltong* is Afrikaans for 'rump strip'. It's similar to the American beef jerky but *biltong* isn't sweet and is cured in chunks rather than slices. I used to give a stick to the children when they were teething; it would keep them happy for ages."

I helped myself to another slice, my new addiction.

Of course, eating well and having servants weren't the only aspects of life in the Karoo. As land owners and keepers of livestock, the Southeys had their share of anxieties. In a semi-desert, droughts are a constant threat. They can last for months or, in worst situations, for years. The consequences for farmers and their animals are devastating. Coming from Canada, which has the largest surface freshwater supply in the world, I tried to imagine an existence with little rainfall and limited ground water. The Karoo was teaching me to appreciate the blessing of this precious resource.

The fact that there hadn't been any rain in weeks was an ongoing cause for concern in the Southey household and a major topic of conversation at lunch one day.

"If something doesn't happen soon, we're buggered," Geoff worried. "The weather report still isn't positive."

"We get most of our rain in the winter," Bonnie told me. Her sores had healed and she was her animated self again. "We've had a couple of bad years, so it's particularly important that we have decent rain this year."

"You might not have to wait too long," I announced. Everyone gave me their full attention. "Grannie Scott says that when the leaves turn inside out, it's going to rain. She's never been wrong. I noticed that the trees look silvery today. Maybe the change in the wind direction means rain is coming."

No one said anything for a moment as they allowed themselves to be caught in my net of hope. Finally Percy spoke.

"I've never heard that before. Let's hope you're right, my girl."

Eventually the dry spell broke but not until well after I had left. Grannie's forecasting methods evidently didn't apply to Karoo conditions.

As much as I would like to have stayed on, after a remarkable week I knew it was time to bring my prolonged holiday to a close and report to work in Johannesburg. I contacted Professor Hahlo to let him know of my arrival.

Leaving *Southford* wasn't easy. Bonnie and I had solidified our friendship and her family had taken me in like one of their own.

"Here you are, my girlie," Val said as she handed me a wrapped package when we were about to say goodbye.

I looked at her questioningly.

"It's a supply of crunchies," she said with a broad smile. "I know how much you love them. Don't think I haven't noticed you raiding the crunchie tin on a regular basis! Let us know when you're coming again and I'll be sure to make an extra batch."

These sweet oatmeal bars were yet another food discovery I had made during my week with the Southeys. I gave Val a tight hug and promised to return soon if Bonnie could put up with me. Bonnie gave me a playful nudge and rolled her eyes.

"Chop-chop, Kath. You'll miss your train if you don't get a move on. I don't intend to be a bloody saint and put up with you forever."

Not for the first time, I reflected on how fortunate I was that good people had come into my life, enhancing my adventure. I couldn't imagine university being as much fun, or even as educational.

CHAPTER 9

I am not the same, having seen the moon shine
on the other side of the world.
Mary Anne Radmacher

The big old steam engine screeched to a final halt. After more than eight thousand miles and six weeks of travel by plane, boat, bus and train, I had arrived at my ultimate destination.

Johannesburg's covered station trapped the train's bilious coal smoke that rose to the roof and then settled on the crowds below. I accepted the offer of a porter's assistance and hurried to the exit to escape the cloying smell of the sooty smog.

So this is the 'wicked, money-hungry' capital of South Africa, I mused. No one I met who knew Johannesburg had a good word to say about the place, but in the clear, crisp winter air it appeared unthreatening. I hoped I would see the city's good side—if it had one.

Not wanting to interfere with Professor Hahlo's busy schedule, I had insisted on taking a taxi to his home in Craighall Park. As we passed Witwatersrand University, I turned to have another look. This was where Professor Hahlo held the lofty position of Dean of the Faculty of Law.

A man frantically waving in the car behind caught my attention. Good grief! It was Professor Hahlo. I asked the driver to stop as soon as possible. Professor Hahlo pulled in behind us. We ran towards each other.

"What are you doing here? You're supposed to be at work!"

"I couldn't let you arrive in Johannesburg for the first time and not have a welcome party. You were too fast leaving the station. I couldn't catch you. Come, I'll take you the rest of the way."

The taxi driver transferred the luggage.

"It seems you've had a pleasant journey?"

"Oh, yes! It just kept getting better and better."

"Dear Douglas and his family are enchanted by you," Professor Hahlo said with a smile.

"The feeling is mutual. What lovely, hospitable people. I could have stayed there forever but I really do need to get back to work."

"You can start whenever you like," he said as we drove north of the city centre. "Don't be surprised if you feel tired and have headaches for the first few days. Johannesburg is nearly six thousand feet above sea level, just over a mile. The air is thinner at this height, less oxygen."

"I feel fine so far," I said, certain my young, healthy body would be invincible to this impediment.

"Wait and see," was Professor Hahlo's only comment.

Along the way, he pointed to tall, grassy hills that had an almost uniform, flat-topped shape.

"Those are slag heaps. Waste from the gold mines. They plant grass on them to make them look better. Johannesburg's success was founded on the gold and diamond industries. Although the city has matured in the last hundred years, it still has mining town perils and instabilities."

"I have to admit, everyone offers their sympathy when they learn I'm going to live in Johannesburg."

"Yet people come here like pins drawn to a magnet. Where there's money there's greed." Professor Hahlo gave a resigned shrug.

We entered a leafy suburb with attractive houses and well-tended gardens. Professor Hahlo turned into his driveway and parked outside the garage.

The reserved, bird-like Mrs Hahlo was waiting for us. It had been evident when we first met in Montreal that having her husband's secretary live in her home for an indefinite period was not her situation of choice. Nevertheless, she had agreed—or had been persuaded to agree—to the arrangement. If she had hoped the trip would fall through, that hope was now dashed. Here I was on her doorstep.

My arrival elicited little more than a forced smile. Being back in South Africa after her sabbatical in Canada hadn't mellowed Mrs Hahlo's dour disposition. I missed the mothering warmth of Susie Duncan and Val Southey.

Mrs Hahlo showed me to my bedroom and bathroom and then took me around the rest of the moderately sized but beautifully decorated house. Paintings, sculptures and ceramics filled the rooms. Many of the attractive pottery displays had been done by Mrs Hahlo herself, a potter of some renown. I loved the artistic environment.

The grand tour included detailed instructions on the setting of burglar alarms in the evening.

"This is one of the oldest—and best—neighbourhoods," Mrs Hahlo said, allowing her nose to rise ever so slightly. "It's well patrolled and safer than most but one must always exercise caution. Vandalism and worse is rife in Johannesburg. Once the alarms have been set you cannot open any windows or doors until the system has been turned off."

She gave me a piercing look to make sure this important directive had been properly absorbed. I could only nod and pray I wouldn't inadvertently be the cause of police descending on the house under false pretences.

"Why is there so much crime here?" I asked.

"Because of the flood of black mine workers, tensions in Johannesburg are more fraught than in other parts of the country. Here, high levels of serious crime are the rule rather than the exception. Never, ever walk in the streets after dark," Professor Hahlo warned.

"And never go to any rough areas, even during the day," Mrs Hahlo added.

I nodded again, sobered by these pronouncements and thinking about the contrast with my own city. I could wander the streets of Montreal at any time of the day or night with no fear of assault. No one I knew had a burglar alarm.

Once I got past the anxiety of fitting into the Hahlo household, life developed a comfortable rhythm. Whenever possible, the Hahlos included me in their interesting social life. It might be Sunday lunch at the exclusive Bryanston Country Club or dinner with diplomats. An invitation to lunch at the home of Bertha Solomon merited an expanded briefing from Professor Hahlo.

"Bertha was one of South Africa's first female lawyers and is the country's foremost advocate of women's rights. Thanks to her campaigns, South African women now have entitlements in marriage. Bertha used to be a prominent parliamentarian until she retired about ten years ago. She's still a daunting personality," he said with a chuckle. "You're privileged to have the opportunity to socialise with one of South Africa's national treasures."

I never had heard of Bertha Solomon so I had to pretend enthusiasm about this supposed honour.

Although Bertha was gracious in her welcome, I felt overwhelmed by her intense energy. Being in her presence was like getting caught in a powerful intellectual current. It soon became apparent that Bertha was a character of the first order and had strong views about anything that mattered to her ... which covered quite a range. She probably won a lot of her landmark battles simply because she wore down the opposition.

On the day of our invitation, Bertha's company included writers, sculptors, painters and political and legal luminaries. I was the youngest guest and the only one who had not achieved a measure of fame, but I was made to feel welcome by the group. The stimulating, animated discussions gave me thoughts and theories to ponder long after the lunch. This, I decided that day, was the type of eclectic atmosphere I wanted to emulate when I eventually had my own social gatherings.

***

Thanks to Dear Douglas's connections, I had employment as soon as I got to Johannesburg. Thanks to Professor Hahlo's recommendations, my salary was at the top end of the scale. These foregone conclusions didn't endear me to the man who had to put me on his payroll.

"I can't use you!" announced a short, grey-haired man who barely gave me a passing glance as he blew into the cramped, three-room office in downtown Johannesburg on my first day of work. "What's the point of taking the time to train you if you plan to return to Canada in a few months?"

This was my unconventional introduction to Dr Hillel A Shapiro. I stood wide-eyed, too stunned to give a response. Only now did it occur to me that Dr Shapiro wouldn't want his staffing dictated by others.

Just as I was about to offer to look for another job, Dr Shapiro apologised for his outburst. He gruffly briefed me on my duties and then disappeared into the seclusion of his office, firmly closing the door behind him. I slumped into the chair at my assigned desk, shell-shocked.

"He's not the easiest person," one of the office girls said in a low voice, "but he's not unfair. He respects anyone who works hard."

"And makes life unbearable for under-performers," the other woman warned.

Now that Dr Shapiro had given his grudging approval, my co-workers introduced themselves and brought me up to speed on office routines.

Three days after starting work, Dr Shapiro announced he was keeping me full time.

"I thought I already was full time," I said.

"I'm sure you were led to believe that." He rubbed the back of his neck. "Professor Hahlo offered to take you twice a week if I didn't have enough for you to do. You're working out well, though. It will be easier if I keep you here."

Once again, Professor Hahlo had been busy behind the scenes on my behalf, like an employment guardian angel.

A couple of weeks later, to everyone's surprise, Dr Shapiro promoted me from general dogsbody to being his private secretary in charge of advertising for his medical journals and of looking after the office during his many absences. Dr Shapiro's bark had been worse than his bite.

I never got excited about secretarial work but involvement in the production of monthly journals captivated me. As well as dealing with the advertisers—and sometimes convincing them to place larger or more expensively positioned ads—I was required to do layouts. Instead of keeping to traditional placements, I experimented with moving the articles and ads around. This sometimes resulted in interesting white spaces that made the pages look more visually appealing. The exercise awoke in me a nascent creative talent.

Dr Shapiro, pleased with the results, was generous enough to show it. When I told him I would be going to visit Bonnie for the weekend, he gave me an extra day and a half off work.

"It's a long trip," he said as he rearranged stacks of papers on his desk. "You might as well make it worth your while." With a hint of a smile, he added, "Enjoy the break. The Karoo is a beautiful part of the world."

The train journey was three hundred seventy miles, so I was grateful to have the extra time.

It was wonderful to be back at *Southford Stud*. Bonnie's brother Dave had returned from Europe the day before my arrival so the house had a festive atmosphere. Of the three siblings, Dave seemed to possess the solitary sensible gene, although he also exhibited the zany traits of his younger brother and sister. He welcomed me as sincerely and enthusiastically as the rest of the family. I was in love with each and every one of them.

The comfortable Southey home embraced the weekend's planned and unexpected drop-ins. Dave McQuoid-Mason, Bonnie's romantic interest from the ship, made a surprise appearance. Dave was as fun-loving and personable on land as he had been at sea. He and Bonnie made a beautiful couple. Liz Chapman, an Australian whom Bonnie and her brother Dave had met in England, also showed up. Liz is one of life's ultra capable creatures. Being around her made me feel less competent. She didn't have a warm, fuzzy personality but I admired her self-assurance.

In addition to the house guests, there were constant comings and goings of local friends and relatives. The weekend was awash with parties and laughter. I was grateful for the additional leave Dr Shapiro had given me.

The most positive outcome of the long weekend at *Southford* was that Bonnie announced she would join me in Jo'burg and try to get work. The timing was good. I needed to stop imposing on the hospitality of the Hahlos and find my own accommodation. When I mentioned a move to Dr Shapiro, he suggested contacting his former secretary, a Mrs McKenzie, who had a spare room to rent. This solution would be more economical than leasing an apartment, especially since I didn't know how long I would stay in Johannesburg.

Mrs McKenzie lived in Rosebank. Jo'burg's Rosebank wasn't as exclusive as the Cape Town Rosebank where the Duncans lived but it was nevertheless a lovely neighbourhood in the safer northern suburbs. My new landlady charged an affordable rent and provided a bright, spacious room. She agreed Bonnie could live there as well.

Mrs M, a tall, slender, middle-aged woman was pleasant enough but she tended towards the aloof Mrs Hahlo personality. Maybe there was something in the Jo'burg air that made people less open, more suspicious. Despite her reserve, we had developed an enjoyable routine of sitting on the *stoep* after work and chatting. She volunteered little information about herself—for example, where was the mysterious Mr McKenzie?—but I mined many nuggets of local lore from her. These evening conversations helped expand my knowledge of South African history, geography, flora and fauna but fell short on the political scale. What little Mrs M said on the subject indicated she was anti-apartheid but, like a number of individuals I had met, she chose not to be outspoken with people she didn't know well. I had heard murmurings about a repressive police force and assumed such caution was well-founded.

"I have a nephew your age," Mrs M announced one evening. "His name is Tim Everett. Tim's mother is my sister. Would you like to meet him?"

I evidently had passed her scrutiny during my settling-in period.

"That would be great," I replied. "I haven't met any young people in the city."

Nor was I likely to if I continued my limited office/home routine.

Aside from being in steady saving mode to pay for ongoing travel, I had no inclination to explore Johannesburg's nightlife which, by all accounts, could be dangerous.

Tim joined us for drinks the following evening. I liked him right away. He looked sporty enough to be able to row across the Atlantic or ski down Everest and sophisticated enough to be comfortable on the deck of a yacht with a martini in his hand. The clincher, though, was the twinkle in the eye. It seemed from his easy conversation and disinclination to leave that he liked me too. Not boyfriend-girlfriend like but good friends like, which is what we became.

Tim lived with his parents and older brother in a large, thatched-roof house in Sandton, a nearby suburb that seemed to specialise in estate-like properties. The Everetts had a clay court where Tim tried to teach me how to play tennis. I would never have Tim's expertise but that didn't make me less passionate about the game. Tim also insisted on giving me driving lessons. My skill set was expanding almost faster than I could cope.

Bonnie's arrival a couple of weeks later made the picture complete, especially when she took to Tim as easily as I had.

"He's a *lekker ou*," Bonnie said approvingly.

I had learned this description meant 'great guy'.

The friendships were sorted but Bonnie still needed a job. She had never worked, so finding employment that interested her was a challenge. I turned to Dear Douglas. Perhaps he could steer Bonnie in the right direction via his web of contacts.

"Don't worry, Kathy," Douglas assured me. "We'll find her something at Juta's bookshop. They can always use an extra pair of hands. The store isn't far from where you work, so you girls can meet up during your lunch breaks."

Bonnie's artistic temperament wasn't cut out for the tedium of a desk job but she gave it a good try … usually.

"It's not a life sentence, Bon. It's a temporary job that pays your bills. Suck it up, girl," I had to remind her. She had every blessing in the book. It wouldn't hurt her to come down to my level and do an honest day's work.

The arrival in Jo'burg of Bonnie's brother Dave broke the period of monotony Bonnie was suffering. Horse business had brought him to town for a few days. As a treat, he offered to take us to the races, another new experience for me.

We followed Dave around the enclosures, paying close attention to comments he made as he scrutinised each horse and discussed details with trainers and riders.

"C'mon, Kath, forget budgeting for one day. We have to place a bet," Bonnie chided.

"Fine, but this is your world. You'll have to show me what to do."

"There's nothing to it. We pick a horse—preferably a winner—hand our money to the bookie, get a ticket and watch the race. I'll take care of it for you."

Dave had no insider tips for us so I persuaded Bonnie to bet on a horse based on name rather than form. She took my money and came back with our receipt. We returned to the stands.

As the starting bell clanged, I felt my heartbeat increase to match the rhythm of the pounding hoofs. For much of the race, our chosen horse performed with steady mediocrity. Then, in the final stretch, his speed suddenly increased. The other horses were inhaling his dust.

"Oh my god," I shouted in disbelief as he crossed the finish line. "We've won! That's the horse we chose!"

"Talk about beginner's luck," Bonnie grinned as we hugged each other excitedly.

We hurried to the betting area to claim our win.

"Sorry, luv," the teller said as he checked our ticket. "You accidentally picked the stall number, not the horse's number." He pointed to the correct column on the list. "Better luck next time."

Bonnie and I looked at each other in astonishment.

"Oops. Sorry, Kath."

How could Bonnie have slipped up on something so basic? Then we both laughed.

"Why am I surprised?" I asked, shaking my head.

Life was always a little more complex when Bonnie was around.

Kathy Cuddihy

CHAPTER 10

Sometimes when you're in a dark place you think
you've been buried but you've actually been planted.
Christine Caine

Once again, I had taken the opportunity to escape from Johannesburg for another exceptional weekend at *Southford Stud*. Now, Sunday lunch marked the approaching end. The tell-tale buzz of a small aircraft flying low over the house interrupted the pleasant flow of conversation. The sound lessened for a minute then returned at full volume.

"That might be for me," I announced excitedly as we all jumped up from the table to see what was going on. Everyone stopped and gave me a mystified look. "Hurry, let's check it out," I said rushing out the door before having to answer awkward questions.

Once he saw people outside, the pilot tipped his wings up and down in an aeronautical greeting. Then he dropped a tiny parachute from his side window. Without hesitation, I raced across the thorn-covered ground. My high emotional state overruled any complaints from my bare feet. I retrieved the prize and ran back to the house. Breathlessly, I read the message to the curious gathering: *Hello, Gorgeous. Can you come for a spin later? If not, have a good trip back to Jo'burg and I'll see you the next time you're here.*

Bonnie cocked her head, waiting for an explanation. We had reached the stage where we shared every detail of our lives. How, she must have wondered, did she not know about this unexpected and dramatic development? The rest of the Southey family looked equally bemused.

"His name's Ken," I said with a blush. "He's a Rhodesian I met at the club last night."

"Evidently you impressed him," Val said with a laugh.

I did more than create an impression. What began as an innocent night out ended in a loss of innocence.

I replayed in my mind the events of the previous evening. The country club's fun Saturday night atmosphere beckoned. Bonnie and her brothers felt exhausted from party overdose but I didn't want to waste a moment of my precious weekend with the Southeys. Finally I persuaded Dave Southey to take his girlfriend and me dancing.

We met up with other friends. Then, Ken, a stranger in his mid twenties, introduced himself into our group—apparently so he could meet me. I quickly sized him up as 'medium': medium height, medium-brown hair and medium attraction. He excelled, however, at perseverance. Eventually his charming persistence eroded my reserve. We danced and chatted for the rest of the evening.

When Dave signalled that it was time to leave, Ken quickly intervened.

"Don't worry, I'll take Kathy home."

And take me home he did. But first we made a detour to his home. We had a drink, we had a chat and suddenly we were in the midst of having ... sex.

Every virgin dreams of or dreads The First Time. I had visions of being swept off my feet by The One whose adoration and masterful seduction would seal the bonds of our love. Or some such thing.

Alas, the reality bore no resemblance to the fantasy. Ken didn't quite belong to the wham-bam-thank-you-ma'am school of sex but neither did he exhibit any enticing love-making skills. Or perhaps I was too distracted by the nagging thoughts swirling in my head: *You're about to lose your virginity. Are you ready? Is this the guy you want to deflower you?* Then, while weighing possible answers, the deed was done. It was technically uninspiring and, for me at least, anti-climatic ... literally. *What was all the fuss about?*

I didn't have to worry about pregnancy: girl gossip had been explicit that there were no risks the first time. "It's like having a free pass, to see if you like it or not," I remembered someone saying—and no one contradicting.

The only positive to come out of this non-event, I mused before falling asleep, was that the burden of chastity had been lifted.

But getting over one hurdle presented another. Would everyone know I had had sex? Irrational concerns dominated my fertile imagination. Would I have a bow-legged stance? Would my face break out in pimples? Would I smell different? Act different? These worries put a damper on any feeling of accomplishment.

At breakfast I kept alert for glances which screamed *I know what you've been up to*. Or double-edged comments. Nothing. Absolutely nothing. Had everyone been doing what I had been doing and no one wanted to cast the first stone? Or was having premarital sex less deplorable than the Catholic Church had led me to believe? It came as no small relief that the after-effects were no more noteworthy than the event itself.

"So what's the answer, Kath?" Bonnie asked, interrupting my reverie.

I looked at her blankly, not having registered the question.

"Are you going to take Ken up on his offer?"

"I think I will," I replied. "Would you like to come along?"

"Sure, if you don't think I'll cramp your style."

"No worries, Bon," I said with conviction.

After lunch, Bonnie and I went to the nearby flying club.

"Hello, ladies," Ken said, winking at me. Thankfully he made no reference to our late-night activities. "I'm about to take someone up for a lesson but you're welcome to come along."

"Would it be better if we come back later?" I felt my cheeks burning.

"It's not a problem, I promise. As long as you don't distract me." This last statement was accompanied by a conspiratorial smile and yet another wink in my direction.

Taking off in Ken's four-seater Cessna brought back fond memories of flying with my parents who both had private pilot licenses. After a brief taxi along the dirt strip, we soared above the Karoo's beige terrain. Within minutes we escaped all evidence of civilisation. Long-necked ostriches stared up at us and then scattered to some imaginary safety; springbok, more organised in their flight, veered left and then right in an attempt to evade this unfamiliar threat. I felt like I was part of a National Geographic film crew.

We carried on over hilltops and across plains. And then the unthinkable happened.

Shifting my glance from the side window to the front, I realised I could see the blades of the propeller. They were still going pretty fast, but each blade should *not* have been distinguishable. Then the revolutions became slower ... and slower. I took another look at the beautiful but desolate Karoo and wondered if anyone would find the plane wreckage. Would my parents have a body to bury? I had promised not to distract Ken so I said nothing. Presumably he, too, had seen the problem. Screams from me wouldn't help. In lieu of suffering the trauma of the upcoming crash, I passed out.

"Kath, wake up. What's the matter with you?" Bonnie said as she shook my slumped body.

Slowly my eyes refocused.

"Everything OK back there?" Ken asked, turning in his seat.

"I saw the propellers stop turning," I said, astonished we were still airborne, and that the propellers were once again a reassuring blur.

"Sorry, I should have told you beforehand. Today's lesson was how to recover from a stall. We stop the engine and restart it."

I nodded, feeling a little foolish—and much relieved to be alive to tell the tale.

As we chatted over drinks in the club afterwards, I once again saw Ken exactly as I had first seen him: in tones of medium. He had attracted me with *his* attention but he had nothing of substance to hold *my* attention.

"So, Kath," Bonnie said on the way back to *Southford*, "is this the man of the moment?"

"No, Bon. This was just a flight of fancy."

***

During my fourth month in Johannesburg, I had a searing premonition of a bad car accident. Intuition told me there would be no fatalities but knowing I would be the main victim and would be seriously injured made me paranoid about making unnecessary car journeys. After two weeks, I had had enough.

"I'm going stir-crazy, Bonnie. I need to get out of the house. If an accident's going to happen, it's going to happen. I'm probably just delaying the inevitable."

"Great. Let's give Tim a call. We can go into town for a drink," she replied, already heading towards the telephone.

Twenty minutes later, Tim knocked at the door.

"I'm going to take you girls to a smart hotel bar in the city," he announced. "You've been cooped up too long. We need to celebrate your release."

We piled into Tim's Volkswagen. I sat in the back, as usual, because Bonnie claimed she needed the extra leg room offered in the front seat. Tim dropped us off at the door of the hotel and parked nearby. For the next two hours we enjoyed the elegant surroundings and each others' company. It felt good to get out. The disquiet seemed to be receding, as though it had exhausted itself.

Then, three unusual events allowed Fate to play her hand. First, in a moment of mischief, Tim and Bonnie ran ahead to the car and drove off. They were gone only a couple of minutes while Tim drove around the block but those minutes made a difference. When the car pulled up beside me, Bonnie opened the door and insisted that I get in the front seat with her. This wasn't something she normally would suggest. Nor would I usually agree to the three of us cramming into the front. Yet I gave in easily enough. The third event came a few minutes later. As the song *Those Were The Days* played on the radio, I thought that these really were the best days of my life, living the adventure I had dreamed about. Out of the corner of my eye, I saw a speeding car headed towards us from a cross street. Tim swerved so his side would take the brunt of the crash. I braced myself against the dashboard. The last thing I remember before we were hit was relief: the strain of the premonition instantly disappeared.

I became aware of someone opening my door. *Why is a man trying to get into the car? Is this a carjacking or a robbery? And what am I doing on the floor instead of on the seat? Where are Bonnie and Tim?* The stranger scooped me into his arms. I didn't protest.

"There's a theatre across the street. Take her there," I heard someone say.

The man gently lay me on a table. *If this is a theatre, am I on stage?* Then, somehow, I was in an ambulance. I have no recollection of moving between the two locations. Bonnie was by my side, holding my hand and looking worried. It seemed she wasn't injured.

"Don't let them give me stitches, Bon. Promise me you won't let them give me stitches." I squeezed her hand tightly to reinforce the importance of this request. She looked at me with agony in her eyes. "Promise me, Bon, *please.*"

"I'll do what I can, Kath," she finally agreed.

For some reason, I put my hand to my face ... and lifted off half my nose. The problem was more serious than I had imagined. Now I understood Bonnie's reluctance to promise the impossible.

As they wheeled me into Emergency, one doctor said to the other, "This one should have been DOA."

Television hadn't arrived in South Africa so there was no regimen of popular doctor shows to expand the population's medical vocabulary. Presumably the doctor figured I wouldn't understand the abbreviation. Wrong. I became so angry at his unchecked words and premature pronouncement that it put the fight back in me.

"What the bloody hell do you mean 'dead on arrival'? It will take more than a goddam car accident to kill me."

I spewed a slew of expletives—words I had heard or read but previously never uttered—and told him to concentrate on keeping me alive instead of wondering why I wasn't dead. The outburst got their surprised attention; we now worked as a team to save me.

"Make sure she's under observation for the next twenty-four hours," the doctor instructed his nurse after he finished stitching me up. "If she gets past that, she'll probably make it."

South African doctors certainly didn't make much of an effort at discretion in front of their patients. An orderly wheeled me from Emergency to a ward.

A middle-aged nurse with curly yellow hair and a pasty, pockmarked complexion placed a chair beside my bed and took up residence. Evidently 'close observation' meant exactly that. Here they didn't rely on multi-tasking bodies monitoring machines from an isolated nursing station.

"Were you wearing a seat belt?" my watcher asked tersely.

"No," I mumbled, offended by her aggressive approach towards a defenseless patient who might be dead in a few hours.

She gave me a lecture about how this wouldn't have happened with a seatbelt. I couldn't disagree but I also suspected that even a seatbelt might have been useless against the course of Fate. As my eyelids began to lose the battle with fatigue, I wondered if I would wake up. Would my determination to survive be enough?

The noise of hospital activity dragged me back to a state of consciousness: the clanking of carts delivering meals and medications, announcements on the public address system and the beeping of various pieces of life-saving machinery, none of which was attached to me. I opened my eyes to bright sunlight pouring into the ward. Nurse Grumpy still sat stoically in her chair. Now she was reading the morning paper.

"Good morning," she said in a more pleasant tone than she had used during our previous conversation. "How are you feeling?"

I thought about that for a second. Was she asking if I was remorseful for not wearing a seatbelt? I decided to answer along medical lines.

"Sore, I guess. I have a headache but otherwise I seem to be fine. Have I made it past the twenty-four hours? Am I going to survive?"

"You're about halfway there but I don't think there's any doubt you'll make it. The doctors are impressed with your spirit. It's what saved your life. Still, you lost a lot of blood and had a bad concussion. Recovery will take awhile."

Bonnie and Tim came to see me as soon as they were allowed. They assured me neither of them had anything worse than a few bad bruises to show for the accident. When I pressed them, I learned that Tim had torn the ligaments in his shoulder and that Bonnie had flattened the gear lever with her knee. Bruises indeed!

However, the fact they were alive and relatively well tallied with my premonition that I would suffer the worst injuries.

Visitors tried to hide any sign of dismay but I could see in their eyes that I must have looked worse than I felt. When I finally had the courage to look in the mirror, I understood their angst. A monster stared back at me. Large black stitches, laid out like sleepers on a railway line, secured my nose onto my face. Two more sets went from the outer corner and the middle of the top of my right eye socket, up my forehead and into my scalp. Dried blood crusted around the wound areas. Why hadn't anyone cleaned me? As I examined my face more closely, I noticed a few small bumps on my bloated cheeks. Gently picking at them, I released pieces of glass.

After the initial shock diminished, one of my first thoughts was the stark certainty that no one would want to marry me. I was surprisingly acceptant of this realisation, already understanding it wouldn't do any good to dwell on negatives. *People will have to like me for who I am, not for how I look.* I knew I had to learn to accept the new me. If I couldn't do this, how could I expect it of others?

Bonnie, my most frequent visitor, explained what had caused the accident.

"It was an eighteen-year-old girl who drove through the stop sign. Instead of braking, she put her foot on the accelerator. You went through the windscreen and came back again. It's lucky you didn't lose your eye ... or worse."

I didn't feel lucky. In fact, I might have sunk into an abyss of self-pity had it not been for the patient across from me. She sat in a chair beside her bed. There was an easel in front of her—and a paintbrush in her mouth. When I got up to have a look at what she was doing, she bent her head and released the brush onto the table.

"Car crash," she explained. "I'm paralysed from the neck down. I used to be a successful artist. The accident took almost everything from me. I refuse to let it take my talent as well. I'm learning to paint with my mouth."

Her quiet strength compelled me to feel less sorry for myself and recognise my good fortune.

After numerous entreaties, I persuaded the doctors not only to release me several days earlier than planned but also to let me return to work.

At first, sudden, blinding headaches prevented me from spending more than a brief time at the office each day. Dr Shapiro kept a close eye on me and subtly tested for neurological damage.

"Would you mind bringing me a sharp pencil, my printer's phone number and a copy of last month's medical journal?"

Invariably, I would arrive at my desk and forget one or two of the requested items.

"You suffered serious head injury," he said. "Because you're young and healthy you'll make a good recovery but it won't be one hundred per cent."

Dr Shapiro didn't mince words. I thought of the paralysed artist and decided I had got off lightly with moderately impaired mental acuity.

Getting used to radically altered features wasn't easy. On my lunch break when I was in a department store, a little girl saw me and screamed. When her mother turned to see what the problem was, her hand flew to her mouth and she pulled her daughter closer to her. Their reactions reminded me I had the face of a freak. I left the crowded shop, my enthusiasm for browsing spoiled.

Outside, a one-legged black man on crutches came toward me. Ordinarily I might have averted my gaze but that's something people were doing to me these days and I didn't like it. *Look beyond appearance,* I wanted to shout, but most people, I realised, wouldn't listen. The black man and I made eye contact and smiled. In this mute exchange we expressed the message that our physical aspects may have altered but we were whole inside.

***

Johannesburg had chewed me up and spit me out. With the exception of Tim and Bonnie, I had no friends my age and no compelling reason to remain in the city. Professor Hahlo, of course, was a comforting presence but, despite his good intentions, his wife made it clear I wasn't part of their world. Dr Shapiro had come to value me and allowed me much creative freedom. He was disappointed but understanding when I gave him my resignation. A part of me hated to quit what had become an interesting job but another part of me knew it was time to move on. But to where?

Bonnie and I chatted on Mrs M's verandah one evening after work. I watched her perform the soothing ritual of putting tobacco on a cigarette paper, neatly rolling it and licking the paper shut. I never had smoked and had no desire to start the habit, but I enjoyed the feeling of calm from the aroma.

"So, Kath, what's next?" she asked after exhaling her first satisfying drag.

"Durban is next," I said.

The idea of a trip to Durban had been inspired by my shipboard acquaintance Dirk Caney. On impulse, I contacted him to see if he still felt inclined to have the pair of us as guests. His positive response would allow us to see a different part of the country.

"Not that next, man," she said, refusing to be sidetracked. "I'm talking about after Durban and after Christmas."

"I don't know. This accident has stifled my get-up-and-go. Maybe it's time to go home."

"No way, man. You promised you'd think about Australia. Geoff had a great time there. He has tons of contacts and says it wouldn't be any problem to get jobs. You can't go home yet. Your adventure isn't over."

Bonnie's brother Geoff had regaled us with endless cattle and sheep station stories. The idea of experiencing that life ourselves appealed to both of us. As tempted as I was to return home, Bonnie had a point. If I could find the courage to continue, my adventure didn't have to end just yet. Besides, if I was ever going to look Grannie Daley in the eye again, I had better get myself around the world.

"I tell you what, Bon," I said, still undecided. "Let's flip a coin. If it's heads, we go to Canada, tails we go to Australia. Deal?"

"Deal," Bonnie said.

She produced a coin and did the honours. We watched it spin

upwards and descend, the author of our destiny.

"Tails!" Bonnie shouted triumphantly.

One of my mother's pithy quotes came into my head: *he who hesitates is lost.*

"Tails it is," I acknowledged with resignation. "I guess we should start planning."

CHAPTER 11

If you're too comfortable, it's time to move on.
Terrified of what's next? You're on the right track.
Susan Fales-Hill

"**W**hat do you mean we can't get a booking?" Bonnie exclaimed.

"There's absolutely nothing available," I confirmed with a shrug. "I've gone to several travel agents. They've looked at everything, from freighters to liners. It seems everyone wants to go to Australia at the same time we do."

Because we had had such a good time on the voyage to South Africa, we hoped to repeat the experience by sailing to Australia. Flying, we agreed, was too conventional.

"So it looks like that coin we flipped is still in the air," Bonnie said philosophically. "Let's let Fate be the guide. Things will work out as they're meant to work out. In the meantime, we can focus on going to Durban and then having a great Christmas with the family."

"Since there aren't any evident options at the moment, we don't have a choice," I pointed out.

After the accident that had nearly taken my life, the pull of Canada had become stronger. Part of me yearned for the familiarity and security that family and friends could offer. Yet, the unwounded side of me, the adventurous side, was disappointed that Australia no longer seemed to be on the cards. If I went home now, I would never achieve my ambition to travel around the world before I turned twenty-one. It was easier to adopt Bonnie's reasoning and not worry about situations we couldn't influence. We had plenty to keep us busy for the coming weeks.

As keen as I was to visit Dirk Caney and see a different part of

South Africa, I wondered if I was being fiscally reckless. Now that I was unemployed, I needed to spend cautiously. The unexpected arrival of Bonnie's brother Dave in Johannesburg a couple of days before our planned departure made it tempting to abandon the trip to Durban and get a free ride back to the Karoo.

"The final decision is yours, Bon. Once you decide, though, don't change your mind. Repeatedly."

Bonnie's lack of response was an admission of her occasional indecisiveness.

We tied up loose ends in Johannesburg, said our goodbyes and got ready to leave ... to wherever. As we sat having a coffee on Mrs M's verandah, Tim pulled into the driveway.

"Give me your bags, girls," he announced. "No more flip-flopping about what you're going to do and where you're going to go. It's decision time. I'm taking you to the station. Being there might prompt you to catch the Durban train—which is what I think you should do and what Dave thinks you're doing. If you change your mind, you can always go back with him tomorrow."

We discussed the pros and cons all the way to the station and were still debating as we stood on the platform. In case the outcome was Durban, I loaded the luggage onto the train.

"No, Kath, I honestly think it's better to go home," Bonnie announced firmly.

Off came the luggage.

"Bonnie, this is a good opportunity to see something different. How many sugar plantations have you visited? If Dirk's behaviour on the ship is anything to go by, he will be a great host. We can go to *Southford* later," I argued.

Bonnie paced.

"OK. You're probably right," she said with reluctance.

On went the luggage. Bonnie, however, remained on the platform, still dithering.

A piercing whistle and the noisy release of the train's brakes settled the dispute. The luggage and I were on our way to Durban. Bonnie sprinted along the platform and reached for my outstretched hand.

"Why is everything you do punctuated with a dose of drama," I asked as Bonnie clambered on board.

We found two seats and sat back to catch our breath and enjoy the journey. When the conductor arrived, he took longer than normal to examine our tickets.

"There seems to be a misunderstanding, ladies," he said. "My list shows no reservations in your names. When did you buy the tickets?"

"A few minutes ago," I answered.

Fate, it seemed, had put us on the train but had not attended to the paperwork! The conductor scowled at the administrative error. He remedied the situation by giving us a vacant private compartment. Our holiday was off to a nice start.

***

"Welcome to Durban," Dirk said. "It's great to see you both again."

As Dirk approached to give us each a hug he did an involuntary double-take when he noticed the angry scars on my face. "What happened, Kathy?"

"Car accident in Jo'burg," I said self-consciously. "This is a big improvement over what I looked like a few weeks ago." Then, trying to make light of the moment, I added, "When you warned me about the dangers of the city, I didn't think you meant inexperienced drivers."

"Hell, Kath. What bad luck. In time I'm sure you'll make a full recovery. It can't be easy, though." Dirk gave me a comforting hug and a gentle kiss on the forehead.

"Come on, you two. Let's go home. It's about half an hour's drive to the house."

Once we left the city, Bonnie and I marvelled at the beautiful countryside. The rolling green hills were a sharp contrast to anything I had seen in South Africa.

"Natal is called the garden province," Dirk remarked.

"Do people here have more gardens than elsewhere in the country?" I asked.

"I don't think so," Dirk replied. "Garden refers to the fact that just about anything grows here. The coastal area is subtropical. Inland it's rich agricultural land. As you know," he said, looking at Bonnie, "much of the country is semi-desert. Natal is a welcome exception to the rule."

Soon we arrived at *Tongaat*. Fields of leggy stalks of sugar cane bordered the drive to the house and stretched as far as the eye could see.

"What does Tongaat mean?" Bonnie asked from the back seat. Since Dirk was my contact, I got the rare honour of sitting in the front.

"It comes from the Zulu word for the trees that grow along a local river, the Tongati. This land is part of the Zulu Nation."

"Aren't Zulus fierce warriors?" I asked.

"True," Dirk chuckled. "Zulus are famed for their fighting skills. And for their tall good looks."

As the car pulled up to the house, a very tall, very fit, very good-looking black man appeared at the door. If he was representative of the rest of the Zulu Nation, no wonder they had such a reputation.

"This is Nduduzo," Dirk said. "His name means 'make one feel better', which is what I hope he does while you're here." Dirk looked directly at me and gave a cheeky smile, waylaying the concerns about being in proximity to a warrior that had floated into my imagination. "Nduduzo looks after the house. If you need anything, just ask him."

After lunch Dirk suggested a tour of the estate.

"This is what the canes look like when they're ready to be cut." Dirk stopped the car and we got out to walk along a row of green vegetation that stood more than six feet. It was hard to imagine these thick, fibrous stalks with grassy leaves morphing into a bag of supermarket sugar. "In order to harvest the cane, we burn the fields. This gets rid of most of the snakes and other vermin but leaves the stalks undamaged."

We returned to the car and drove to another part of the estate where hundreds of black men laboured in the large field.

"Workers grab a handful of stalks, bend them and cut them

with machetes," Dirk explained. "The stalks are processed within twenty-four hours of cutting and then sent to Durban for refining."

The task looked hard, dirty and potentially dangerous. Not a single man acknowledged our arrival or broke the grab-bend-cut rhythm.

"They have a quota to fill," Dirk explained. "It's usually between one hundred thirty and one hundred sixty rows each day. A skilled worker can harvest about one thousand pounds an hour. Labourers who don't meet the quota have their pay docked. It's long hours, usually without a break."

"But it must be well compensated," I stated. Surely there was a rainbow at the end of each back-breaking day.

"They get minimum wage and have food and housing provided."

"Aren't those costs deducted from their salaries?" Bonnie asked.

Was she trying to stir the political pot? I assumed Dirk sat on the liberal side of the fence but perhaps Bonnie suspected otherwise.

"True," Dirk admitted. He seemed unperturbed by Bonnie's question. "It's not ideal but the workers at *Tongaat* are better off than on a lot of estates."

We weren't taken to the workers' housing area. After Bonnie's remark, this was probably by design. Dirk's firm but respectful attitude towards the men assured me he wasn't an abusive employer but it still upset me to see conditions that exploited the black population and enriched the whites. I had heard pro-apartheid arguments about the paternalistic way whites looked after the natives. Although I never witnessed examples to the contrary, there were plenty of disturbing stories. On a corporate level, oppression evidently flourished. This was a side to the otherwise idyllic society I couldn't condone.

Our two enjoyable days at *Tongaat* broadened my knowledge of both the sugar industry and the plight of native workers. The clash between big business and human dignity made me more aware of the true cost of some products.

Shortly before we left, Dirk made a suggestion.

"My step-brother Ian lives in Durban. He's a couple of years older than you girls. I could ask him to give you a call and set something up."

"Sounds good to me," Bonnie replied immediately. She looked at me to back up her decision.

"Thanks, Dirk," I agreed. "We have a few days in Durban, so it would be nice to have a contact."

As promised, Ian phoned our hotel and invited us out for a night on the town.

"It's probably easiest if my friend and I meet you in your lobby. Would 8:00 pm suit you?"

Sure enough, at the appointed hour, two fellows approached us.

"Are you Ian?" I asked the one who walked straight up to me.

"That's right, luv. And this here's Andy."

Bonnie and I introduced ourselves and exchanged uneasy glances. Telephone Ian had sounded more refined.

"What say we go upstairs to the bar for a get-to-know-ya drink?" Ian suggested.

We ordered drinks and 'got to know' each other. As the conversation progressed, I found the behaviour of this burly brute increasingly offensive. *How could Dirk have done this to us?* Bonnie was faring no better with her partner. In the course of the conversation, it transpired that Ian didn't have a clue who Dirk was! Bonnie and I quickly excused ourselves from their company.

"But you promised to come back to the ship with us," they bullied in loud voices.

We fled down the stairs, not daring to risk getting stuck in the antique elevator.

There in the lobby, waiting patiently for us, were two beautiful, clean-cut young men. We rushed up to them and hastily asked them to identify themselves. To our relief, it was the real Ian and his friend.

"We arrived just as you were going off with those other fellows," Ian said. "We didn't know whether you were leaving by choice or mistake. We figured if it was a mistake, you'd be back here pretty soon."

"And if it was choice," added Ian's friend Mark,"then it would have been our loss."

This was more like it! We quickly left the hotel before the rowdy sailors had a chance to further disrupt our evening.

The beach during the day and a glut of parties at night with Ian, Mark and their friends kept us well occupied for the rest of our stay in Durban. We left the city with good suntans, happy memories and the lesson to listen to our instincts when meeting strangers.

***

When Bonnie and I got back to *Southford*, preparations for Christmas were in full swing. This had always been my favourite time of the year but I never had stopped to think why. Perhaps it was the peaceful atmosphere of our living room lit with candles. Or the excitement of being able to open one present each before my sister and I went to bed on Christmas eve. Now that I was at the other end of the world where the seasons were reversed, I realised that Christmas also involved the anticipation of the first snowfall which, of course, had to arrive before Christmas morning; it meant runny noses when entering warm stores from cold streets in the rush to do last-minute gift shopping; it was cups of marshmallow-topped hot chocolate to sustain me while I wrapped presents. South Africa could provide none of these familiar physical comforts on my first Christmas away from home but, in the company of the wonderful Southeys, there was plenty of consolation.

The Southeys always spend Christmas at their second home in Port Alfred, a small Indian Ocean holiday town at the mouth of the Kowie River. In mid December, Bonnie, her parents and I migrated from the bone-dry Karoo to the subtropical climate of Port Alfred. The Southeys' back garden, a riot of colourful bird and plant life, slipped gently into the river where they kept a motorboat moored at a wooden dock.

Although the Christmas spirit had not yet touched me, everyone else's lively mood soon became infectious. Val relegated herself to the kitchen to prepare seasonal treats while Bonnie and I cultivated our tans at the nearby beaches. By the time brothers Geoff and Dave arrived immediately before Christmas, the house was bursting with a warm, holiday atmosphere. On Christmas day we opened presents and ate far too much of Val's exceptional lunch: turkey and all the trimmings, just like we had in Canada. The only difference was the refreshing fruit salad and ice cream for dessert. Then we all went to the beach. In the evening, a crowd of neighbours and relatives showed up for drinks and supper. It was a perfect day. Christmas, I learned, was not just about weather.

The downside of this otherwise stellar holiday was New Year's eve, the worst night of the year, as far as I was concerned. Only losers had no date. At least that's what my schoolgirl chums had instilled in me. I never had had a New Year's eve date so I carried this unfair stigma.

This year was no different. Bonnie, on the other hand, had accepted three invitations.

"What do you mean you're going to the dinner-dance with Tom?" I asked. "Yesterday you said you'd go to a party with Malcolm and before we left Norval's Pont you accepted a New Year's invitation from Roger Biggs. Do you *deliberately* get yourself into all these mix-ups?"

My disapproval of her behaviour masked my own frustration that no man had showed the slightest interest in inviting me to a New Year's event. It could be emotionally taxing being the relatively plain friend of a beautiful, vivacious female.

Bonnie and I each had made an evening dress in anticipation of a crush of parties and gatherings in Port Alfred over the holidays. I was determined to wear my creation, even if it was just to go fishing with Bonnie's parents.

In the end, everything worked out. Bonnie returned to the Karoo to honour the invitation from Roger, the first in line. I went to a formal dinner-dance-cabaret with the family and some friends. This New Year's eve, finally, I did not feel like a social loser.

***

After the holiday period, it was time to get serious about plotting our next move. There still were no available bookings to Australia but it was easy to get a ship to England. After much debating, we decided that if we couldn't get on the boat leaving for Australia on the twenty-first of January, we would sail to England on the twenty-ninth and then fly to Montreal. In either case, Cape Town would be our departure point. This would give me an opportunity to spend time with the Duncans.

Having committed ourselves to a plan of action, we revealed our options to the family at dinner.

"Australia? Canada? What's all this talk about?" Val exclaimed. She placed her knife and fork on her plate and gave Bonnie a hard stare. "This is the first we've heard of such intentions."

Percy, equally surprised, nodded in agreement and added sternly "Do you think money grows on trees and you can just flit around the world?"

"We're planning to work," Bonnie said proudly. "In case we go to Australia, Geoff has already written to Jane Edkins. She says I can have a job as a governess on their station outside Perth. She's going to ask around to find something for Kathy."

"Don't worry, Mom and Dad," Geoff chipped in, "I've given Bon my list of contacts. They're all good people and they'll pass the girls on to other good people. They'll be fine."

"If we end up in Canada," I volunteered, "it'll be easy enough for Bonnie to get work. My family will make sure she's OK."

"Well," Val conceded, "I guess it's some consolation that you'll have each other."

"That may not be the best situation," Geoff teased. "There's a possibility Kath will influence Bon to be more sensible but how do we know Bon won't tempt Kath to follow her dippy schemes?"

The comment lightened the mood but Val and Percy weren't happy to lose their daughter so soon after she'd returned from a lengthy stay in Europe. Nevertheless, they were wise enough to give their thoroughbred her head.

The next day, Geoff, not trusting our booking skills, drove to Grahamstown, about thirty miles from Port Alfred, to see a travel agent. He came back defeated: there were no available berths on ships going to Australia.

"I admit the prospects for Oz don't look good," Geoff said, "but don't give up hope, girls. Something tells me you're going to overcome this hurdle. I suggest you stand on the dock with your thumb out. Someone's sure to give you a ride."

My sharp look warned Bonnie not to contemplate this scenario.

Val and Percy closed up the Port Alfred house and we returned to *Southford* in the middle of January. Knowing I probably wouldn't be back this way any time soon, I drank in the sights, sounds and smells of this stark land where I had had some of the happiest days of my life. I took long, reflective walks in the veld, delighted when I encountered ostriches or saw springbok bounding in the distance. They reminded me of my first impression that nothing could live in such a landscape. So many of my preconceived notions had been dispelled on this trip.

The evening before my departure was bittersweet, none of us knowing when—or if— we would meet again. After a light supper we retired to the living room. I let Dave persuade me to sample a concoction called a brandy and ginger: a generous shot of brandy benignly masked with ginger ale.

"This is surprisingly good," I said after a couple of sips.

When I drained the first glass, Dave happily mixed me a second.

"Brandy and gingers have a way of sneaking up on you" Percy warned.

"But in the meantime, enjoy," Geoff said with a laugh.

Breakfast the next morning was a sombre affair, the sadness of the imminent farewell exacerbated by a queasy stomach and sore head. Percy had been right. Those brandy and gingers were sneaky.

Too soon, it was time to go to the train station. Although Bonnie and I would be sailing together, for now she remained at *Southford* until we knew where we were going. I said goodbye to the surrogate family whose love and laughter had allowed me to flourish. My feeling of loss might have been more intense except for a quote by Goethe I came across: *The world is so empty if one thinks only of mountains, rivers and cities; but to know someone here and there who thinks and feels with us and who, though distant, is close to us in spirit, this makes the earth for us an inhabited garden.* I knew I had discovered a garden and that I would carry this garden with me wherever I went.

CHAPTER 12

Anything is possible if you've got enough nerve.
JK Rowling

The journey south to Cape Town took nearly twenty-four hours. There was nothing to see except endless miles of desolate landscape relieved only by the many small stations at which we stopped. A lack of drinking water and ventilation made the temperature that exceeded one hundred degrees Fahrenheit unbearable. Meditative thoughts of cool streams and fresh breezes allowed me to sleep fitfully for a few hours at a time.

The light at the end of this dark tunnel was Dear Douglas waiting patiently on the platform at Cape Town.

"How lovely to see you again, Kathy," he said as we hugged and kissed. Then he held me at arm's length in order to better examine my face. "Susie and I were devastated to hear of your accident. What a relief to see how well the scars are healing."

"Thank you, Douglas. And thank you for making a comment about my face. I feel like a freak when people look away from me."

"You're far from freakish, my dear. They probably don't want to offend you by drawing attention to the injury."

"You're right," I admitted. "I would have done the same thing myself once."

In the car on the way home, Douglas caught up with my news.

"You really don't know where you're going next?" he asked, taking his eyes off the road for a moment to give me a surprised look.

"The preferred destination is Australia but we've been trying to get a sailing for ages. Anything that floats is fully booked."

"Would you like me to look into it for you?" Douglas offered.

"If it's not too much trouble, I won't say no. Thank you."

At home, Susie was no less effusive in her greeting than Douglas had been. She, too, gave me a critical once-over.

"At this rate of recovery, you'll be like new in no time." She punctuated these words with another tight hug.

Douglas returned to the office, leaving me to enjoy the mothering attentions of Susie and Isabella. No sooner had I got settled in than Isabella presented me with one of her potions.

"Put this on the scars. It will soften them."

She stood at the bathroom door waiting for me to apply the greasy but fragrant and soothing paste. Perhaps she suspected, correctly, that I was doing nothing more than letting nature handle the healing process.

When Douglas returned from work, he had a spring to his step. Part way through dinner he tapped his wine glass. The clear pings of the crystal brought conversation to a halt.

"You'll be pleased to know, Kathy, that you and Bonnie are going to Australia." Douglas beamed at his achievement. "The ship sails in five days. You mentioned Bonnie having a job outside Perth so you'll probably want to disembark at Fremantle, the port in Western Australia."

Susie and the three Duncan siblings applauded. I sat in stunned silence.

"That's amazing," was all I could say. At first, I didn't know whether to be pleased or disappointed. The trip to Australia meant a delay in going home but it also represented a unique opportunity. I accepted the push Fate had given me.

"I do have to warn you," Douglas added, "unlike the luxurious SA *Vaal*, this is a tourist-class ship. It's smaller and it won't be as comfortable."

"That's fine, as long as there's decent food and accommodation. Stabilisers also would be useful," I said. Then excitement began to wash over me. "How on earth did you do it? It's been impossible to get a booking for weeks."

Douglas wouldn't say more than, "I know a few people."

Immediately after dinner I called Bonnie to tell her she needed to get herself to Cape Town lickety-split.

"You're kidding! That's amazing news, Kath. I'm not sure how the folks will take it but Geoff will be pleased."

Bonnie promised to call when arrangements at her end had been made.

In the meantime, I enjoyed life with the Duncans. Beavan Duncan, Susie and Tom's older brother, had recently returned from studying printing in England. It fascinated me that after all this education, he instead chose to earn his living as a professional salvage diver.

"I think the ideal is to have three careers in a person's life," Beavan explained. "The first should be doing something you really love, the second should be something that will provide for a family, and the third, again, should be something you love. I love diving. I have no family to support, so now's the time to get this out of my system."

Beavan was given the task of squiring me around Cape Town. Sometimes we went on mainstream outings, such as to the top of Table Mountain to admire the brightly lit semi-circle of the city and harbour far below. Usually, though, he showed me a side of Cape Town that tourists seldom see. I particularly loved horseback riding along Blaauberg Strand followed by a barbecue—what South Africans call a *braaivleis*—on the beach with friends.

His parents certainly wouldn't have approved of our excursion into District Six. This inner-city suburb was inhabited mostly by Cape Coloureds. It was portrayed as a dangerous, vice-ridden slum that whites were advised to avoid.

"It's true there's crime here and it can be risky for whites," Beavan explained, "but those conditions aren't exclusive to District Six. A lot of people believe the government exaggerates the situation because they want an excuse to expropriate the land for redevelopment. By their reckoning, prime real estate shouldn't be populated by Coloureds. Apartheid is an ugly beast."

We proceeded without incident through the streets. I could see evidence of deprivation in small shanty houses and businesses but I also saw lively bars and nightclubs and groups of people chatting on street corners or on narrow *stoeps*. Common hardship had forged a bond within the community. Surely the government would face serious and perhaps violent opposition if they tried to remove these people from their homes and neighbourhoods. Or perhaps not. If I had learned nothing else in South Africa, it was that politics could be vicious.

***

Bonnie and her family arrived in Cape Town a couple of days before sailing. One of the first things we did together was to go to the travel agent. I was still unsure about travelling to Australia. Bonnie, as usual, had a way of rationalising the decision.

"My grandfather always said, *When a pessimist thinks he's taking a chance, the optimist is grasping an opportunity*. We're grasping an opportunity."

"Fine, Bon, I'm all for that. A big problem, though, is that I'm almost out of money and there's no guarantee I'll have a job when we get to Australia."

"Don't worry about money, Kath," Bonnie assured me. "I'll lend you what you need. You can pay me back when you're working. And you will be working," she added with conviction.

There was no escaping Bonnie's determination. I signed the last of my travellers' cheques and bought a one-way ticket to uncertainty.

"You have to be on board the ship by 3:00 pm tomorrow," the agent instructed as she handed us our travel documents. "If you like, you can disembark after the paperwork has been completed. She sails at 8:00 am the following morning. Bon voyage, ladies."

This time there was no asking if it was my first voyage. Had I at last acquired a patina of world travel?

The Duncan household came to the fore in getting me ready for the trip. Isabella, impatient with watching my struggles at dressmaking, stepped in and finished the job in masterly fashion. Douglas insisted on mailing several boxes of books and other collected treasures to Canada for me. Too soon, it was time to take leave of *Vredenburg*.

"We say good-bye to you more often than we like, Kathy," Susie said as she held me tightly. "Don't forget us. We certainly won't forget you."

Isabella, too, stood in line for a sad farewell. How I would miss these marvellous people.

The chauffeur cleared his throat to remind us that we had to get to the docks before 3:00 pm.

Bonnie and I met on the ship, got our boarding passes and then joined her family for a final few hours in Cape Town. The emotional parting at the docks that evening was wrenching. The Southeys had been unstinting in their affections and generous in their hospitality.

Bonnie's grandfather was right about risk versus opportunity. This realisation made it easier to keep taking those sometimes difficult but always necessary next steps.

***

At 8:00 am on Saturday 25 January 1970, the MV *Akaroa* raised her anchor and dockers cast off moorings. With muted dignity, she steamed out of Cape Town's protected harbour and headed up South Africa's east coast to Durban, the final stop before reaching Fremantle, Australia.

During this two-day journey Bonnie and I familiarised ourselves with the ship. Our cupboard-sized cabin had little room for storage. Fortunately, Bonnie now travelled with a substantially reduced wardrobe. Nor did we have the luxury of bottom bunks. These had been claimed by two frumpish British dowagers who had boarded in Southampton.

We checked out the dining room and other public areas. Everything was clean but the spaces felt tired and uninspiring.

"This sure isn't the *Vaal*," Bonnie muttered.

"The passengers don't look great either," I observed.

No diamond heiresses or finishing school graduates were apparent in this lot. Instead, the decks were solidly sprinkled with elderly, spindly-legged Brits sitting in deck chairs enjoying the sea air and soaking up the sun. They seemed to be representative of our four hundred shipmates.

"Don't young people want to go to Australia?" Bonnie asked, dismay in her voice.

The one-day stop in Durban gave us the opportunity to phone Bonnie's folks. What should have been straightforward was unbelievably difficult. Durban was the only city in South Africa with its own telephone system. Annoyingly, it didn't sync with the rest of the country. We had to wait most of the morning for our call to go through and then we were cut off twice during the conversation. It was an exercise in frustration but we were grateful for a last chance to talk with the family.

"Let's head to the Indian market," Bonnie suggested when we completed our call. "Everything that opens and shuts is sold there but you must bargain. It's good fun."

We never got there. Along the way we bumped into one of the fellows we had met during our previous visit to Durban. He invited us for a cool drink. I thought he meant something trendy but it was just the South African way of saying cold drink, a refreshing beverage to relieve the effects of the heat and humidity. In the early evening we met Bonnie's cousin Richard for drinks.

"Where do you want to go for dinner?" I asked when we left Richard. My stomach grumbled for more than liquid nourishment.

"There's a huge Indian population here. Let's have one of Durban's famous curries."

We found an open-air restaurant in the market we'd missed visiting earlier in the day. The venue was already crowded with eager diners.

I'd never eaten curry, so I relied on Bonnie's recommendations. Soon the waiter placed two attractive copper pots in front of us. One held chunks of beef in a steaming, stew-like gravy; the other contained a mound of white rice. Several small bowls of condiments, including raita and chutney, and two types of flatbread accompanied the meal. The aroma from the beef made my mouth water. I mixed a generous portion of the beef with the rice and helped myself to a large forkful.

"Oh. My. God." I guzzled a glass of water, signalling the waiter for an urgent refill. "I think the roof of my mouth has third-degree burns."

"I guess I shouldn't have ordered the extra hot version," Bonnie laughed.

"I have to admit, the flavour's pretty addictive," I said, wiping tears from my eyes once the fire had died.

"This will stop us getting scurvy on the ship," Bonnie announced. "Chilies are really high in vitamin C."

I didn't know whether or not Bonnie was serious but I didn't care. Now that I had adjusted to the spicy blast, I couldn't get enough of the delicious meal.

After dinner we walked along the beach in the rain, arriving back at the ship well in advance of the midnight sailing.

Shipboard life improved after Durban. Geriatrics still outnumbered vigorous youth but now, thanks to some passengers disembarking and others boarding, there were enough lively individuals to make things interesting.

An invitation to the officers' bar for what was supposed to be an evening of conversation expanded our social horizons. The somber tone of the invitation, however, inspired rebellion in fun-loving Bonnie.

"Bugger that for a joke," Bonnie said. "There's too much conversation on this ship and not enough action. Let's remedy the situation."

The respectable gathering soon turned into a party. At one stage, I announced I was going to spend the night in a lifeboat.

"That's probably not a great idea, Kathy. There's a boat drill first thing tomorrow morning."

This piece of advice came from Mac, an engineer from northern England who had attached himself to me during the evening.

"Then just let me check it out," I pleaded.

Mac sighed and ran his fingers through his short, curly brown hair, as though this action would help him arrive at the right decision. He seemed torn between trying to impress me and not wanting to do something he shouldn't be doing.

"I suppose it's better that I'm with you if you're going to try that stunt," he said finally.

We headed to the lifeboat deck. With Mac's resigned assistance, I clambered into one of the wooden boats.

"It's a bit Spartan, isn't it? I wouldn't like to be adrift in one of these for any length of time."

"They're built for survival, not comfort," Mac replied. "Let's hope we never have to use them."

Amen to that. We returned to the bar, my curiosity satisfied and Mac no doubt relieved not to have been caught breaking rules.

Days and nights on the *Akaroa* quickly fell into a rhythm. The only disagreeable routine was early morning cabin inspection six days a week. This ensured that passengers were out of their bunks in time for breakfast, not somewhere we wanted to be after being out all night. The rest of each relaxing day we spent sunbathing in balmy temperatures, playing table tennis or deck games, going to the cinema, reading and eating.

As with prisoners, meals were a focal point. No one went hungry but neither was there the satisfaction that results from fine ingredients, talented cooking and artful presentation. Each three-course meal had variety but lacked inspiration. I didn't count ice cream with wafers or tinned fruit as culinary innovation. Although the quantity was sufficient, we couldn't always say the same about the quality. Bonnie once found a worm in her salad.

"Don't complain, Bon, it's fresh meat for a change," I teased before carefully checking my own salad for signs of activity.

Night life centred around drinking, dancing and staff-organised entertainment. Bonnie's twentieth birthday at the end of January coincided with Roaring Twenties Night. One fellow was having too much of a good time: he tried to jump 'over the wall'. A quick-thinking companion caught him by the ankle just before he went overboard. This near tragedy sobered everyone except the jumper who was dragged into a lounge and guarded for the rest of the night.

After partying with the general population, Bonnie and I usually hung out in the officers' bar. We each had a steady fellow. Hers, in typical Bonnie style, was a dashing heartthrob of a man. I had hooked up with Mac, my lifeboat guide. This sweet but shy person wasn't a show stopper but he had eyes only for me. No longer having virginity to worry about gave me a sense of liberation.

Our first tentative kisses soon evolved into more passionate embraces. I tried not to flinch as Mac's fingers brushed over my still-sensitive scars. When he whispered "Let's go to my cabin," I willingly followed, all the while trying to ignore Grannie Daley's smug voice saying *I told you so.*

Officers were allowed to commiserate with passengers but they weren't permitted to have them in their cabins—or in their narrow bunks. Few obeyed this regulation, of course. The protocol of knocking gave a moment's warning, allowing a guest time to hide. I had to go through this performance twice one night when the telltale knock sent me hastily grabbing bits of my scattered clothing and scurrying into a narrow, airless closet. I couldn't hear the question asked by the officer but Mac's answer made me smile.

"No, Sir, just having a quiet night."

***

Everyone knew Bonnie and I were planning to work in the outback.

"You have to have a swaggie hat on a station," an Aussie called Sam said with the trademark Australian twang.

"What's a swaggie hat?" Bonnie and I wanted to know.

"A swaggie is someone who carries his belongings in a bundle. I can't say I've ever seen a swaggie with a swaggie hat but that's where the name comes from."

"But what *is* a swaggie hat?" I asked again.

"It's a clevva invention to keep the flies away. They's a million of them buggas so you need something special. Basically it's a brimmed hat with corks hanging from it. Simple but effective."

"I don't know, Kath. It sounds a bit fishy," Bonnie said. "Geoff never mentioned anything about fly-deterring hats."

"It makes sense, though," I said, intrigued with the idea. "I'm going to give it a go."

No one contradicted Sam's story. On the contrary, lots of people assisted in the unusual undertaking. Someone found a man's felt hat on board. With step-by-step instructions from Sam, we soaked it, stretched it over a bottle to achieve the 'ideal' shape and then dried it in the sun. Contributions of corks came from young and old volunteers. At first it was mainly wine bottle corks but then a stylish woman upped the game.

"No, dear, if you're going to do it, do it with class," she declared. "You need champagne corks."

She became a regular contributor of this item. I hung the corks from long threads around the rim and then modelled my creation to all and sundry, many of whom had participated in some way to bring the project to its conclusion.

"I'd say you're now prepared to meet the Aussie outback head on," Sam declared with approval.

Each day, the Aussie outback came closer. The ship made steady progress through the calm waters of the Indian Ocean. The crew told us we averaged eighteen or nineteen knots per hour.

"What's a knot in relation to land speed?" I asked Mac one evening.

"It's just over a mile an hour. Knot refers to the way speed and distance used to be calculated. A knotted line was released into the water from the stern of the boat. The knots were counted within a specific time period. Sailors could then calculate how fast and how far they were travelling."

"So we're averaging about four hundred miles each day?" I asked, doing a quick calculation.

"That would be about right," Mac agreed.

"It doesn't seem like a lot of distance in twenty-four hours."

Mac looked affronted, as though my comment was irreverent.

"You try pulling a few thousand tons of metal through water and see how you go."

"Point taken," I said with a new appreciation of the speed at which ships travel.

The important thing was that we stayed on course and on schedule. The weather remained cloudless and warm and the sea hypnotically flat. There were no sightings of boats or birds, not even a playful porpoise to remind us of other life.

Thirteen days after we had embarked in Cape Town, the west coast of Australia came into view. Our cabin mates woke us at

3:45 am to make sure we participated in the excitement of landfall. Bonnie and I weren't impressed. The shoreline was too distant to be anything more than a black smudge on the horizon. We returned to the comfort of our beds.

By the time the steward got us up, the ship was buzzing. Bonnie and I joined a crowd of passengers on deck to observe our approach into the port of Fremantle.

"Fremantle's been a colony for about one hundred and fifty years," our Aussie friend Sam explained. "It's been a proper port since the end of the 19th century. It was particularly important in the gold rush days. Now it serves as the western gateway to Australia."

There was no horseshoe harbour or charming coastal backdrop, just a long stretch of cranes, containers and other port-related paraphernalia interspersed with boxy buildings.

"It doesn't have the scenic glory of Cape Town and Table Mountain," I said.

"No," Sam admitted, "but the town has an interesting architectural heritage and an important history. But you girls should make your way straight to Perth. That's the main city."

As passengers started the process of disembarkation, we bid a final farewell to our shipboard friends. Saying goodbye to Mac was harder than I expected. I would miss his comforting decency. We promised to keep in touch.

"Well, girl, here we go," Bonnie said with a grin as we headed down the gangway.

I nodded. Then I, too, smiled. The fear of the unknown that had gripped me when I left Canada was now noticeably absent. In its place was simply an eagerness to face the next adventure.

CHAPTER 13

I don't know where I'm going, but I'm on my way.
Carl Sandburg

I'm not sure what I expected when we disembarked in Fremantle but it certainly wasn't the thorough interrogation and inspection that we and our luggage received from Customs authorities on behalf of the Department of Agriculture. Australia has strict policies to try to keep out pests and diseases that could devastate their agricultural industry. Our recent time at *Southford Stud* resulted in us being subjected to an extraordinary level of scrutiny. Every piece of footwear we owned had to be sterilised. With dismay, I rifled through my tightly-packed suitcase, retrieving and handing over offending items. Haste made the job messy. Books, toiletries and clothes were laid onto the counter. Not for the first time, I recognised that travelling with less would be easier. But less, as always, was for another day.

Finally we were released. Somehow I managed to repack everything and close the suitcase. We put the agro behind us and made our way to the bus that would take us from the port to Perth, a distance of about ten miles. Sand beaches and the Indian ocean flanked one side of the highway, scrub land bordered the other. The effects of summer's reduced rainfall were evident on the thirsty vegetation.

In Perth we made our way to the recommended Wentworth Hotel. We had no reservation but there was no problem getting a room.

"Welcome to Western Australia, Australia's largest state, and to Perth, Australia's sunniest city."

The greeting of the hotel receptionist was both friendly and informative. We knew Western Australia was large—approximately one-third the size of Australia and bigger than all of western Europe —but we didn't know we were in the city with the most hours of sunshine per year. This was welcome news to two sun-worshipping females.

We completed the registration form and paid the required four dollars and fifty cents for the room.

"Be sure to visit Kings Park," the receptionist said as he handed us our keys. "It's more than one thousand acres on top of Mount Eliza in the centre of the city. The botanical gardens are lovely but there's also bushland and parks and spectacular views of Perth, Swan River and the mountains. Here's a few brochures on things to see and do in the area."

He could have been a representative for the Australian Tourist Board.

We headed upstairs. This was a budget hotel so we weren't expecting luxury but, after nearly two weeks in a pokey cabin, the brightness and spaciousness of our otherwise ordinary room made it appear 5-star.

"It's nice having beds that don't require a ladder to get into," I remarked, testing the mattress and giving it a thumbs up.

We unpacked and then I curled up on the bed with the newspaper I had picked up at reception. While I combed through the classifieds, Bonnie rolled and lit a cigarette. The tranquillising smell of tobacco made me feel less stressed about unemployment.

"I'm going down to the lobby to phone Jane Edkins and let her know we've arrived," Bonnie said a few minutes later. She stubbed out her cigarette, extinguishing my source of calm. "Let's hope she hasn't changed her mind about offering me work."

I had no doubt Bonnie would have a job, but what would I do? This time, there was no cushy secretarial position being handed to me on a silver platter. Nor did I have my own well-connected contacts. I depended on Bonnie and her address book filled with names of people we didn't know. What had I been thinking? Geoff Southey's assurance of 'plenty of jobs' now seemed cavalier, especially as I scanned the Help Wanted section and noticed there were no jobs for which I was remotely qualified. Before I got too caught up in my worries, Bonnie returned to the room.

"We have to be in Arthur River on Thursday," Bonnie announced.

"We?" I echoed, looking up from the newspaper.

"Yes. You've got a job as well. On a neighbouring station."

"Doing what?" I asked suspiciously. Bonnie was acting a little too offhand.

"I didn't ask. But, as someone once said to me, 'It's not a life sentence. It's a temporary job that pays your bills. Suck it up, girl.'"

"You're right," I said with a sigh. I ignored my inclination to press for specifics and threw the newspaper into the bin. We were on an adventure, not a career path.

Like Johannesburg, Perth owed much of its economic success to the mining industry, most of which occurs in the northern part of the state. Unlike Johannesburg, this didn't translate into an explosion of criminal activity. Instead, Perth had a sleepy, colonial atmosphere and was more like a large town than a city. The place shut down completely on Sundays and then took a couple of days to rev up for the next work week.

With job hunting out of the way, we went shopping. Someone on the ship had stolen the top to Bonnie's bathing suit and the bottom to mine. We spotted a department store that hopefully would rectify the problem. When Bonnie asked if they had 'costumes', as they're called in South Africa, the saleslady took us to the section that sold suits for older women.

"No, we're looking for bathing suits," I said, thinking she might understand the Canadian term.

"Oh, you mean bathers. Come this way."

None of the selection appealed to us so we tried another store.

"Can you please tell us where your bathers are?" we asked, feeling pleased with our new fluency.

"Who?" the saleslady said.

Hand gestures and descriptions finally made our request understood.

"Oh, you mean cozzies."

Eventually, we each got a bathing suit—and acquired new words for our Aussie vocabulary.

Although full-time employment was imminent, after a couple of nights we downgraded from the Wentworth Hotel. The Cloisters, a 19th century, convict-built building, was now a hostel that charged only two dollars and fifty cents a night. The savings allowed us to take an occasional tour and visit some local sites. During a trip to the Yanchep National Park and Caves just outside Perth, we inadvertently broadcast our economic concerns. Coming to a wishing well at the end of the tour, and forgetting the cave magnified voices, I whispered to Bonnie, "Do you have change for two cents?" There was laughter but no donations.

***

Nearly a week after our arrival, we took the bus to Arthur River, just over one hundred twenty-four miles southeast of the state capital. The further we got from Perth, the rougher and less populated the terrain became.

After nearly three hours, the driver told us we had arrived at our destination. The only signs of habitation at this stop in the middle of nowhere were a store/post office and a scruffy service station. Jane Edkins, an Englishwoman turned pioneer wife, met us as we stepped off the bus.

"Welcome to the Australian outback." Jane seemed amused at our surprised expressions. "It's good you brought Kathy with you, Bonnie." Jane turned to face me. "I mentioned you to some friends yesterday and they're willing to take you on. I think they need a cook for the shearers."

I turned to Bonnie, mouth slack, eyes wide. She responded with a sheepish grin.

"So I was a little premature about your employment status," she whispered. "The important thing is that you have a job. Be happy."

"I can barely cook for myself. How am I going to produce satisfying meals for a bunch of hungry shearers?" I hissed, angry and fearful in equal measure.

"It'll work out, Kath," Bonnie said confidently.

"Easy for you to say," I snapped.

I stewed over my predicament until we arrived at the Edkins home, an attractive one-storey house with a covered verandah that wrapped around the front and two sides of the building. Two little boys rushed out to meet us.

"You'll be looking after the children and the house," Jane said to Bonnie. "Do you think you can manage?"

"No problem," Bon replied with a self-assurance she couldn't possibly have felt.

I had to turn away; if I caught Bonnie's eye, I would burst out laughing. For a girl brought up with a fleet of servants, housekeeping had to be a job for which my friend had little aptitude and less inclination.

The following day, Jane left Bonnie with a pile of ironing and drove me to the neighbouring station where I would work for Peter and Viv Rex, one of the biggest land owners in Western Australia. 'Neighbour' in this part of the world had a different meaning to what I was used to.

I was apprehensive about committing to living with strangers who expected me to do their chores. Of course, this was what 'odd jobs' was all about but now that push had come to shove I thought longingly of the benefits of secretarial work.

Peter and Viv were a handsome, friendly couple in their early thirties. They welcomed me into their home, an unremarkable bungalow. It didn't have the level of refinement of the Edkins' home, but neither did it have the air of British correctness. I knew I could be comfortable here.

"You have your own room," Viv said, showing me to a cosy space with tasteful furnishings, "but you might want to keep your door closed or you'll be bugged by the kids all the time.

After getting settled in, Viv and I sat in the kitchen and had a cup of tea.

"The shearing's been delayed," she announced. "I'm grateful for help with the house and kids. The two older ones are at school. Michael's seven and Sally's five. This little nipper," she said, holding up a wriggling toddler, "is two-year-old Robbie."

Robbie pointed a stubby finger at me, smiled, and said 'Lady'.

"I told him a lady would be staying with us," Viv explained. "After that he kept asking when Lady was coming. Now that you're here, you're Lady."

I never had had much to do with young kids and wasn't interested in changing this track record ... until I met Robbie. This beautiful blond child stole my heart and made the child-minding part of the job a joy.

Housework, the main focus of my chores, was as uninspiring as the salary of twenty Australian dollars a week. But it was a job. I had arrived at Arthur River with only three dollars and eighty-nine cents in my pocket. Back in South Africa, when my decreasing funds put our trip in jeopardy, Bonnie had lent me the equivalent of one hundred and twenty-eight Australian dollars. The sooner I could repay this debt, the happier I would be. Twenty dollars a week with board and lodging was a route to solvency.

"Where are all the horses?" I asked Peter a few days into my stay.

"We don't have any."

"You don't have *any* horses? Not a single one?"

This news scuppered my dream of herding cattle on horseback, like cowboys did in Western movies.

"We've got more than five thousand acres. It makes more sense to have motor bikes," Peter said as he grabbed two quart bottles of Swan lager out of the fridge and handed me one.

Aussies didn't do their drinking in half measures. Although I hadn't been a beer drinker up to this point, Western Australia's hot, dusty climate gave this cold, refreshing beverage unimaginable appeal.

I followed Peter into the living room. We sank into two comfortable chairs and took our first swigs.

"Have you ever ridden a bike?"

"Only the pedal variety," I answered, trying to mask my lack of enthusiasm for machinery I associated more with gangs than with sheep stations.

"It's easy. I'll teach you. Viv still expects some help but she's agreed to let you work with me as a land girl."

My face lit up. As much as I loved being with Robbie, the outdoors appealed more than housework. We raised our bottles to seal the deal.

Being a land girl was a lot more physical than doing housework. Sometimes it involved helping to unload half a ton of timber or super-phosphate. Other times I might go out with the government surveyor to mark contour banks, a system designed to minimise soil erosion on slopes. Whatever the job, it was always made un-comfortable due to temperatures that lingered around one hundred degrees Fahrenheit and plenty of flies that crawled all over the face looking for any bit of moisture.

One afternoon Viv announced we would take tea to the men supervising a burn on one hundred sixty acres. Landowners had these carefully-monitored fires each year to clear old, dense growth and promote new vegetation. This, surely, would be the perfect op-portunity to christen my swaggie hat.

Viv's eyes widened when she saw my unusual get-up but she made no comment. The reaction was less discreet at the burn site. Conversation stopped as sixteen men stared at my practical but unfashionable—and unfamiliar—apparel.

"You look like a Pommie's version of a dinkum Aussie," one of the men ventured. "Can't say as I've ever seen a real person in such a contraption."

"It's meant to keep the flies away," I explained. *Why didn't they already know this?*

"We just give the Aussie salute: a backhand swing to the face to brush off the buggas."

I realised I was probably the only person in Western Australia —probably in all of Australia—with a champagne-corked swag-gie. My gullibility caused only momentary embarrassment. It may have looked foolish but the hat worked. Nevertheless, because it wasn't always practical to wear the swaggie hat, I quickly mastered the Aussie salute.

***

Peter taught me how to drive a tractor and his trusty little motor bike. The bike and I didn't always have a happy relationship. On the first day, I burned my leg on the exhaust pipe. Another time, climbing to the top of a hill in the full glare of the sun, I drove into a wire fence. Fortunately, the only injury was to my pride. I untangled myself and the bike and continued my journey, never breathing a word of the mishap.

Every day I learned something new. The most unconventional lesson was how to skin a sheep.

"First you flip the animal onto its back," Peter said, positioning the recently-slaughtered beast. "We always start at the back end. Hold one of the legs between your legs, lift the wool and cut through the skin from the hoof to the ass."

Peter swiftly cut the tendons and muscle from the skin and repeated the process with the other leg. He then broke the legs in order to more easily remove the skin from the hooves, and repeated the process with the front legs.

When he got to the belly region, Peter lay down his knife and hung the sheep by the back legs from a short wooden hanger.

"OK, Kath, your turn. Make a fist and, with a rolling motion, separate the skin. It's like punching," he said as he demonstrated. "Don't be afraid to put a bit of muscle into the action."

My first couple of efforts were timid. I was afraid of breaking through the membrane and finding my fist in a pool of steaming guts.

"You'll never get the skin off if you dance around like that. Push!"

I took a deep breath and punched. It worked! I kept up the pace until a naked sheep hung before me. Peter finished the job by using his knife to release the skin from around the anus and the head.

"Gudonya, mate. You've just skinned your first jumbuck," Peter announced as he held up the pelt.

I felt inordinate pride.

"This will be a talking point on my resume."

Although I preferred working outside, household duties, too, expanded my skill set. I helped Viv prepare meals and occasionally took on the task by myself. I enjoyed browsing through her cookbooks and trying recipes, many of which I'd never heard of and so didn't know how they were meant to turn out. The family was enthusiastic about my successes. Failures suffered the censure of the kids.

"What *is* this?" Michael said as he poked his fork into my attempt at stuffed cabbage rolls with tomato sauce. "It smells like dirty socks and looks like bloody turds."

"Not a big hit, then?" I asked him.

"I only like your biscuits," he said. The verdict was seconded by Sally.

Through trial and error, I discovered that sweets were my forte. Viv shared her family recipes. She also taught me how to bottle pears and make fresh lemonade. I loved picking the fruit off the tree and then preparing or preserving it. It occurred to me that I hadn't seen a supermarket since arriving in Arthur River. No wonder people in this part of the world cooked well: they had no instant meals to come to the rescue.

***

Despite considerable distances between properties, a sparse population and the scarcity of towns, people here enjoyed an active social life. Peter made a valiant effort to introduce me to the area's bachelor population.

"There's a real shortage of sheilas in this part of the world. You and your mate won't lack male company," Peter assured me.

'Sheilas' sounded like it could be a derogatory term but I never heard anyone use it in a disrespectful fashion. It was simply what Aussie men called women. The men, we learned, were called blokes. The term suited the rough and ready nature and appearance of outback men. They weren't like any Bonnie and I had come across. This crowd was most comfortable in the company of men, preferably with a cold bottle of lager in hand. At parties, the blokes huddled together on one side of the room and the sheilas gathered on the other side, each group furtively eyeing the other. Sometimes Bonnie and I would join the men but our boldness didn't always meet with the approval of other women, especially married women who didn't know us and who suspected these two mini-skirted strangers might have eyes on their husbands—or vice versa.

The best way to interact with blokes was to participate in one of their favourite pastimes: hunting.

"I've organised a 'roo shoot for Friday night," Peter announced after work one evening. "It'll be a new moon, so conditions'll be good."

"What does the moon have to do with hunting kangaroos?" I asked.

"We hunt with spotlights mounted on the vehicles. When we see a 'roo, we shine the light in its eyes. It stuns him and he sits down. It's easier to get a clean shot that way. A full moon gives too much light."

"Do you go on 'roo shoots often?" I asked.

"As often as we need to. 'Roos are vermin. They compete with livestock for grazing. Farmers don't mind having a few families on the land but they have to be culled regularly to keep the numbers manageable."

After dark on the appointed night, four neighbouring blokes, Peter and myself, piled into a Land Rover and headed off to the bush: vast acres of undeveloped scrub land. I was nominated to manipulate the spotlight but with Peter careening across the bumpy terrain and making sudden, sharp turns when a 'roo was sighted, my dexterity left much to be desired. Nevertheless, by the end of the evening, the lads had shot ten kangaroos.

"We'll skin one for you, Kath," Peter said.

"Do you eat the meat?" I asked. It seemed a waste to kill the animals and then leave them where they fell.

"Not usually," Peter admitted. "It's meant to be pretty good for you, though, because it's so lean. I know you can make soup with the tail."

"Would you mind cutting me some steaks and saving a tail for me? I'd like to try it."

The next morning I drowsily opened the fridge to get milk for my coffee. A snake-like creature unwound itself like a spring and flew into my face. I screamed long and loud. Peter and Viv rushed into the kitchen to see what had happened. They found me picking a kangaroo tail off the floor.

"Therein lies a tale," Peter said with a laugh.

"Let's make the soup right away," Viv suggested. "We don't need a repeat performance."

We cut the tail into sections, placed it into a large pot with plenty of vegetables, added water and let it cook. The finished result was a pleasant-tasting broth but I decided it would be easier to stick to making old favourites like tomato soup.

The 'roo steaks were less dramatic. The meat was dry and stringy the first day but the longer the meat sat, the better it tasted. The difference between the first steak, a day after the kill, and the third steak, about a week later, was noticeable. Now I understood why butchers hang meat.

Another souvenir of the kangaroo shoot was a skin. After removing it from the body, the fellows nailed it to the door of the shearing shed to dry. There wasn't time before my departure to tan it so, until the process could be completed, I had nothing more exciting than a stiff, furry animal shape.

Not all hunting ventures were successful or even particularly enjoyable. When the guys invited me to go on a wild boar shoot, no one mentioned the potential dangers. At least, not until we were at the site of the hunt, a scrubby, lightly wooded area.

"Always stay close to someone with a raffle," one of the lads warned.

"What's a raffle?" I asked.

"Raffle," he repeated impatiently. "You know: bang, bang."

Aha. I had to stay close to someone with a rifle.

"These pigs are vicious when cornered or when there are piglets," he explained. "They won't hesitate to charge. A combination of razor-sharp tusks, phenomenal strength and an ornery attitude can do serious and sometimes fatal damage. And if that weren't enough," he added, "they're one of the smartest bloody animals around. Keep on your guard."

Well, that little lecture sure took a lot of fun out of the exercise. Fortunately, we came across the feral beasts only rarely. Their short-legged, hairy bodies, topped by a large, snouted head and small, piggy eyes didn't inspire empathy. It was the fact that they destructively rooted up the ground, ate crops and could spread disease to livestock that made them a prime target for land owners. Our outing resulted in no kills and no charges. I was relieved to get home without incident.

An afternoon of horseback riding at a neighbour's station evolved into supper and a party. Apropos of nothing, someone suggested we go rabbit hunting. Shooting, evidently, is never far from the outback man's mind. Because it was dark and there were too many of us to risk using guns, the chase would be on foot. We piled into a vehicle and headed off. I bounced around in the open back with five fellows and a dog. When a rabbit appeared in the beam of the spotlight, everyone jumped out and chased after the poor thing. The fast-paced antics were comical to watch and exhausting to participate in. Captured rabbits were killed and thrown in the back of the 'ute', Australian slang for utility or pickup truck. A stray sheep maxed out the crowd of live and dead bodies and brought the hunt to an end.

I didn't like to kill animals. My outings so far had been 'justified' because kangaroos, boars and rabbits needed to be culled. An invitation to go duck hunting was simply sport. The universe must have been displeased with my ethical compromise because it made the experience one I never wanted to repeat.

Used to walking in bare feet much of the time, it didn't occur to me to put on shoes for the duck hunt. I regretted this decision when I had to walk through scrub brush and across pin grass to reach our destination: a swamp. My companion strode along in his thigh-high boots while I tagged after him. With every hesitant step I sank further into the muck. He shot a couple of ducks and then tilted his head in the direction of the fall. I was the bird dog, for goodness sake. I was able to fetch and find three of five shot ducks. We ended up with the best haul. I evidently had talent as a retriever.

CHAPTER 14

Keep going because you did not come this far
just to come this far.
mollyhostudio

"**W**e hate to let you go," Peter told me as we quaffed our cold Swans after work. "This has been a treat for Viv and me but our budget is stretched."

I knew all about stretched budgets. The Rexes already had kept me on for a week longer than the expected two weeks. I had grown close to everyone in the family but leaving little Robbie would hurt the most. His devotion to me had awakened a mothering instinct I didn't know I possessed.

The good news was that Peter had found me a job with Liz and Owen Dare. It was time for the annual shearing and the Dares needed an extra pair of hands. Not with the shearing, of course. That is done by professionals who travel from station to station and work all day every day until the job is done. An experienced shearer not only works fast—it might take less than two minutes per sheep— but he works efficiently: the fleece is removed in one piece without any nicks to the sheep or injury to the shearer. The event is timed to happen about a month before lambing and when there is no risk of cold weather.

"Tell me about my new employers."

"They're a good family. Well respected in the area. They have two daughters at school and lots of sheep. No horses," Peter added before I could get the question out. "Their station is a few miles down the road."

Peter drove me to the Dares' farm the next morning. Like he had said, they seemed like good people. They laughed easily and were warm in their welcome.

Liz and Owen wanted me to help with the additional cooking and do odd jobs in the shearing shed. This included sweeping the floor of discards and skirting the fleece, the process of removing unwanted bits.

"This is high quality wool," Owen said as he tossed a freshly-shorn fleece, cut-side down, onto the large, slatted skirting table. A skin could weigh as much as ten pounds but tall, lanky Owen made the throw look easy. "To get the best prices, pelts have to be as free of defects as possible." He deftly 'skirted' his way around the table, rapidly removing undesirables. "Pay special attention to the edges, the belly and around the tail. Sheep can pick up debris from anything they eat, lie in, rub against or eliminate."

Skirting fleeces was a job with benefits. Removing accumulated plant matter, faeces, urine stains and matted wool left a residue of skin-softening lanolin on my hands.

Once the shearers left, the station returned to normal routines revolving around the large numbers of sheep. Dogs played a vital role in herding. I marvelled at the simplicity of Owen's commands and the intelligence and intuition of his black-and-white English sheep dog Rexy.

"I need you to bring this mob to the pen," Owen said as he drove up to a large paddock that contained a sea of undulating white wool. Rexy barked excitedly and jumped out of the back of the ute. "Don't worry, Rexy will do all the work for you. She's a ringer stock dog."

I stared at seven hundred yellow-eyed creatures who, despite their limited brain power, surely had sized me up as an amateur. Owen gave me the string of commands for the dog that would send him in any necessary direction and do any required task. Then Owen disappeared in the cloud of dust kicked up by his retreat.

It should have been straightforward, but remembering lists had been difficult since my accident. Until now, I hadn't needed this skill. When the sheep began to fan out, Rexy looked at me expect-antly. The one or two commands I retained got us on our way in a messy fashion. Arriving at a marsh shattered this feeble suggestion of order. The sheep split into groups of twos and threes and dispersed in all possible directions. I shouted every logical command I could think of but none had any effect. Rexy barked and herded but without my guidance it was nothing more than an unruly mob going in circles. I did the only thing left to do: I sat on the ground and cried.

Eventually Owen showed up looking for his lost shepherdess.

"No worries, Kath. Rexy'll round them up in no time."

Owen's calm, succinct directives quickly got the stampede under control.

"It's as much the tone of voice as the words that the dog understands," Owen counselled, as though he knew I had been reduced to bellowing and wailing.

As soon as the sheep were delivered safely to the pen, Rexy disappeared for a well-deserved break.

Then five sheep escaped down the road.

"Off you go," Owen said with a mischievous grin.

I was on my own. The challenge seemed manageable. After all, there were only five, not seven hundred. It soon became apparent that small numbers dart and dodge just like large numbers. Finally, after fifteen minutes of hot pursuit, I had the little buggers back where they belonged. Like Rexy, I needed a break.

***

As much as I was enjoying these new experiences, I missed home. Everyone had been good about keeping in touch but in this part of the world post was delivered only once a week. It was difficult to endure a week without mail. On those infrequent occasions, I would take old letters and find a shady gum tree under which to sit. As I hungrily reread all the news, I imagined myself caught up in familiar routines with friends: shopping along Montreal's famous St Catherine Street on a Saturday morning, going for a pizza after a movie or simply hanging out and talking about life and loves. Yet, I wasn't discontented to be sitting in a dusty paddock in Western Australia. I accepted that achieving goals often requires compromise.

During a rare gloomy period, I decided to use some of my limited cash to phone home. We hadn't spoken in the nearly nine months since I had left Canada. Long-distance calls, especially to the other end of the world, were expensive, planned events. Now, I decided, it was time to plan such an event.

The distance between Montreal and Western Australia was reinforced by the fifteen-hour time difference: when I phoned home on Thursday evening, my day was over and their Thursday was just beginning.

To my surprise, I noticed my parents and sister had accents! Except for the Canadian woman I had met in Ireland at the start of my trip, I hadn't had contact with any Canadians. Now my family's pronunciation sounded unfamiliar … foreign. Did they think the same about me? Surely not, I told myself. I spoke like I always had spoken, certainly not with the flat Australian twang. Yet, on more than one occasion, my parents asked me to repeat what I had said because they couldn't understand!

Accents or no, it was wonderful to hear their voices. I felt connected once again.

"I'm so happy you called," my sister Liz said, emotion in her voice. "I didn't realise how much I miss you. I want to sing with you. That's what I miss about you most."

"I miss you, too, Liz. I'll be home soon enough."

"How soon?" she pressed.

"I honestly haven't got a clue but at least I'm travelling in the right direction," I said, trying to put a positive spin on the situation.

I couldn't afford more than a three-minute call. The poor connection spoiling the beginning of the conversation turned into a blessing.

"I'm giving you an extra five minutes to compensate for earlier static," the operator announced as the three-minute mark approached.

I thanked her sincerely, suspecting kindness and consideration had overruled company policy.

***

On the morning of the twentieth of March young Gillian and Meryl Dare woke me with a rousing chorus of *Happy Birthday* and laid a prettily wrapped gift on the bed.

"How did you know?" I asked as I removed the paper to reveal a packet of writing paper.

"Bonnie phoned a couple of days ago and told my mom," Gillian answered.

Only Bonnie knew I faced my twentieth birthday with apprehension. I no longer would be a carefree teenager. Pretty daunting stuff to face with no family and friends around to cheer me out of my low spirits. Bonnie had wanted to make sure the occasion wouldn't go unnoticed.

Liz and the girls did their best to make the day special. When the girls came home from school, we all went to Dumbleyung, the nearest town. The girls bought me a lovely bar of lemon soap. Their thoughtfulness made my concerns about ageing seem petty.

At home, we all sat around the kitchen table for a cup of afternoon tea. Liz cut thick slices of homemade bread.

"Help yourself to strawberry jam and cream. The strawberries are out of the garden and the cream and butter are fresh from the cow."

"I know what to do with the bread, the butter and the jam," I said reaching for the fragrant preserve, "but what am I supposed to do with the whipped cream?"

"Put it on top of the jam, of course," Liz said. She looked astonished that I would have to ask such a question.

"I've heard of strawberries and cream but not on bread. A cream sandwich is a step too far for me."

"Try it," Liz urged. "You might be surprised at how good it tastes."

Reluctantly, I desecrated the jam with a timid dollop of thick cream. Liz laughed as she watched my eyes widen.

"It's delicious," I said, greedily adding more cream. "Absolutely delicious. This combination of flavours might have been made in heaven."

After dinner, Liz surprised me with a sponge cake with whipped cream and passionfruit seeds in the centre. Everyone sang *Happy Birthday* to Owen's piano accompaniment. The Dares' celebratory mood soon got the better of me. What the heck, I thought, it's just a birthday. I'm attaching more drama to the event than this transition into the next decade of my life deserves. I accepted another piece of the tempting cake and joined the fun.

***

Staying employed wasn't easy. Money everywhere was tight and temporary labour was expendable. Like the Rexes, the Dares offered to keep me on until I could find other work but it would have to be at half wages. If I was ever going to get out of debt, this level of income couldn't continue.

Bonnie and I talked on the phone most days and met up with each other at social events. A day after I had conveyed news of my impending unemployment, she called with a solution.

"Jane's found a job for you," Bonnie announced. "It's cleaning at the roadhouse in Arthur River. Jane says you can stay with us and she'll lend you a bicycle for transport. What do you think?"

"There's not a lot of choice, is there? I can't afford to be picky—and I can't afford to be on half wages … or no wages. It's just for a week. I'm sure I'll survive."

The work was hard: washing windows, scrubbing floors, cleaning storerooms. This began and ended with a two-mile cycle. To someone with sedate secretarial skills, the new regimen took getting used to. Only the combination of an income and Bonnie's company made the efforts worthwhile.

One evening when I returned to the Edkins', Bonnie had an unusual invitation for us.

"What on earth is marroning?" I asked, digesting yet another new word.

"It's fishing for what the Aussies call marron or yabbies; you might know them as crayfish. We'll go out after dusk tomorrow."

"Aussies seem to do most of their hunting or fishing at night, don't they?" I remarked.

A couple of the lads picked us up after work. We drove sixty-five miles to a reservoir outside the town of Collie, an area known for its dense forests and coal mining.

"Tie a chunk of meat to each of these pieces of string," John Humphries said. He had a bucket of raw meat and a pile of three-foot-long strands. "Throw the baited end into the water and stick a rock on top of the other end on the shore."

Everyone busied themselves with this task. Our area covered a quarter of a mile. Once all the strings were in place, John got another bucket from the car.

"These are grower's pellets," he explained as he sprinkled them between the lines of string. "We feed them to young chooks but yabbies go crazy for them. They're illegal to use this way but everyone does it."

"Law enforcement's slack in these parts?" I asked sarcastically.

After dusk we checked the lines. Our scoop nets revealed mostly young marron, which we threw back. The lines were re-baited and extended. The second effort netted nearly three times as many marron and all of them were large. Each time, the lines went a bit farther into the water, which meant we had farther to wade. It was nearly midnight before we could persuade the fellows that the campfire wasn't enough to keep us warm and dry us off between collections. We divided the catch and went home.

The next evening, Bonnie made a delicious paella with our share. Her domesticity impressed me.

"Who said you can't teach an old dog new tricks," I teased.

"You haven't done too badly yourself," she replied. "All sorts of acquired skills, not least of which is skinning sheep."

I smiled at the memory.

"It's been an interesting few weeks, hasn't it?"

"That it has," Bonnie agreed, "but it's time to move on. We seem to have exhausted the job opportunities around here." Bonnie took another serving of paella. "Tom Hollingsworth has offered his place as a party venue so we can say goodbye to everyone."

The gathering was big and gregarious. I was surprised we knew so many people! As usual, the blokes outnumbered the sheilas by five to one. At first, Bon and I were the only two single women. Eventually, three more showed up.

"You know that Western Australia isn't just the biggest state, it's the best," Tony Scott said. He put his arm across Bonnie's shoulders. "Are you sure you want to leave all this?"

"Don't make it harder than it already is, Tony," Bonnie replied, giving his hand a squeeze.

I observed the interaction, wondering how attached the two of them had become. Bonnie hadn't revealed to me any romantic connections so perhaps poor Tony was simply another victim. Bonnie had a knack of leaving a trail of broken hearts in her wake.

"You'll be right, girls," Tom piped up. "You've both got a spirit of adventure. Just try not to forget your many friends in WA. We certainly won't forget you."

Shortly before midnight, a barbecue got underway. Coals were tended and slabs of meat and links of sausages were thrown onto the grill. It was good to have food to soak up some of the alcohol.

After eating, dancing and sad farewells, we shot home at 6:00 am to pack and leave for Perth by 7:30. We had a train to catch.

CHAPTER 15

Travel makes you realise that no matter how much you know,
there's always more to learn.
Nyssa P Chopra

By the time we arrived at the station in Perth, we felt more than a little tetchy from lack of sleep. An unexpected run-in with officialdom, therefore, didn't go down well.

"Sorry, luv, that 'roo skin has to stay behind," the agent said, pointing to my board-stiff trophy. His words were polite but his demeanour suggested he wouldn't take any nonsense.

"Why?"

"It's not tanned and it hasn't been passed by the Department of Agriculture."

Remembering my Department of Agriculture encounter in Fremantle, I decided that this branch of government and I were on a collision course.

"Please," I begged, too weary to fight.

"No way. The skin stays here. Your choice if you want to stay with it."

Reluctantly, I surrendered the pelt and accepted the train ticket.

When we got to the platform, I blinked in disbelief at the line of old-fashioned carriages, each of which had a small balcony at the end.

"It's like a relic from the Wild West."

"I know the clocks move forward one and a half hours between here and Adelaide," Bonnie said, "but it seems we have to go back in time to get there."

As we walked through our carriage, I glanced at my fellow travellers. There was no one our age and relatively few women. We settled in for the nearly three hundred seventy-five-mile journey to Kalgoorlie, a former boom town that came to prominence in 1893 when gold was discovered. It remains an important centre for mining.

Travelling from Perth to Adelaide would involve two changes of train because of inconsistent track gauges between Western Australia and South Australia. It would take the better part of three days to reach our destination.

The steady clickety-clack of the wheels and the gentle swaying of the carriage soon eased us into a much-needed sleep. We woke a few hours later feeling stiff but in better humour.

At Kalgoorlie, we disembarked and followed passengers to the connecting train. Judging from the fast pace everyone adopted, it seemed there wasn't much time between connections.

"Chop-chop, Kath," Bonnie called to me from a couple of yards ahead. "We don't want to miss the train."

Too breathless to remind Bonnie that she was usually the cause for late arrivals or indecisions at trains, I struggled to keep up. Finally I got to the appointed platform. But where was Bonnie? I peered at the crowd, trying to spot her long black hair. Suddenly her head popped out a carriage window.

"In here," she called, attracting hopeful glances from passing male passengers. "I've got seats for us."

In sharp contrast to the outdated train from Perth, this was a sleek, modern Japanese design, famed for its compactness, cleanliness and excellent food. It would have been nice to experience fine dining but we had to make do with a more economical meal of fresh fruit and a stale sandwich.

The one thousand two hundred eight-mile portion of the journey between Kalgoorlie and Port Pirie includes the longest, straightest stretch of railway line in the world: nearly three hundred miles. The twenty-hour journey might have been deadly boring except for the grizzled travelling companion sitting across the aisle from us. He looked like a relic from gold-rush days. My hope that he might be a source of information and distraction wasn't misplaced. It didn't take much prodding to get Billy, a retired miner, to open up about himself. After regaling us with stories of his prospecting adventures, Billy pointed out the window.

"That's the Nullarbor Plain," he said, almost with affection.

Bonnie and I looked at the parched, treeless landscape.

"What does Nullarbor mean?" I asked.

"Nothing," Billy's partially toothless mouth informed us.

"Nothing? It doesn't come from some Aboriginal word or something?" I persisted.

"No, it means 'nothing'. Or close enough. It's from Latin meaning 'no tree'. That's what I've been told."

The place was aptly named.

"What's more interesting, though, is the geology," he continued with enthusiasm. "The whole thing's one bloody great piece of limestone. Largest in the world. Twelve and a half thousand square miles of it."

From the vantage point of a speeding train, there was little opportunity to appreciate the phenomenon.

We were about to indulge in another nap when Bonnie noticed everyone getting off the train with their luggage. We had arrived in Port Pirie. The mining town first settled in the mid 1800s sits on the eastern shore of the Spencer Gulf. We gathered our belongings and made a marathon dash to change trains for the final one hundred forty miles to Adelaide.

Liz Chapman, a friend of Bonnie and David Southey whom I had met at *Southford*, welcomed us at the train station. We piled our luggage into her souped-up Mini and got our first look at Adelaide. It was as though we had stepped into another world. There was no whiff of outback to this cosmopolitan capital of South Australia. The planned city, designed with wide avenues and an abundance of green spaces, felt immensely liveable.

Liz lived with her mother, a woman of svelte good looks. I sensed that her impeccable manners concealed an uncompromising attachment to old-fashioned tradition.

Their home, a stately mansion in a suitably upmarket suburb, represented an awesome contrast to our accommodation up to this point.

"Let me know if you need anything," Liz said as she showed us to our room. "You're welcome to stay as long as you like. Freshen up and then I'll show you the rest of the house."

As soon as Liz left the room, Bonnie and I raised our eyebrows at our good fortune.

"Haven't we just landed on our feet," I said, admiring the room's tasteful decor.

"I can't imagine we'll be staying in too many places like this on our travels. Let's enjoy it while we can."

We washed and changed and then joined Liz for the grand tour. The house lent itself to entertaining. One elegant reception area led to another. The large kitchen could cater for crowds.

"The location's convenient," Liz explained, "because I can exercise my horses in the park across the street."

Of course. Weren't on-site stables and a convenient riding park what every home buyer looked for?

"Speaking of horses," Liz continued, "you'll be getting your fill of them while you're here. We'll be going to a gymkhana, polo matches and races. We leave on Friday to drive north. In the meantime, you have a temporary job starting first thing tomorrow."

Job? Bonnie looked as nonplussed as I felt, so evidently this wasn't another of her employment surprises.

"Doing what?" I asked.

"Grooming and exercising polo ponies."

The opportunity to earn quick cash met with my approval but Bonnie didn't look thrilled. Ironically for a girl from a horse-breeding family, she wasn't comfortable around horses. To her credit, Bonnie 'sucked it up', as we liked to say.

The next morning, Liz drove us to the local polo club. A groom nodded at us and said simply, "Here's your bridle, there's your horse" and left us to fend for ourselves. The bridle looked like an unduly complicated piece of machinery. I never had had to 'install' one because every horse I had ridden came ready to go.

"They don't look like ponies to me," Bonnie muttered as we figured out how to saddle and bridle our assigned mounts.

"I think pony refers to their youthful agility," I replied, guiding my horse out of the stable area.

We had been told to do nothing more than go at a quick trot, my least favourite gait but not disagreeable once I settled into the rhythm. Even Bonnie admitted that the early morning ride in the cool air was pleasant. We circled the long, sandy track several times. The first day we only had to cover six miles; in a couple of days we were doing ten miles. Before we achieved the usual requirement of fifteen miles of trotting, we were on the road again.

On Good Friday, four days after we arrived in Adelaide, Liz, Bonnie and I drove to *The Selection*, a station in New South Wales. We had been invited to use the homestead as a base when we attended the gymkhana.

Much of the four hundred thirty-five-mile journey was over dusty, unpaved road. After making a couple of rest stops we reached our destination after dark.

I thought the properties we had been on in Western Australia were big but *The Selection's* eighty-six thousand acres dwarfed them. The driveway alone is seven miles!

The thing that impressed me most about the station was its large transceiver.

"With such immense distances between neighbours and to emergency services, this is a vital communication resource in rural communities," our hostess Anne Laurie said.

Anne showed us how the set-up worked by tuning in to the Flying Doctor clinic.

"I used to watch that show on TV every week!" I said, surprised that such a service wasn't a figment of Hollywood's imagination.

"Every station has a well-equipped box of clearly-numbered medicines," Anne explained. "Symptoms are relayed to the clinic and the doctor treats them by referring to the numbers in the medicine box. For the most serious cases, medical staff will fly to the patient."

"What happens if they're too far away?" I asked.

"Occasionally a doctor won't be able to make it in time," Anne said with a shrug. "In those situations, he guides the station hand through the operation."

"I wouldn't want to be the patient—or the amateur suddenly

having to perform surgery," I said, appalled at such a possibility.

"No one wants that," Anne agreed, "but we have to be prepared for every eventuality."

I had a growing admiration for outback people.

By 10:00 am, everyone was heading to *Packsaddle* station for the annual gymkhana, the reason for our journey to this remote area. There were plenty of horse-related events for all ages of participants and audiences. The skill level of even the youngest riders in the many races and timed games impressed me. It was dusty and dirty but lots of fun.

The first evening marked the start of the famous Wool Shed Ball, a social gathering which lasts a couple of days. I associated 'ball' with a grand occasion that demanded long gowns and tuxedos. The wool shed venue didn't fit. Then I reminded myself that this is the Australian outback. My humble wardrobe gave me no cause for embarrassment.

It was a wonderful party. I danced almost continuously until 4:30 am and only quit because the band took a well-earned break. We found out later that more than five hundred gallons of beer were consumed during the weekend!

Most people camped out. It was nice to know we had comfortable beds to fall into. On the way back to *The Selection*, our driver and fellow party goer Geoff Goddard suddenly pulled to the side of the road.

"Sorry, ladies, I need a kip."

Liz took the wheel. Geoff passed out almost as soon as he switched seats. Fortunately, Liz was as good at driving as she was at everything else she tackled. Her quick reaction on two separate occasions avoided hitting kangaroos that appeared out of nowhere.

"That's why vehicles in this part of the world have 'roo bars on the front fenders," she said, showing no signs of anxiety at the near misses.

It was good to get back to *The Selection* safely.

Before leaving on Sunday afternoon, Anne gave Bonnie and me beautiful teal emu eggs.

"This would make some omelet," I said, feeling the weight of the egg, which I judged to be well over a pound. I was determined to fit this treasure into my suitcase, despite its melon-like size.

"Yes," Anne laughed. "They're equivalent to about twelve chicken eggs but there's more yolk in an emu egg. The abos are very good at turning them into artwork. They paint or carve on the thick shells. The layer of white under the blue makes for effective contrasts."

We returned to Adelaide for a full night's sleep before heading off to yet another horsey event the following day, Easter Monday. This time the destination was just outside the city at a revered club called Oakbank, founded in 1876. Easter weekend is the occasion of the famous Oakbank Carnival, the world's biggest picnic race meeting.

The turf is usually reserved for racing but on this occasion it is given over to crowds of happy race goers. I marvelled at the sight of hundreds of people in their finery sitting on picnic rugs in the middle of the race course divvying out packed lunches. Men in neatly creased trousers and smart blazers poured champagne for women in silks and pearls. What a civilised tradition.

In the evening we went to a pub called *The Feathers*. By 10:00 pm everyone was hungry again, so one of the fellows invited us for a steak dinner. Liz had a party at her place afterwards. Exhausted after the busy weekend, I gave up the ghost at 2:00 am, wondering how these horsy people kept the pace!

***

While we had no permanent address, Bon and I availed of the excellent service called *poste restante*. Letters are held in main post offices in alphabetised pigeon holes for up to a month.

In Adelaide, I hit pay dirt: four letters in one day! Happily, one included a cheque from Grannie Scott for my birthday. This was the first financial assistance I had received from home. At last, I could beef up my wardrobe. By this stage, I was down to only one dress.

Marilyn Hawkins's chatty letter revealed that many of our friends were either engaged to be married or were touring Europe. In the space of less than a year, international travel had become the norm within my peer group. Because Marilyn continued to soldier on at university, she complained of being 'unfulfilled'. I was grateful not to know that feeling.

Mom's letter brought me up to date with all the family goings-on. This included the dramatic news that they had completed the sale of the house in Montreal and bought a farm about an hour away, near a town called Hawkesbury. There had been talk of my dad leaving his executive position and opting for the life of a gentleman farmer. He had even gone to agricultural college to become familiar with techniques and trends. I told myself only their surroundings had changed, the family was the same. Still, I couldn't erase the niggling disquiet at the back of my mind. My travels involved adapting to new circumstances nearly every day. I counted on familiarity when I returned to Canada. That no longer would be the case.

Last but not least was a letter from Mac, the officer from the MV *Akaroa*. Bonnie and I had booked passage to New Zealand in September. By coincidence, the ship was the MV *Akaroa*!

"I wonder what Mac'll say when he finds out he has to put up with you again?" Bonnie teased.

"Maybe he'll have a new dolly-bird by that time."

"I don't know. He was pretty smitten with you. And he's still writing."

"True," I admitted. "But will I be interested in him?"

"Any port in a storm," Bonnie said with a cheeky grin.

***

After Oakbank we had two days to build up stamina for the next event. On Thursday morning we were off to Wentworth for a weekend of polo. Horses seemed to be the all-consuming existence of these people. Did no one have a regular job?

"Do you mind travelling with Rob Radford?" Liz asked me. She pointed to a lean hunk standing beside a hay-loaded ute. "It's a long drive that's best done with company. Bonnie can come with me."

"No problem at all," I said, pleased.

Rob took the arrangement in stride, displaying none of the awkward bashfulness of the blokes we had met in Western Australia. He checked that the bales were secure and then we got on our way.

"What's so special about Wentworth?" I asked once we were outside the city.

"Not sure it's special." Rob thought for a moment. "It sits on the junction of the Murray and Darling rivers. It used to be one of the country's busiest ports in the paddle-steamer era of the late 1800s. That might count as special," he said with a smile. "The abos met there for thousands of years for their corroborees and special ceremonies."

"What's a corroboree?"

"It's a traditional gathering where there's lots of song and dance, music, that sort of thing."

"Do they still do it?"

"Sure, but I haven't been to one. It's an abo thing."

It wasn't the Aussie custom to mix with the indigenous population. I saw this as a missed opportunity. What little I had learned of the Aboriginal culture sounded fascinating. I loved that they are in tune with nature and the spirit world and that their survival in a harsh environment depends on this harmony. There must be so much to learn from this ancient people but all the Australians I had met regarded the 'blacks' as being primitive and inferior and treated them as social problems rather than sources of accumulated knowledge.

We made good time until we reached the Murray River, the fourth longest river in the world. We had to wait for fifty minutes until a punt arrived to take us across. During the pause, I learned from Rob that the first race meeting in Wentworth had occurred more than one hundred years earlier and was run down the main street. It mystified me why Australians were obsessed with horses. It seemed that to qualify as a town, a community had to have a pub and a racetrack.

Ninety miles outside Wentworth we met up with Brian Purdy, the person transporting the horses to the match. I switched to Brian's van in order to help him when we arrived at the polo grounds. We unloaded and fed the horses amidst a scourge of midges before going to a dinner party at Mike Keenan's nearby home, where we were staying.

Mike was a well-heeled bachelor who lived in stylish comfort and had the time and the income to indulge his passion for polo.

"I hear you girls are going to be strappers this weekend," Mike said as he poured us pre-dinner drinks.

We had been told of our role the day before.

"That's a new word in our vocabulary. We're not sure what to do," I confessed.

"Strappers are grooms with a difference. In addition to helping care for the horses, your most important job is between chukkas: you have to unsaddle and wash the horse that's been ridden and saddle a fresh horse, all within the tight schedule of eight minutes. Think you can do it?"

"Sure," Bonnie said quickly.

I was still doing time calculations. It was possible the exacting demands would exceed our capabilities. How did we get ourselves into these situations?

The next day, I learned how focused the mind becomes under pressure. Following the lead of more experienced strappers, we soon got the knack and consistently were able to complete the tasks with time to spare.

In addition to strapping for Mike, I did a stint for an ex-racing driver who was reputed to be the best polo player in the country. Between chukkas, I overheard him talking to another player about a 'done' horse. I didn't know a lot about polo, but I did know that horses weren't allowed to be disguised by dyeing their coats. I divulged the conversation to Mike, who looked suitably alarmed at the news. He discreetly looked into the matter and reported back to me.

"Dun, Kathy. The horse is dun. It's a colour. A natural colour, no dye involved."

He gave me a pat on the shoulder and thanked me for letting him know.

The social side of the weekend was no less demanding than

strapping. After the Friday match, Mike had another dinner party, this time for fifty guests. I enjoyed chatting with my dinner companion Keith Forster. When he learned Bonnie and I were working our way around Australia, he invited us to stay with his wife Pauline and himself on their citrus farm for a few days. I knew nothing about picking oranges but I welcomed a change from the high-energy work of looking after polo ponies.

On Saturday night there was a dinner-dance at the Wintersun Hotel in Mildura. Because the hotel was located in Victoria, they had to get special permission to stay open after 11:00 pm. Based on the Australian proclivity for alcohol, I wondered how such a law could have been passed! They relaxed the rules and shut off the lights at 11:45. That didn't stop this hard-drinking crowd. Everyone crossed the border back into South Australia and went to the Grand Hotel to drink with the Melbourne team. We got back to Mike's at 3:30 am. Hopefully life in the orange groves would be less hectic.

***

Over the course of the weekend, Rob Radford and I had frequent interactions. His was a friendly face in a crowd of strangers. Sunday, the final day of polo, he asked to take me out when we got back to Adelaide.

I liked Rob. It would have been nice to get to know him better but I needed the job more than I needed romance. Nor did I want to become embedded, so to speak, in one place and miss out on seeing the rest of the country.

Bonnie returned to Adelaide with Liz for a few days. She would collect my gear and we would meet up at the Forsters' on Thursday.

Pauline Forster took me home to *Bulpunga* with her after the last match. Along the way, we stopped at her friend's place for coffee and damper, another one of those Australian specialties immortalised in song and poem.

"The simple ingredients—flour and water and sometimes a bit of milk—make the bread popular with swaggies and drovers," the friend explained. "They flatten the ashes of the camp fire and put the dough on top to cook for about ten minutes. Then they cover it with ashes and cook it for another twenty or thirty minutes. When the bread has a hollow sound when it's tapped, it's cooked."

"The dressed-up version is called cocky's joy," Pauline added. "That's when you eat it with dried or cooked meat and a splash of golden syrup."

It didn't sound appetising but neither had strawberry jam and cream sandwiches. I sampled the damper and came to the conclusion I would have to be a hungry swaggy to fully appreciate it.

The next day I started work. Although I was pretty fit after all the riding and grooming, that type of exercise hadn't prepared me for the backbreaking rigours of picking oranges. The first day I worked for seven hours and picked two and a half crates, each of which was four foot seven inches by three foot nine by three foot nine. This was double what everyone thought I would achieve. Keith paid three dollars a crate, so I needed to up my quota if I wanted to earn proper money.

This first batch of oranges went to a lab to test the sugar and acid content. It failed to meet the requirements, so further picking was delayed for a few days. In the meantime, Pauline and I collected oranges that had fallen off the trees and split. These we squeezed into twenty pints of juice. Delicious.

The days off gave me an opportunity to make a dress with the material I had bought with some of my birthday money. Like Isabella in Cape Town, Pauline soon felt obliged to rescue me.

"I'll work on the dress if you make biscuits," she offered.

I certainly got the better deal.

Bonnie arrived during this lull. It was great catching up with her.

On Saturday we got together with three other families for a picnic. I made hamburgers, an unfamiliar item at an Australian barbecue. They were the hit of the party.

By Sunday we were back picking. We got two crates each before lunch but then I had to take the rest of the day off. A severe headache served as a reminder that the effects of the car accident were still with me. The intense spasms that centred on the scar on the right side of my forehead had become less frequent but no less severe.

On Monday Bonnie and I picked until dark. Tuesday was our last day. Thank goodness. Every muscle in my body ached and I smelled like oranges, mandarins and grapefruit. It wasn't a job opportunity I would jump at again. Still, the money wasn't bad. For three and a half days' work I earned twenty-four dollars, more than double my usual earnings for this amount of time. I was leaving in worse physical but better financial shape than when I arrived.

CHAPTER 16

All that is gold does not glitter,
not all those who wander are lost.
JRR Tolkien

Our itinerary across Australia corresponded to entries in our address books. Bonnie's brother Geoff had passed on his contacts and we had picked up quite a few of our own. The downside was that we relied on people wanting to invite us into their homes. Sometimes we wrote, other times we phoned, always hoping our potential hosts would initiate an invitation without undue persuasion.

"It's your turn to make the phone call, Kath," Bonnie said a couple of days before we were scheduled to leave *Bulpunga*.

"No, Bon. It's definitely your turn," I insisted.

Bonnie remained silent as she rolled a cigarette. I guessed she was figuring out a way to cajole me into making the approach rather than thinking of what to say during the call.

"C'mon, Bon, it's not that difficult. Just give them our usual patter: 'You don't know me, but …'. It's the outback. Everyone seems to welcome strangers arriving on their doorsteps."

Bonnie took a deep drag and exhaled slowly, apparently contemplating the argument.

"Fine," she said eventually.

She returned a short while later with a smile that signalled success. Bill and Julia McBratney had 'invited' us to stay.

"They're going to meet us in a town called Hay," Bonnie said.

We learned this was in southwestern New South Wales.

"It's part of the Riverina," Keith explained, "a prosperous, agriculturally-diverse region located approximately midway between Adelaide and Sydney. Pauline and I can give you a lift if you like."

"That would be great," I said immediately, thankful to save transportation costs.

"How far is it?" the more diplomatic Bonnie asked.

"About two hundred and fifty miles," Keith said without missing a beat.

Travelling great distances apparently was the norm in this great land. Bonnie and I looked uncertain but succumbed to Keith's and Pauline's insistence that it was no bother.

"Beaut. We'll take you girls for a slap-up lunch and then stop with friends on the way home. Pauline will enjoy the opportunity to do some shopping in the big smoke. It's ANZAC Day tomorrow, so you'll be able to see the celebrations."

"What's ANZAC day?" we asked.

"ANZAC stands for Australian and New Zealand Army Corps. Each year on April 25th, Australians commemorate the soldiers who fought and died at Gallipoli in 1915."

Because Bill and Julia would be overnighting in Hay, Bonnie and I checked into an inexpensive hotel. After lunch the Forsters handed us over to the McBratneys. Like the majority of our hosts, the couple was welcoming and thoughtful.

"Sorry about the hotel," Julia said. "I need to take the opportunity to spend time with my mother. We'll take you out to dinner and then Mom's invited you to coffee."

It was a good day for eating and for meeting nice people.

"Do you realise this is the first hotel we'd been in since Perth?" Bonnie asked when we got to our room that evening. "We've been so lucky getting passed from one person to another."

"It must be the charming words you use in your introduction phone calls," I replied. "I'm happy to hand over that job to you."

"Nice try, Kath. It's not going to happen."

The following day we watched the ANZAC parade and wreath-laying with the McBratneys before travelling with them to *Bringagee*, their station about thirty miles from Hay. Bill took us on a tour of the twenty-two thousand-acre property.

"This is magnificent," I said admiring the bucolic beauty of a river wending its way past leafy gum trees. Birdsong provided pleasant background music. "It's the lushest green I've seen in months."

"It's the lushest green we've seen in decades," Bill said. "We recently had the first good rainfall in forty years."

As we headed back to the car, a large snake crossed the road. Bill got a gun, shot it and then hit it over the head.

"These buggas are supposed to be hibernating at this time of the year but the warm spell has brought them out again. They're deadly poisonous, so never go near one."

No fear of that! Due to a traumatic childhood experience when a boy stuffed a wriggling reptile down the back of my T-shirt, I found it upsetting even to look at a picture of a snake. I quickly got into the car and tried to get a grip on my phobia.

Back at the house, Bill and Julia's daughter Wendy had arrived home for the weekend with three friends. Dinner was a lively affair. One of the fellows had lived in Montreal for four months. It was interesting to hear a foreigner's impression of my city. His enthusiastic descriptions gave me a twinge of homesickness for Montreal's fine restaurants, stylish boutiques and bilingual culture which made it famous.

The weekend's main event was a duck shoot at a neighbouring station. I gave an involuntary shudder. This one, I convinced myself, couldn't possibly be as bad as the one in Western Australia.

"This'll be the last one of the season," Bill told us. "Not that we have many seasons. Shoots are rare because the area usually suffers drought. The recent heavy rains have recreated the swampy terrain ducks love."

The local hunters were suitably attired in thigh-high rubber boots. My jeans and running shoes provided little protection against the sucking mud. Periodically I sank to my waist and had to be pulled out. If that wasn't bad enough, Bonnie and I were expected to fetch the felled birds—an annoying repeat of our previous duck-hunting experience.

"They have dogs for this sort of thing where I come from," I said to Bonnie as she pulled me out of another hole.

"Look at it as exercise. This is sure to burn a few calories," Bonnie replied with her glass-half-full optimism.

We certainly needed to burn calories ... and eat and drink less. Australia had been deadly to my waistline. I blamed Peter Rex in Western Australia for getting me started on daily quarts of Swan lager. After a hot day's hard work, they went down smoothly and settled happily. Treats like strawberry jam and whipped cream sandwiches didn't help either. We worked hard but we ate heartily, too heartily. Accepting the need for exercise, I focused on finding the bloody birds.

By the end of the day, the men had shot nearly two hundred ducks. At dusk, everyone chipped in to cut, pluck and gut the haul.

"Cut the wings off first," one of the men advised. He supervised my initial attempt. "Closer to the body," he said. "Now take the feet off just below the knee." When I had done that correctly, he showed me the next step. "Take the feathers off in small clumps. They're easier to remove that way."

The chore was tedious. Pin feathers were the worst, requiring a tweezer to remove them. Faster hands soon made short work of the pile of bodies.

Once the job was done everyone headed off to *Mungadal* station. At one hundred thousand acres and with twenty-five thousand sheep, this is one of the largest sheep studs in Australia. They are famous for the quality of their merino wool. Judging by the happy crowd, it seemed they were no less accomplished at throwing great parties and big barbecues.

One of the guests was a fellow called John Clark. He had stayed at *Southford* when he visited South Africa. Now he offered to repay the hospitality by inviting us to stay at his home for a few days. John's brother Dave added to the appeal as far as Bonnie was concerned. This suited me just fine since John was the one who had grabbed my attention. His mop of blue-black hair set off his cornflower blue eyes to perfection. Electric currents in my body fired excitedly, alerting me to the potential for romance. Judging by John's lingering glances and his excuses to be near me, the attraction was mutual.

Early the following morning, Bill McBratney drove us to *Merri-*

ola.

"Welcome," John said, helping Bill unload our bags. "We'll get you settled in shortly. Right now we need to check on lambing maiden ewes. Are you girls up for some station work?"

"Absolutely," I said with enthusiasm.

By 9:30 am we were galloping across the range. At last I was living my cowgirl dream. We were on a mission to check for fly-blow among the ewes. This is a condition where flies lay their eggs in the soiled wool or in open wounds. When the maggots hatch, they burrow into the wool and eventually into the animal's flesh.

"We dip the sheep regularly to prevent this sort of thing," John explained, "but it's a big problem. If the larvae get a chance to develop, the cycle continues."

We were on horseback for five and a half hours before taking a break.

"There are more meal times than meals with this job," John said with an engaging smile.

For once, I didn't care. My stomach was already full—with butterflies! Despite my determination not to let romance interfere with travel, I was helpless in the face of John's charm.

After we unsaddled and tended to the horses, we went to John's place, separate from the main house which we saw only from a distance because his parents were away.

John's accommodation was bereft of decoration or anything beyond rudimentary comforts. The kitchen, immediately to the right of the entrance, had basic appliances and a sink. There was little cupboard or counter space. The Spartan living/dining room took up the rest of the open area. To the left of the entrance was a small bedroom and bathroom. I noticed how neat everything was: bed made, no build-up of dirty laundry on the floor, none of the mess I would expect to find in the bedroom of a bachelor—unless he was expecting a visitor.

That evening, I played my guitar and sang for the Clarks, Bonnie and two station hands. Finally, everyone went their separate ways. Bonnie and Dave disappeared to Dave's bachelor hideaway and the station hands shuffled off to their bunkhouse. John and I were alone.

It wasn't long before we found ourselves in John's single bed. John, I realised, was my first 'love' affair. Making love with him wasn't unexpected or a matter of convenience, like it had been with my first two partners. With John it happened as a result of a deep emotion I never had experienced. When he cradled me in his arms afterwards, I felt safe, cherished and at peace.

Neither of us had brought up the subject of protection beforehand. On the ship, Mac had a ready supply of condoms—to be expected with a globe-trotting sailor. Evidently, outback farmers don't get the same volume of traffic.

John tried to be helpful when I belatedly raised my concern about pregnancy but he only could update me on sheep cycles, which occur every seventeen days. Not useful. As naive as I was, I knew human cycles were monthly. But I never could remember exactly at what point the 'danger zone' occurred. I wished my mother had had 'the talk' with me, but sex education in the 1960s was rare in general and totally absent in my household. Based on the date of my last period, I figured I was safe for another ten days —even by sheep cycles.

To lighten the mood, John offered a snippet of local wisdom.

"Australian women take the pill and LSD together."

My eyes widened. Drugs were definitely not part of my routine.

"Why?" I asked, walking into the trap.

"So they can take a trip without the kids."

We laughed at the silliness but I admonished myself to pay closer attention to birth control.

The time spent with John at *Merriola* couldn't be described as domestic bliss. There was hard work to be done and difficult horses to ride. One morning after breakfast I had to go to one of the paddocks and drive the tractor back so they could pull a pipe out of the river and repair the water pump. Another day, Bonnie and I had to muster Dorset rams. Bonnie was given Trump Fire, a former race horse. He began to buck as soon as the saddle was put on. He eventually calmed down but Bonnie persuaded me to switch horses with her. On the ride home, Trump Fire reared and pranced and jumped around. A couple of fellows saw what was happening and raced over in the ute. What a relief to dismount from the monster.

"It's past lunch time. Let's grab a bite," John suggested, discretely giving me a chance to calm my nerves.

Not only were meal times irregular on the station, they could be unusual.

"Ever eaten sheep's brains?" John asked when we got to his place.

"I can't say I have. And I'm not sure I want to start."

"They're delicious. I'll cook some for you. We have a new batch."

I watched John heat the blackened frying pan on his two-burner stove, throw in some butter and then add the knot of brains.

"You only want to eat brains from healthy sheep," John warned. "If they're infected, your own brain can go spongy, or some such thing."

"That's a great sales pitch," I said, now adding health worries to my squeamishness about eating this part of the animal.

"Where's your sense of culinary adventure?" John teased.

In fact, the brains were surprisingly tasty. I suspected, however, this would be my first and last such experience. They're not a supermarket item in Canada.

Bonnie and I had agreed we would limit our stay to four days. Emotionally, this was a wise decision. I was becoming increasingly fond of John. A full-time commitment to the hardships of outback life didn't appeal but John had qualities that attracted me: a sense of responsibility, intelligence, kindness and humour. A combination like that was hard to dismiss. *Say goodbye now, while it's still relatively easy*, I told myself. Reluctantly, I listened to my head instead of my heart.

"You're not the first fling I've had," John said as we snuggled in bed on our final morning, "but you're the most difficult to let go."

His gentle kiss on my forehead threatened to melt my resolve.

"We'll write, won't we?" I asked, putting a little physical distance between us.

"We'll write. And we'll remember."

One last time, the physical distance disappeared.

Later, as I packed, John suggested that we spend a day or two with another outback bachelor and go wild pig hunting.

"Thanks but no thanks, John," I said firmly. "Hunting is never a good experience for us. Besides," I added, smoothing my hand over his stubbled cheek, "I don't need another bachelor in my life at the moment."

***

We had an invitation to visit Brian and Joy Jones in the strangely named Wagga Wagga. This is the largest inland city in New South Wales and a major metropolis of the Riverina. The plan had been to get a ride on a mail truck going to Wagga but that lead fell through.

"I'll drive you girls," John offered.

"How far is it?" I asked.

"About a hundred and sixty-five miles."

"No way. You have too much to do here."

"Then let me at least drive you into Hay. Maybe there's a bus you can catch."

We accepted this arrangement. It would give me an extra couple of hours with John.

It turned out there were no buses going to Wagga within our time frame. We decided to hitch. Reluctantly, John left us at a service station on the outskirts of town. We can't have looked appealing with our suitcases, a guitar and a large, curly-horned ram's skull I had collected along the way. Eventually a man driving a roomy station wagon got us to where we were going.

The Joneses had taken a bit of persuading to act as hosts. It seemed they weren't used to having strangers as house guests. The first evening, their idea of entertaining was to show us a couple of exceedingly dreary hours of holiday videos. As nice as it was to have a break from riding crazy horses, plucking ducks, picking fruit and doing myriad other difficult or monotonous chores for little or no money, home movies was a steep price to pay for a bed.

The next day, Joy Jones took us to a nearby poultry farm that had a gem-polishing sideline. After observing the process and chatting with the owner, Bonnie came to the conclusion that we should go opal mining in Lightning Ridge.

"Jeez, Bon, there's no requirement to have *every* Australian experience," I moaned.

"Think of the adventure, man," she insisted.

"That's exactly what I'm thinking of, and I'm not sure it's something I want. Besides," I added hopefully, "a mining town like Lightning Ridge has got to be way off our itinerary."

"We don't have an itinerary," Bonnie reminded me. "Think about it."

There was nothing to think about. Not when Bonnie got her teeth into an idea. I made no further objections, gambling that a new, outrageous idea soon would replace Bonnie's current enthusiasm for opal mining.

"Fine, but first we have to get to Canberra. The Sages are expecting us today."

Bonnie decided we needed to step up our hitch-hiking efforts. She made a *Canberra or Bust* sign to let potential rides know where we were headed. After an hour of standing by the roadside with our thumbs out, a bearded wonder called Paul Harvey picked us up. I was wary at first but he turned out to be considerate, knowledgeable and generous with his time. When we arrived in Canberra he gave us an informed tour of the city, took us to Kay and Charles Sage's house in the suburbs to drop our luggage and then brought us back into the centre so we could explore on foot.

We didn't like Canberra. In 1908, with Sydney and Melbourne vying to be the seat of federal government, it was decided to build to plan a compromise capital. Canberra is located within the specially-created territory called the ACT (Australian Capital Territory). The architecture is impressive and the city's layout features many interesting geometric motifs and green spaces but the relatively young city lacked atmosphere.

On our second and final night, the Sages had a dinner party for us. Mike Keenan, the fellow with whom we stayed during the Wentworth polo matches, showed up with three friends. It was lovely to see him again.

"Does everyone know one another in this country?" I asked, astonished at the web of connections I kept coming across.

"There's a small population for enormous distances," Mike said with a smile. "We tend to build networks and keep in touch. I never go anywhere without my address book."

Bonnie and I laughed. We weren't alone in our reliance on contacts.

Three days after arriving in Canberra, we were on our way to Sydney. This time we splashed out and took the train. Crossing the continent, from Perth to Sydney, had cost me a grand total of forty-three dollars and ninety-three cents in transportation. The scenery and distances were the same whether we travelled first class or budget, I told myself, trying not to long for the comfort and convenience of luxury travel.

The final stretch of our continental journey took eight hours. In between the frequent stops at small stations I had plenty of time to reflect. By now I had been away from home for ten eventful months. I was no longer the innocent who had been determined but terrified to step into the unknown. Now I did that almost every day without giving the matter a thought. Travel had expanded my mind and allowed me to see and do things I couldn't have imagined a short time ago. The pleasures far outweighed the setbacks and hardships. Moreover, I was fortunate to be making these discoveries in the company of a loyal friend whose impulsiveness and sense of fun kept me on my toes and ensured life was never dull.

CHAPTER 17

A mind that is stretched by a new experience
can never go back to its old dimensions.
Oliver Wendell Holmes

Jack Mitchell, one of Geoff Southey's contacts, met us at the train station.

"Welcome to Sydney," Jack said, shaking hands. His tall, slender figure bent to pick up our two suitcases. He observed the ram's head without comment. "It'll take a bit longer than usual to get home. It's rush-hour."

"That's something we haven't seen for a long time," I remarked.

"You haven't missed anything, I promise," Jack said, leading us towards the exit.

'Rush' hour, in fact, was 'deadly slow' hour but the snail-like movement gave us a chance to study the cityscape. We drove through a canyon of towering glass and steel. After the open spaces of the outback, the environment felt claustrophobic.

"Not long now," Jack said, as we finally picked up speed.

Geoff hadn't told us much about the Mitchells but when we pulled into their drive, I knew our stay would be comfortable. The Mitchells lived in a northern suburb called Avalon Beach. The area had an idyllic quality about it: expensive, architect-designed homes with lush gardens and spectacular views. The Mitchell house was the most modern residence I ever had been in. Large windows, stylish furniture and expensive art featured prominently. Each room looked like it had been staged for a photo shoot. The atmosphere wasn't warm but there was no denying its elegance.

"This is my wife, Janice," Jack said, introducing us to an equally tall, equally slender woman.

I admired Janice's coordinated, smart-casual clothing and her flattering use of makeup. It occurred to me that makeup was another thing I hadn't seen much of in a long time. Women in the bush used little more than moisturiser.

Janice showed us to our room and then offered drinks and hors d'oeuvres before dinner. I could get used to this.

Jack and Janice were an agreeable, sophisticated couple. Jack described himself as a lawyer. I mentally added 'successful', based on his lifestyle and the fact that he owned one thousand square *miles* of land in northern Queensland.

"It's not as impressive as it sounds," Jack said modestly. "It's mostly scrub."

To me, it was as impressive as it sounded. His bit of scrub land was bigger than some countries.

I wondered what the Mitchells thought of us. Did they admire our initiative to see the world? Or did they consider us reckless and naive to embark on such an expedition with little cash and no experience? Perhaps our gumption made them wish they had had the courage to have similar adventures before settling down. Their words and expressions revealed nothing. I helped myself to more cheese and crackers, relegating philosophical meanderings to another time and place.

The next day, Janice showed us the surrounding area. Except for the Barrenjoey Head lighthouse, there were no major landmarks in the northern suburbs, but the scenery of tropical vegetation and the sea lapping at sandy beaches was picture-postcard perfect.

Janice dropped us at the Manly ferry. The thirty-minute service that would take us into Sydney has been operating since the mid-19th century.

"What a sight!" I leaned on the ferry railing and admired a view of bridges and skyscrapers sprinkled with plenty of greenery.

"Not bad for a former penal colony," Bonnie remarked.

The outpost situated on the world's largest natural harbour had grown into a global centre of commerce and culture. The throb of Sydney's pulse could be felt even from this distance.

Up close, the city didn't disappoint. I had seen more beautiful places, less crowded places but the intense energy of this particular city took hold of me and didn't want to let go. I had loved South Africa deeply but quietly, my feelings tempered by a political slant that ran contrary to how I believed people should be treated. Sydney, on the other hand, aroused passion. I never had encountered such vibrancy. This was somewhere I could live.

Our first destination was the headquarters of Dr Scholl's, the world-famous specialists in footwear and foot care. Bonnie needed a new strap for her sandals.

"These are great shoes," I said to the man assigned to help us. "I've come all the way from Canada in them and will go the rest of the way around the world if they hold up."

The man looked at the stained, worn examples of his company's product. I wrapped one foot around my ankle, instinctively attempting to hide evidence of the demands I had placed on these sturdy clogs.

"You girls are the best advertisements for Dr Scholl's that I've seen for a long time. I'd like to give you each a complimentary pair of sandals. And there won't be any charge for the extra strap," he added with a broad grin.

Bonnie and I turned to look at each other. Our astonishment quickly turned to delight.

"Really? Free shoes? Thank you so much." I said, casting my eyes over the well-soled, clean selection.

It was hard to know who got more pleasure from the transaction, him or us.

Our next stops were transportation- and job-related. We dropped in at the offices of Dalgety's, a national shipping agent. It had been suggested that we might be able to get a ride to northern Queensland with one of their drivers. The harried office manager seemed surprised we would approach the company with such a request.

"We transport goods, not people," he said sharply.

Evidently he never had had to be creative about getting from point A to point B. His terse rejection perplexed me.

"It wasn't such an unreasonable request," I grumbled to Bonnie as we returned to the noisy sidewalk outside the office. "They have trucks travelling with empty passenger seats and we're willing passengers who need to get to a new destination at minimal cost. What's the big deal?"

The job hunt proved no more successful. We had heard good things about Hay Island, a luxury resort on the Great Barrier Reef off the northern-most coast of Queensland.

"Try again when you get farther north," the company receptionist advised, "but don't hold your breath. We have more requests than openings."

This piece of news probably would please Mom. She had written in a recent letter, *Take it easy on the Great Barrier Reef. I hear it is slowly disintegrating because something is destroying the coral-making animals.*

Good old Mom. Ever the pessimist. It was just as well she didn't know everything Bonnie and I were getting up to or her negativity gene would have gone into overdrive.

Errands done, we were free to explore the city. We headed straight for King's Cross or The Cross, as locals call it. It had a mixed reputation as the red-light district and a centre for crime but also as a quarter favoured by artists and entertainers. It was therefore a tourist draw. The less attractive visuals—neon signs and seedy places of business—were interspersed with trendy shops, galleries and funky restaurants. We preferred the upmarket retail area in central Sydney.

"We should get a small present for the Mitchells," Bonnie reminded me as we pressed our noses against shop windows. "Any ideas?"

On our budget, house gifts for our hosts couldn't be expensive but we tried to inject originality into each offering. But what to give the Mitchells? They were millionaires living in Australia's biggest city. They had or could get anything they needed or wanted.

"Food's always a good idea. They don't have to dust it or put it on display," I said.

"Chocolates?" Bonnie suggested.

"No, that's too mundane for people like the Mitchells."

"What are you suggesting?"

"I'm not sure yet. A gourmet shop's a good starting point."

We found just the place we were looking for. Steering away from elaborate gift baskets, we headed to luxury grocery.

"Perfect!" I said, picking up tins of smoked octopus and smoked oysters.

"You've got to be kidding!" Bonnie exclaimed.

"They can serve these at their fancy drinks parties."

Bonnie allowed herself to be persuaded.

A startled look crossed Janice Mitchell's face before she thanked us graciously.

"You didn't have to do this," she said.

Now, I realise, she probably wished we hadn't.

***

On Saturday, Jack Mitchell took us for lunch at the local sailing club. From the dining room window, I admired the flock of puffed sails as weekend mariners tacked out to open water.

"So what are your plans?" Jack asked once we had ordered and after the waiter had poured glasses of chilled sauvignon blanc.

Plans? That concept was alien to our current existence. Of course, I wasn't about to confess the shortfalls of our migrant lifestyle.

"We're heading north to work on stations," I said with false confidence.

"Jim and Mary Grant, former employers of Geoff's, live near Dalby, Queensland. They're expecting us," Bonnie added. "In fact, we should probably be on our way later today."

I tried not to mirror Jack's surprised reaction. I hadn't expected our departure to be imminent.

"That's rather sudden, isn't it?" Jack asked.

"These types of decisions are usually sudden with Bonnie," I said with a frown in her direction. She could have warned me, and she certainly should have given the Mitchells a bit more notice. "We don't want to appear ungrateful, but cities eat cash. We need to start working again. Stations are more willing to take on temporary help than city businesses. In order to make it around Australia within our time frame, we don't stay anywhere for too long."

"I understand," Jack said. "Let's enjoy lunch. Judging from some of the stories you've told us, this could be your last good meal for a while."

After a hurried job of packing and saying goodbye to the Mitchells, we caught the bus and train that would take us to central Sydney. Cash dictated distance. We bought a ticket to Quirindi, a nonentity of a town about two hundred fifty miles north of Sydney. The stop-start journey got us to the station at 4:00 am, a fact we hadn't taken into consideration when booking. We were the only passengers to disembark.

"It's unlikely there'll be any sort of accommodation open at this hour of the morning—if this bump in the road even has accommodation," I said grimly. "What do you want to do?"

Bonnie walked over to the waiting room and tried the handle. The door opened.

"Let me show you to your room, Madam," she said with a bow and a sweep of her arm.

At that moment, we saw the solid frame of the station master heading in our direction.

"Planning to spend the night?" he asked.

We nodded, waiting to be evicted.

"This isn't a hotel, so we don't have blankets or other creature comforts but I can offer you these mail sacks as some protection against the cold," he said, handing us smelly canvas bags.

We each chose a bench, covered it with one bag and crawled into another bag. The supplement of coats and sweaters kept the worst of the cold at bay. At least we had a roof over our heads.

When I opened my eyes the next morning, I saw a window full of faces staring at us. Passengers who otherwise would have waited inside had let us continue sleeping. We nodded our thanks as we went out to the ladies' toilet.

When we returned to the waiting room, the area manager of the railway introduced himself and offered to drive us to Werris Creek.

"It's only thirteen miles away but it's a major junction," he explained. "I'll try to get you onto a goods train to take you further north."

"Goods train?" I asked. "You mean in a box car with no seats? Like hobos travel?"

"Well, we might be able to offer you something a little better," the man said with a laugh.

It turned out there were no goods trains going in our direction until that night. We decided to hitch-hike. The manager dropped us at a local service station. Half an hour later, he showed up to check on our progress ... or lack of it.

"Hop in," he said, opening the passenger door, "I can take you a hundred miles up the road."

This got us to a place called Armidale, a small inland city halfway between Sydney and Brisbane. We had been travelling for nearly a day and we were still in New South Wales.

We got picked up by a truck driver glad of company. Bonnie carried much of the conversation burden. My god, that girl is good at talking about nothing. I would doze off until a sharp elbow in the ribs reminded me I was supposed to help out.

For our next ride, Bonnie went in one truck and I followed in a second. When my driver got drowsy, he pulled to the side of the road, explained the nine gears and told me to drive. He was foolish to suggest such a thing. Since I didn't have a driving license and couldn't remember lists of instructions, I was even more foolish to agree! Changing four gears on a car was a challenge for me; nine on a truck was beyond my immediate comprehension, especially since I was so tired. Manoeuvring a groaning vehicle overloaded with potatoes around sharp bends and up steep hills was not an experience I want to repeat. Only the tunnels of light thrown off by the truck's headlights pierced the curtain of blackness. I concentrated intensely, praying I wouldn't have to brake if an animal suddenly appeared, or swerve sharply to make room for an oncoming vehicle. Fortunately, we met no traffic. After a harrowing descent down a twisty road, I persuaded the driver it was safer to let me talk and him drive. I suspect many of my sentences were incomplete or inane but I had the wherewithal to make sure his eyelids didn't droop.

Bonnie and I arrived in Warwick at 11:00 pm. Unable to face more driving, we went into an all-night café. Not even strong coffee could keep me awake. I lay my head on the table and slept until I felt a large hand shaking me at 2:00 am.

"Do your parents know you're here?" the equally large owner of the hand wanted to know.

We convinced the policeman that, although our parents had absolutely no idea of our whereabouts, our intentions were honourable.

At 5:00 am a truck laden with apples took us further along the road to Toowoomba. We enjoyed delicious apples for breakfast but for this I had to endure the driver's hand on my knee. I pretended to be asleep, silently cursing bloody Southey who always made me get into the trucks first so I sat beside the drivers!

From Toowoomba it was easy to get a ride for the fifty miles to Dalby. We phoned the Grants, to let them know we had arrived. Jim Grant came to collect us.

We liked the Grants immediately. Mary had the warmth of Mother Earth. She immediately took her two bedraggled guests under her wing. After a satisfying lunch, she sent us to our room.

"You girls look like you're asleep on your feet. Go have a rest."

We accepted her suggestion with gratitude—and napped until supper time. We ate quickly and then returned to our beds. Never again would I take for granted the luxuries of sheets, blankets, a soft pillow and a cosy bed.

By the following day we had caught up on lost sleep. Now we had to find a job. I was down to three dollars.

"Your timing's bad. Queensland is suffering the worst drought in its history," Mary told us. "There's virtually no paid work available. I've asked around but, with money so tight, people aren't taking on help like they used to."

When Mary mentioned that Nan and Jerry Foxton were at the end of their tether with the extra work of having to feed the cattle instead of letting them graze, I volunteered to help for a few days. Grateful for my offer, they insisted on paying me.

My first impression of the Foxtons was 'weathered and worried'.

Gangly, moustachioed Jerry wore glasses that made him look pro-fessorial. His polished vocabulary and erudite manner contributed to this image. Nan's pinched features suggested she carried more cares than her petite frame could bear. I was glad to give them a hand.

The first morning, Jerry knocked on my bedroom door at 6:00 am and left a sandwich and a cup of tea on my bedside table.

"This will keep you going until breakfast," he said. "We'll leave in fifteen minutes."

I wasn't used to eating so early in the day but Jerry hadn't said how long we would be gone. I gobbled down the food and hurriedly got dressed.

As Jerry slowly drove through the cattle paddocks, I balanced precariously on the stacked bales of hay in the back of the large truck. My job was to cut the strings on the bales with an axe and break off three-inch wedges. I distributed these 'biscuits' to the hungry cattle who followed.

"Make sure the strings don't get thrown over because the cattle will eat them," Jerry instructed.

And then you'd have stringy beef.

With all the rapid and strenuous bending and lifting, I was glad I had downed the sandwich and tea before going out. We reloaded the truck and repeated the exercise in a second paddock and then loaded the truck a third time to be ready for the next day's feeding.

After a welcome breakfast, Jerry announced we would go out to put droppers on fences. He elaborated when he saw my quizzical look.

"Droppers reduce the number of posts we need, so it's a less expensive way of fencing. They also strengthen the fence, helping it to withstand cattle and 'roo strikes.

"But what are they?" I asked. "What do they look like? How do you put them on?"

"They're like a long, smooth bolt," Jerry explained. "You attach it between two wires of a fence to keep them apart. It's pretty easy."

Jerry was right. Once I got the hang of it, I moved along at a good pace.

"After lunch we need to fence," he said as we headed back to the house.

He didn't assure me this next chore would be easy. With reason. A digger prepared the holes but the manual work of lugging heavy posts, securing them in the holes and then stringing wire between each of them was tough going. All I could think of was the enormous size of these stations. How much fencing did they need? And was I going to have to do it?

Fortunately, this particular job was limited to one smallish paddock. By the end of the second day, we had completed the task.

"We'll eat in ten minutes," Nan said, when Jerry and I walked in tired, dirty and hungry.

I excused myself to wash and change—and to prepare to face whatever Nan had concocted for dinner. Nan had to be the world's worst cook. If I hadn't been so hungry at each meal, I would have left most of the food on my plate. Now I understood Jerry's praise for a tasty but otherwise ordinary vegetable soup I made and why he encouraged me to experiment in the kitchen.

"The best chefs are inventive," he told me when I suggested adding ingredients not included in a recipe. "Don't be afraid to make a mistake."

Nan had taken this command to heart.

On Saturday, after feeding the cattle earlier than usual, Jerry and I drove to the Bunya mountains to get a load of pumpkins for cattle feed. Bonnie and the Grants were there as well.

"These are part of Australia's Great Dividing Range," Mary Grant explained. "They run for more than two thousand miles through Queensland and New South Wales before petering out in western Victoria.

This was my first experience of a rainforest. I breathed in the musty, moisture-laden atmosphere, a pleasant change from the drought-ridden dryness I had become used to. Unfamiliar bird sounds broke the silence. I wondered what other creatures were listening and watching. Bonnie and I swung from the vines and took short walks on trails through the lush vegetation. I wish there had been more time to explore but Jim Grant was taking us to picnic races and a social at the property of their friends the Bassingth-waightes. I felt guilty about leaving Jerry.

"I'll be right. You go off and enjoy yourself," he insisted. "You've earned it."

It was at the races when Bonnie got another of her hare-brained ideas: we would continue our travels around Australia in a horse and buggy.

"We can barely afford to feed ourselves," I sputtered. "How can we take care of a horse?"

"But we wouldn't have to worry about transportation," Bonnie argued, her brows raised in faux astonishment that I hadn't arrived at this obvious conclusion myself.

I could only stare at this crazy friend of mine. Did Bonnie came up with these schemes just to jar me out of the sensible rut where I felt most comfortable?

Two people actually donated horses for the adventure but it was impossible to find a buggy. Thank heaven for small mercies!

***

Jerry and I did most of our work with the help of the ute. One day I persuaded him to let us do something horse related. Now that I had recovered from my horsey overdose in New South Wales, I missed riding.

"There's some cattle that need mustering. Let's saddle up."

The ride was invigorating. My horse handled well and knew exactly what he was doing. When a mob of cattle on the far side of the herd broke away, Jerry shouted at me to go and get them. My horse flew, determined to bring order to chaos as soon as possible.

The fun outing turned perilous when I found myself travelling at no reduced speed through trees, low branches and dead logs. I pulled on the reins but the horse had a job to do and he wasn't going to let a wuss of a rider stop him. Then, as quickly as it had begun, the danger passed. We were in the open, the cattle had been rounded up and I hadn't been dismounted. My knees felt so watery, I could have relieved the drought. Jerry rode over to me, his face creased with a wide grin.

"Gudonya. You handled the horse well but this isn't the place for dressage. Let me show you how to muster Aussie-style."

We rode back to the dreaded woods.

"Depending on the situation, you can either stand in the stirrups or shorten the reins and lean forward on the neck, like a jockey. The Aussie stock saddle was designed for safety in rough riding conditions. The deep seat makes it more comfortable than English saddles on long rides and also gives more security. Let me show you a few tricks."

Jerry gave an impressive demonstration and then patient instruction. What a difference good technique makes! Stock riding now featured more prominently in our daily routine.

One afternoon after we had unsaddled and watered the horses, Jerry disappeared into the barn. When he returned, he carried two kangaroo hides.

"One for you, one for your mate," he said, handing me the bloody skins. "You need to nail them to the shed wall to dry. Then we'll get them tanned."

"Fantastic," I said, holding up the large pelt. "My last skin got confiscated because it hadn't been treated. I don't want to make that mistake again."

Another day, Jerry presented me with a beautiful leather belt he had made and on which he had tooled my name. The buckle was antique brass.

"Got tired of seeing you use binder twine to hold up your strides," he said shyly.

"Thank you. Thank you so much," accepting the practical and sentimental present.

Once again I was reminded of my good fortune in meeting so many kind people.

Jerry's most significant act of consideration was his determination that I would get a driving license. He was a demanding teacher. I accepted having to achieve the usual level of driving proficiency, but Jerry also instructed me about the inner workings of the vehicle.

"In case you get stuck somewhere, you can fix the problem yourself," Jerry said.

Not bloody likely. This much I have learned about myself: I have no aptitude for mechanics. That didn't stop Jerry from making me as qualified as possible in the short time he had to work with me. He took me on rugged routes, made me start the car on a hill, drive in reverse and parallel park between barrels.

"We've got an appointment in Bell tomorrow for your driving test," he announced one evening.

I paused in the chewing of the shoe-leather stew Nan had prepared.

"Am I ready?"

"You're probably as ready as you'll ever be. They're not going to ask you to change the oil or put in a new carburettor," Jerry said with a smile, "so you should do just fine. Besides, the person who'll give you the test is my cobber."

"Your cobbler, as in shoe maker?"

"No, my *cobber*. That's strine for 'good friend'. He'll see you right."

The 'cobber' was an amiable policeman in a sleepy town. He put me through the required paces, carried out quickly and on empty streets. We saw only one other car.

"Congratulations. You passed," he said when we got back to the station. "You'll get your license in the mail."

"That's it? No written test?"

"No need. If Jerry taught you, you know all you need to know, and then some."

Thank you, Jerry.

He hunted through piles of papers and files on shelves, at last retrieving a small booklet which he handed to me.

"Rules of the road. You might wanna take a squizz at them."

CHAPTER 18

It is not the destination where you end up but the mishaps
and memories you create along the way.
Penelope Riley

My ten days with the Foxtons had been eventful. In addition to gaining new work experiences and an Australian driving license, I had learned more about car engines than I ever wanted to know. I was sorry to leave, except for a niggling concern that Jerry might want to teach me about the innards of other farm machinery. His diligence at sharing his extensive mechanical knowledge far exceeded mine to absorb it.

"Thank you for everything. It's been great." I hugged Nan and Jerry. "Believe it or not, one of the things I'm going to miss most is those delicious sandwiches you bring me each morning, Jerry. What kind of cheese is it?"

Jerry frowned and looked at Nan. She shrugged.

"I've never made you a cheese sandwich," he said.

Now it was my turn to frown.

"Of course you have. You wake me up with a cup of tea and a sandwich."

"That's just bread and butter. A thick slab of butter, I admit, but butter."

My stomach did a small flip at the thought of ingesting all that fat but then my taste buds reminded me that this particular fat tasted pretty damn good.

"My expanded waist and I thank you," I said with a laugh.

"We're sorry to see you go," Jerry said. "You've been a great help."

"I hate to leave but Bonnie and I have a lot of territory to cover before we leave in September."

"Are you headed home then?" Nan asked.

"Eventually. First we'll go to New Zealand for a few weeks."

"Safe travels, Kathy. I know you'll get where you're going," Jerry said enigmatically.

The arrival of Bonnie and Val Bassingthwaighte brought our goodbyes to a close.

A week earlier we had been invited to tea and tennis at the lofty sandstone manor known as Jimbour House.

"This is definitely not your typical Aussie homestead," I whispered to Bonnie. "This is a fair dinkum stately home, more suited to the English countryside than the Australian outback."

The spacious, high-ceilinged rooms were lavish compared to most residences we had seen. A swimming pool, trampoline and tennis court were also unusual. It was here where one of the first cattle and sheep stations was established in the Darling Downs more than one hundred years earlier.

Since the late 1800s Jimbour has been known as the starting point for the famous dingo fence, the longest such structure in the world. This five thousand five hundred-mile wire mesh barrier was built to keep out the large population of wild dogs that prey on sheep. Although the fence is monitored regularly, young dingoes can work their way through unnoticed holes. The project therefore hasn't enjoyed a complete success rate but sheep losses have been reduced substantially.

Thanks to contacts we made at the tennis party, we now had a job on the station. The large house and property required numerous employees so, for a change, Bonnie and I weren't alone helping with chores. Because we were the only two female hired hands, the property manager invited us to stay with his wife and him in the main house.

The day began with staff breakfast at 6:30. By 7:00 am we were at work mustering or feeding cattle, pitching hay, putting linseed oil on fences, and any number of other chores. The only break until 5:00 pm quitting time was a half hour for lunch.

Mustering was my favourite part of the job. Since Jerry Foxton had taught me how to ride Aussie-style, I was more confident in difficult situations. My competence, however, was far from expert. On one drive, I galloped ahead to open some gates. When I rode too close to the cattle, the herd scattered in unplanned-for directions. Restoring order added nearly half an hour to our outing.

Not all mustering involved huge herds. On our way back from checking fences, I was asked to bring four 'poddies', or calves, from one paddock to another. This should have been pretty straightforward but one little bugger escaped. Every time I tried to make him go where I wanted him to go, he outsmarted me and took his own route. After I had chased him the length of three paddocks Noel, the senior jackeroo, arrived. I felt like I was watching a cowboy movie: as soon as Noel caught up with the calf, he jumped off his horse, wrestled the calf to the ground and twisted his tail, sending a clear signal that the game was over. A lesson learned but not a technique I intended to apply.

Branding is an important annual event on cattle stations. I pushed aside pity for the animals and followed instructions to work the calves through the races and into a cradle where they were locked in and swung on the side. There they had their ears clipped, were injected against blackleg (a fatal spore-forming bacteria), had drops put in their eyes, and were given a number brand and a station brand. After all the calves had been branded, one or two at a time were put into a pen with the cows to 'mother up'. The cow and calf were then sent through another race and I had to record the calf's brand number with the cow's ear number. I nearly got branded myself when I tripped over a rock and fell a hair's breadth away from a hot iron, threatening yet more damage to my poor face.

Another cattle encounter involved an immense prize bull. Bonnie and I had been invited to a picnic at a station belonging to the Homewoods, near Warra. After lunch, we helped them with dipping cattle against ticks. I was asked to keep the animals away from an opening in the yard. As I walked over to take up the required position, I felt hot, humid breathing on my neck. This was followed by a wet nuzzle in my hair. I turned around to face the biggest bovine I ever had seen. He looked like a model for a Stubbs painting. With slow, deliberate movements, I backed away, trying to relocate to another part of the yard. My suitor gave a soulful bellow. His massive body jiggled as his bony legs pranced in my direction. This time his soft, pink slab of a tongue gave my face a robust lick. One of the men moved the rest of the cattle to another part of the yard while a second man put distance between the bull and me, allowing me to make a clean get-away.

"Never seen him go after a two-legged heifer before!" the owner announced.

"Can't say I've ever been admired by a four-legged bull," I replied, relieved the beast hadn't had a chance to be more expressive in his show of affection.

***

Fencing was my least favourite job. One time, we spent all day putting up temporary fencing in a paddock. Jerry Foxton had taught me well. I suggested to Noel that the posts were too far apart to give enough tension to the lighter gauge baling wire we were using instead of proper fencing wire. He assured me it would be fine. After finally getting the job done, we drove the cattle into the paddock and then watched while they walked through the fence as though it wasn't there. Uncharacteristically, I kept my opinions to myself but it took a mighty effort to keep the words *I told you so* behind my teeth.

Despite the hard work and long hours, Bonnie's tendency to prank didn't diminish. One day, on our last run to unload hay, the truck got bogged down in a rare and unexpected downpour.

"You need to push, Kath, or we'll never get out of here."

Since Bonnie already sat in the driver's seat, I got out and looked for rocks to put behind the wheels to give them purchase.

"Give it a go," I shouted.

I stood at the rear and pushed with all my might. Wheels spun and mud splattered. Suddenly the vehicle lurched forward, freed from the rut.

"Great work. Thanks," Bonnie called out the window.

She waved—and continued driving. I was left standing in the

middle of an almighty great paddock in the pouring rain. When I arrived back at the house fifteen minutes later, chilled and drenched, Bonnie greeted me with shameless good humour, an apology and a thick towel.

"Expect payback," I said with a reluctant grin.

Not all our duties were physically strenuous. After approving our initial efforts, our trusting boss left Bonnie and me with the responsibility of naming the new batch of stud cattle. With over one hundred names being required, our imaginations soon became devilish, resulting in decidedly unconventional stud book entries. This didn't go over well with management.

"These unorthodox names might put a smile on some faces at the sales," I suggested meekly.

Only now was the significance of what we had done hitting me. Breeders take names seriously. Initially, we tried to have a link with the sire's or dam's name but sometimes that link was tenuous. I was grateful we had rejected possibilities such as Big Balls Billy and Hamburger Heaven.

Our boss reviewed the lists once again and shook his head. Then he gave a hint of a grin.

"Some of these are original, I'll give you that," he said. "A few are actually quite clever. You may have started a new trend." Then his face became serious. "That's not to say I approve."

Bonnie and I dutifully bowed our heads and apologised.

After our first week, despite our stud-naming stunt, we received a ten percent bonus on our expected pay of twenty dollars. I felt rich after hitting my all-time low of ninety-three cents!

It amused us that we had been classified as jackaroos on the pay stub.

"Don't reckon there's any calling for a female equivalent— which I guess might be jillaroos," Noel said. "Any sheilas that work on stations usually are governesses or cooks. You girls have invaded a male bastion. Gudonya," he said with a wink.

The second week's pay didn't have a bonus attached. This might have been because I had a tractor accident: as I was trying to get the trailer around a sharp corner, the wheel hit the edge of a cement block, got out of control, and drove through a fence.

An unexpected cheque for one hundred dollars in my weekly letter from home left me feeling like I had won the lottery. I was surprised and relieved in equal measure. This was the first time I had received such a large cash gift. Dismissing a temptation to go on a shopping spree, I earmarked the windfall toward the cost of leaving Australia in September.

***

After nearly two weeks at Jimbour House, we said goodbye. It had been arranged that our new employer, Barbara and Hal Fraser, owners of *Greystonlea*, near Kingaroy, would meet us at a tennis social. Bonnie's brother Geoff had worked for them; now they welcomed Bonnie and me. Hal had a large, solid build. He quietly observed the world from under a pair of bushy eyebrows, a man of relatively few words. Barbara's athletic frame reflected her expertise at tennis. She had an energy that implied she got tasks done with compact efficiency. We returned with them to their home that evening.

Our responsibilities at *Greystonlea* were different than anything we had done so far: painting the roof of the house. The bungalow, with an angled wing coming off each side of the long central portion, was large enough to make this a daunting task, especially as we had to scrub and brush the roof before we could start painting it. The paint dust raised from the intense scraping made me feel sick and was murder on my hands. We soon figured out that the quickest way to remove the old paint and limit the fine particles was to wet the roof as we scrubbed.

After three days we were ready to start painting. This job took a week to finish and was not without its hazards. On one occasion, when we finished after dusk, I didn't see that Bonnie had painted past our ladder-marked stopping point. There was no way to get to the ladder except to walk across the wet paint. I slipped on the slick surface. Using my feet as brakes, I came to a halt when my heels had hooked into the eaves.

"Bloody hell, Kath, you could have gone over the edge. Be careful!" Bonnie said.

Shocked and shaking, I glared at my friend, thinking that going over the edge would at least get me out of doing this truly awful job.

On our final day of painting, Hal came to take a picture of us.

"Give us your usual pose, girls: bums in the air," he instructed.

As I stood to get into position, I once again slipped on wet paint, sending the open tins flying. By now I had become an expert at surviving on the roof. A twist and a turn and a judiciously-placed heel saved the day. Bonnie had less spillage in her area, so she suffered little more than extreme surprise. We painted the pooling mess as quickly as possible but we kept slipping. In the end, even I saw the humour in the situation.

In the midst of our painting travails, Barbara and Hal went to Brisbane for a couple of days.

"We have no idea how to look after a station," I said to Barbara, astonished they would consider leaving us in charge.

"There's nothing to worry about," Barbara assured us. "All you have to do is make sure Mike gets three meals a day. There's plenty of food. Mike will help you out if you need anything. You girls'll be fine."

The first morning, the kitchen was in chaos. I had forgotten to put logs in the stove. No fire meant no cooking. Mike the jackeroo wouldn't be happy if he had to start his day on an empty stomach. I dragged up relevant memories of Canadian summers at the cottage. We had a wood stove but my parents tended it. Only campfires were in my repertoire. Surely they followed the same principle: dry kindling to get the fire going, then a steady supply of wood. I prepared and lit a neat stack of twigs and balled paper. In my haste to produce a full-fledged fire, I added too many logs too soon. The flames responded only when I blew and fanned but lost their vigour when I stopped. I hunted through cupboards until I found what I was looking for: lighter fluid. Sometimes cheating is the only solution, especially when it brings instant success.

Meanwhile, Bonnie asked Mike to milk the cow. The poor fellow probably would have a cold breakfast but at least there would be fresh milk.

"Good lord," I said when Mike appeared at the door with two large buckets. "How much milk did that cow give?"

"Reckon it's about four gallons. Bonnie said milk her and bring the milk in, so I milked her and I'm bringing the milk in."

Mike's impudent response indicated he knew we would have more than we could handle. He obviously didn't take kindly to having a couple of young women telling him what to do. Our inexperience exacerbated the problem.

I did a quick calculation. If there are approximately four glasses to a quart and there are four quarts to a gallon, we had the equivalent of sixty-four glasses of milk to try to wade through. And that was just for this morning's milking. Aren't cows also milked in the evening? We filled every container in the house. I never saw Barbara engage in this sort of panicked activity so evidently there was a more orderly method of disposing of the milk, like sending it to a dairy.

Lunch was successful but supper was another let-down. We got stuck into watching *Bellbird*, a favourite Aussie serial, and let the chops overcook.

Mike got his own back the next day. I should have suspected trouble when he handed me the reins of the horse and said 'Good luck'. As I settled into a comfortable canter, the saddle slipped up the horse's neck. I dismounted to tighten the girth. Then, as I was taking a jump, one of the stirrups came off. Rather than tempt fate further, I returned to the house, reminded that Aussies like to test foreigners when it comes to horses. From now on, I would check the gear before mounting!

My horse-riding exploits at *Greystonlea* weren't over. Soon after the Frasers returned from Brisbane, Mike, Hal, Bonnie and I went on a muster. Typically, Bonnie persuaded me to swap horses with the one she had been given: a thoroughbred mare that had been a race horse. She was temperamental and jumpy and would sometimes break into a quick side-step, but I had ridden her before and we had tolerated each other.

There were no problems until we cantered to a far corner of

a large paddock to pick up stray cattle. As this point the mare decided to bolt. Hal rode hard and managed to cut across my path to block the open gate, but that only resulted in a change of direction. I charged through clusters of startled cattle who miraculously reacted quickly enough to get out of my way.

"Pull hard on the inside rein," I heard Hal yell.

Knowing this mare turned sharply, I instead pulled gently. The result was that we galloped flat out in a five-acre circle that only gradually became smaller. Finally we came to a sobering halt.

Bonnie and Hal galloped over to me.

"Hell, Kath, you don't half put on a show," Bonnie said.

I could hear relief in her voice.

"Are you right?" Hal enquired more solicitously.

"I'm good, thanks." My voice was steady but my knees were shaking.

"Gudonya," Hal said with approval. "Let's finish driving these cattle down to the yards."

We accomplished the mission without further incident. My mount now displayed her best stock-horse manners.

"She'll probably try to bolt at the gate," Hal warned on the homeward journey.

I nodded grimly, keeping a firm hold on the reins to make sure the mare stayed in a walk. When we came to a steep hill, she exerted more energy to make the climb. Then she just kept exerting that reclaimed speed. We were off.

My previous experience of her turning sharply at a gate, made me determined not to have a repeat performance. I kept a firm hold on the right rein. On we went, past the gate. Now we had crossed into uncleared terrain that presented hazards everywhere. A felled tree appeared ahead. Over we sailed. No sooner had I congratulated myself on still being in the saddle than the horse was carrying me in the air once again, this time across a gulley. As I ducked under branches, I thanked Jerry Foxton for showing me the tricks of riding through brush. A fast-approaching row of stumps made me suspect they would be joined by wire. Apparently the horse thought so, too. She took the jump. Both my feet, still in the stirrups, relocated to the right side of the saddle. My arms now were firmly wrapped around the horse's neck. I hadn't come off but neither was I on. I looked down at her fast-moving feet. The outcome didn't look good. My mouth was close to her ear so I whispered, "Please stop." Amazingly, the hoofbeats slowed and she came to a gentle halt. I untangled myself from the stirrups and gave her a pat on the neck as she shook out her mane.

Over the hill, a cloud of dust indicated the imminent approach of my rescue party. Hal arrived first, going from gallop directly to stop when he reached me.

"Your mouth's bleeding," he said, jumping out of the saddle to come to my side but otherwise hiding any anxiety he might have had. "Are you hurt anywhere else?"

I put my hand to my mouth and came away with blood-stained fingers.

"That must have been from my face banging against the horse's jaw," I explained.

"'Struth! What was your face ... never mind. It's probably better I don't know. The important thing is that somehow you stayed on." He surveyed the rugged territory we had blasted through and shook his head. "A lot of riders wouldn't have fared so well in those conditions."

"It's that stubborn streak in her," Bonnie said, arriving at the end of the conversation.

She dismounted and looked me over for signs of damage.

"After today's demos, there's no doubt you can ride." The tone of admonishment masked her relief. "We don't need to witness any more displays!" Bonnie gave me a tight hug and smiled. "I can't tell you how glad I am that we switched horses."

The ride back was pedestrian. Only when we arrived home did shock start to set in. As my mind replayed the wild ride, I felt weak and shaky. The day could have ended so differently. *But it didn't*, I said, forcing myself to get a grip. Once again, I gave silent thanks to Jerry Foxton for teaching me stock riding basics—and to the overworked angel who watched over me.

CHAPTER 19

Will it be easy? Nope. Worth it? Absolutely.
Elite Daily

From the time we arrived in Queensland in mid May, we had heard about the Laura races. Now, late June, the famous weekend was imminent.

"You should make an effort to include Laura in your itinerary," Hal insisted. "The event is legendary in this part of the world. It's been running for about seventy years. According to all the stories we hear, it gets better every year."

Hal rummaged through a messy stack of papers he had retrieved from a crowded shelf. Finally he unearthed a dogeared map and laid it out on a table. The three of us pored over it, looking for the mysterious Laura.

"Here it is," he said, pointing to a small-print name on Queensland's northern Cape York peninsula.

"It doesn't look like much of a destination," Bonnie said.

"It looks like it's the *only* destination in that neck of the woods," I observed, wondering what we might be getting ourselves into.

"True enough," Hal confirmed. "That area's mostly thousand-square-mile stations. The annual races swell the town's population from approximately forty to more than four hundred. It's the party of the year. Sounds about right for you girls."

"But how would we get there?" I asked doubtfully. "This place makes the remote areas we've been to so far look like they're smack dab in the centre of civilisation."

"More importantly, where would we stay?" Bonnie asked.

"I've heard a fellow called Greg Watson is the person to contact. He manages one of those big stations."

Hal found out how to get in touch with Greg. We sent a letter explaining who we were, how we came to hear of him, and could we visit.

All the more the merrier. Will require swag, came his tele-grammed response a few days later.

Swag?

"That's the bushman's equivalent of a sleeping bag," Barbara explained. "In other words, you won't have a comfy bed in a private room. It seems like there's going to be quite a crowd."

It might be a fun weekend. First, though, we had to get to Laura. Greg hadn't given directions.

"Reckon you just keep heading north. Your best bet is to get to Cairns. From there, it shouldn't be hard to get a lift on race week-end," Hal said, plotting the route with his finger. "Looks like there's only one road."

Bonnie and I agreed that the adventure of Laura would be worth the effort to get there. As we prepared to leave the Frasers, Hal said they had arranged for us to stay with their friends the Kings at *Kengoon*, a station near Kalbar.

"It'll break the journey," Hal said.

"And we'll feel better knowing you'll have at least a couple of nights with food and shelter," Barbara added.

Hal piled our luggage into the car while we gave Barbara fond hugs.

"We'll be sure to let you know when the roof needs repainting," she teased as she waved us off.

"From here we'll drive about three hours south." Hal explained once we were on our way. "I know you're trying to head north but Kalbar isn't far from Brisbane. You'll have a better chance of getting transportation from a main centre. Besides it will be a nice opportunity for you to meet the cattle king of Australia."

"Is that because of his name or because of the size of his hold-ings?" I asked.

Hal gave me a sideways glance and a small chuckle before de-scribing the family's extensive lands and herds.

"They're good folk," he concluded.

When we arrived at *Kengoon*, the Kings welcomed us.

"Let's get you girls settled," Edwina King said after introductions.

She led us through a comfortable home to our comfortable bedroom, thoughtfully appointed with everything a guest could need. The most impressive aspect was the ensuite bathroom, a rarity at the time in most places, but especially so on stations.

The Kings certainly didn't stint on hospitality. They and the humorous Uncle Wally entertained with style. Of course, beef featured prominently on the King menus. The roast beef at dinner that first night was the best I ever had tasted. And then there was the novelty of having thick, juicy steak for breakfast each day!

After we said goodbye to Hal the following morning, the Kings drove us to another of their super-sized properties. The vastness of these Queensland holdings still amazed me. I stood on a hillock to better see the surroundings. King land stretched as far as the eye could see in three-hundred sixty degrees. There was no hint of humans or their habitations. Canada, too, had expansive tracts of uninhabited land but an abundance of trees in the areas with which I was familiar diminished the sensation of vastness. When I wandered in Canadian woods, I didn't feel alone; there was too much seen and unseen life around me. Here, isolation was more pronounced.

The outing continued to the Moogerah dam, a massive reservoir completed less than a decade earlier, in 1961.

"The catchment area's eighty-eight square miles," Edwina said. "The purpose of the dam is to provide water for irrigation and drinking but, as you can see, it attracts lots of water sports enthusiasts."

As I watched the many speed boats pulling water skiers, I remembered all the summers I had spent at our lakeside cottage perfecting trick skiing techniques.

Our spoiling few days at *Kengoon* was especially nice because we didn't have to muster cattle, ride temperamental horses or paint.

When it came time to leave, Edwina volunteered to drive us to Brisbane, one of Australia's oldest municipalities.

"It's an excuse to do some shopping," she said before we had a chance to object to her going out of her way.

As well as being the capital of Queensland, Brisbane serves as the gateway to the Gold Coast and the Great Barrier Reef islands. After nearly six weeks in the boonies, this was an ideal reintroduction to urban life. Brisbane of the 1960s was more like a large town than a small city. Pleasant, hilly landscape and its location on the Brisbane River gave the place a good feel.

In the tradition of being passed from one contact to another, we were staying with the Browns, friends of the Kings. Their relatively modern home in the suburbs was interspersed with older homes of an architectural style that was prevalent in this part of the country.

"'Queenslander' houses are almost always timber," Ian Brown explained as he drove us around around the neighbourhood on our way into Brisbane the following day. "They sit on stumps, floating them above the ground."

"Does that ventilate the houses?" I asked.

"That's a good part of the reason. It also protects them from termites and the like. As well, being elevated can be useful in times of flooding."

"I guess stumps of varying heights solves the problem if there's uneven ground," Bonnie added.

"That, too," Ian agreed.

"I love the large verandahs," I said.

"That's another reaction to climate. You can see that part is open and part is enclosed. You probably know by now that we Aussies love to live outdoors. When it gets too hot, the closed verandahs allow the feeling of being outside without the discomfort."

Ian dropped us in the middle of town on his way to work. First on our To Do list was taking our kangaroo skins to a tanner. I probably wouldn't have been able to find a tannery on the streets of Montreal but here it wasn't a problem. For three dollars and seventy-five cents, I got the pelt tanned and mailed to Canada. It was good to be relieved of this stiff, awkward burden.

Brisbane offered an opportunity to address the issue of my deteriorating wardrobe. Imitating the choice of every jackeroo I had come across, I bought a pair of moleskins. These beige trousers are the Aussie equivalent of jeans. The thick, hard-wearing cotton fabric feels as soft as chamois. What a treat to have something new, even if it was practical instead of pretty! Sometimes I begrudged never being able to shop without worrying about the expense but then I reminded myself that by skimping I was able to travel. I would have the memories of this adventure long after I would have the new clothes. Every cloud has a silver lining.

The final order of business was to buy train tickets for our departure that evening to Cairns. Our transport would be the famous *Sunlander*. Over a thirty-one-hour period, the train travels eight hundred miles along a route that follows Australia's eastern coastline, from subtropical Brisbane to tropical Cairns, passing beaches, mountains, rain forests, farms and cane fields along the way. For those who could afford it, there were luxurious compartments and an elegant dining car. Bonnie and I travelled at the other end of the scale, spending the journey in economy seats that reclined and feasting on raw carrot sticks and Metrecal, a diet drink that is supposed to fill you up and slim you down. We needed both.

Our tickets allowed us to make stopovers but, typically, we couldn't decide where to break our journey. We had heard that Proserpine was the main hub for the Whitsunday group of Barrier Reef islands and figured this was as good a place as any. Heavy rain forced us to change our plans. The next island gateway was Townsville. The skies were clear so we unloaded our luggage. After breakfast we enquired how to get to Dunk Island. Everyone had a different opinion but the majority thought we had to go further north, to Tully or Innisfail. We frantically threw our luggage onto the nearest coach, still asking people where we should get off. The train pulling out of the station made up our minds. We were off to Tully. It was pouring rain there, so we carried on to Cairns. It seemed we weren't meant to visit the islands on this trip.

Meeting up with a BBC film crew making a documentary about the *Sunlander* added interest to the journey. They filmed us curled up in our seats trying to sleep. Bonnie had lost the scarf off her hair as she ran to get a cup of coffee at one of the stations. A cameramen picked it up but wouldn't return it until she agreed to an interview. Later we received letters from friends who told us they had seen the programme, so they knew where our travels had taken us.

We arrived in Cairns in mid afternoon and checked into the Pacific Hotel.

"It'll be nice to stretch out again," I remarked, eyeing the beds with approval.

After cleaning up, we left the hotel to explore. I saw no building higher than two storeys. Perhaps this contributed to the laid-back feeling of the town.

"The *mañana* atmosphere reminds me of Spain," Bonnie said.

"I think it's like the Wild West. I expect to go around a corner and see a saloon, or gunslingers in the street. Do you notice that every mile north of Brisbane becomes less 'city' and more 'bush'?"

To me, it was one of the best places we had been to in Australia. The Pacific Ocean and Great Barrier Reef fringed the eastern side of Cairns; the Daintree rainforest sat on the western border. It was nice to observe that popular natural attractions hadn't been exploited.

Like many Australian centres, Cairns originally existed for the mining industry. First it catered to miners on their way to the goldfields, then it became a railhead. In time, the busy port served both gold mining and agricultural needs. With such an idyllic location, it wouldn't be long, I suspected, before it catered to an influx of tourists.

***

When we collected our mail at the Cairns *poste restante* there was a letter from our Laura contact Greg Watson instructing us to get in touch with his colleague Kevin Doyle. I called the given number immediately.

"There's a cattle truck leaving tomorrow," Kevin told me. "I'll let you know if the driver can take you."

A smelly cattle truck definitely didn't appeal.

"I was thinking of something more along the lines of a mail plane," Bonnie said when I gave her the news.

"Beggars can't be choosers," I said with a sigh.

I wished we were in a position to do less begging and more choosing. All that first-class travel I had enjoyed at the beginning of my trip was nothing more than a fond memory. I accepted the inevitable downgrade but travelling steerage with steers was a bit much.

"Change of plans," Kevin announced in a later phone call. "I've got you a ride with George Watkins, the Laura publican. You'll still be in a truck but this one will have booze instead of bulls. He'll leave tomorrow afternoon."

"At least if we break down, we won't go thirsty," Bonnie remarked, only slightly mollified.

Breaking down was a distinct possibility. It took eight hours to travel two hundred miles. Of that, half was over a corrugated, dirt surface. We shook and bounced our way to Laura, collecting layers of dust and sweat with every mile. Deep pot holes, blind corners and the odd wild steer plagued the journey.

"Big improvement over last year's conditions," George told us, shifting gears to negotiate a steep incline. "Now there's bridges over some of the creeks."

A short distance further on, we came to one of these new bridges. Bonnie and I glanced at each other nervously as the heavy truck inched its way over the narrow, creaking boards. This seemed more treacherous than forging the shallow water, although cars would find the bridged crossing easier.

"The creeks look tame at the moment but they're pretty wild in flood," George said, as though reading my thoughts. "Don't ever think about going into any of them," he warned. "There's plenty of crocs hereabouts."

Just after midnight, we arrived.

"Welcome to Laura," George said with a hint of pride. "She's not big but she's home."

Not big? The place seemed to consist of a store, a post office and the inevitable pub.

"That dot on the map that marked Laura was definitely an exaggeration," I said in a low voice to Bonnie.

"It's too late for you girls to go out to the camp. You're welcome to spend the night at the pub with my wife and me."

The chance of a decent bed and a roof over our heads was too good an offer to refuse. If this was 'town', what would the camp be like?

We found out first thing the next morning when Greg Webster came to collect us.

"G'day, ladies. I'm Greg," a smiling bloke said in a booming voice as he entered the pub. "Welcome to the thriving metropolis of Laura."

I liked that Greg had a sense of humour. His height and build made me think of a strong, sturdy red cedar. I straightened my spine and elongated my neck, hoping to look less like a stunted sassafras in comparison.

Bonnie and I introduced ourselves and willingly handed ourselves into this gregarious man's care for the next few days.

"We'd best be on our way. We're about three klicks out of town at the Kalpower camp," he said putting our bags into his 4WD vehicle. "We've got a full few days ahead. You don't want to miss anything. Say goodbye to the big smoke. It's a bit rougher where we're going."

We thanked the Watkins for their hospitality and left for the unknown.

"It's Wednesday, so not many people have arrived yet. I've arranged for you to have your own tent in the front row overlooking the race track," Greg said when we arrived at the site. "Toilets are over there," he said, pointing to a row of outhouses, "and the shower is to the left."

"Shower?" I asked. "There are shower facilities here?"

"Don't get your hopes too high, Kathy. It's what we call modified primitive: the pull-the-chain-tip-the-bucket model has been rigged to provide hot and cold water. Just don't stay under for too long. We'll have a lot of users. I'd get your showering done before the crowds arrive on Friday," Greg said. "The big bashes won't get underway for a couple of days but tonight there's a buckjump show."

"What's that?" Bonnie and I asked together.

"Bronco riding," Greg explained.

"Like a rodeo?" I asked.

"Kind of. We aren't very sophisticated up here with all those fancy competitions like in American and Canadian rodeos but we manage to put on a pretty good display. If past years are anything to go by, this year's'll be a ripper."

That was an understatement. There was something for everyone: singing, shooting, whip cracking, wrestling, fire-eating and, of course, buckjumping. What a performance!

In addition to enjoying the various entertainers, the gathering gave us an opportunity to meet some of the early race arrivals. It was a fun group of people. To make the journey to this lost corner of Australia, you had to have a sense of adventure, a trait that appealed to Bonnie and me.

The following day, Greg put us to work painting the gates and posts of the race course enclosure.

"It's like we have this wretched qualification written on our forehead," I complained to Bonnie as we slapped on the emulsion.

"At least our feet are on the ground this time," Bonnie replied, accepting our lot more graciously than I.

Food in the camp was exceptionally good, better than some meals we'd had in urban centres.

"I should think so," Greg said. "We import a Cordon Bleu chef from Cairns for the event."

The buffet-style meals were eaten at long, refectory-style tables in the centre of the dining tent. With each successive meal, small cliques grew larger and more boisterous. The meals themselves were a major social event.

On Friday, we visited the local school, located in a pleasant, treed area in Laura. The one classroom accommodated three primary grades consisting of a total of eight Aboriginal and four white children.

"That's the entire school-age population up here?" I asked, incredulous.

"Life in this part of the world isn't easy for families. Supplies have to be brought in," the school master replied. "For instance, there's no fresh milk. Kids are given calcium tablets."

"All these beef cattle and they can't sneak in a dairy cow?" I asked.

The teacher shrugged and continued with his tour. I must have shown appropriate curiosity and asked all the right questions because the next thing I knew, he was inviting me to take over the class for the rest of the morning.

"The kids would love to see a pretty new face instead of this weather-beaten old mug, wouldn't you, kids?"

The class responded with giggles. Still, I wasn't persuaded. I didn't have a clue about how to teach, let alone how to tackle three grades at once.

"It's pretty straightforward," the teacher assured me. "Start with maths and then move on to English, reading and writing."

"Whoa. Wrong person for the job," I said raising my hands in a 'stop' motion. "Except for mental arithmetic, I'm hopeless at maths. These kids probably know more than I do."

"We use the Cuisenaire system here. It's easy to teach and easy to learn."

He walked me over to his desk and emptied a box of coloured, rectangular rods of varying lengths.

"Each colour corresponds to a specific measurement, from ten centimetres to one centimetre. By manipulating the placement of the rods, students can visualise equations instead of just memorising tables. Let me show you."

He proceeded to give me a crash course in the use of Cuisenaire rods. To my astonishment, understanding them was as simple as he had said. I wasn't a mathematical Neanderthal after all! What a difference this system would have made to my own education.

I would never know what the children thought of their Canadian substitute teacher but I enjoyed the experience immensely. The class was respectful, attentive and curious. It was nice to see the two cultures mixing so easily. I knew this wasn't always the case. The attitudes of most Australians ranged from outright hostility to mild intolerance. Until today, I hadn't seen evidence of mutual understanding and respect. Perhaps these children would help to change future perceptions.

By Friday afternoon, everyone who was coming to Laura for the races had arrived. The official start to the weekend was a dance. Laura's street and open spaces were packed. The festive mood was contagious and not always sober. Eighteen tons of grog—mainly beer—were brought in to quench the thirst of the influx of visitors. For most of the year, peninsula men saw few white women, nor did they get much chance to drink. Annual race time was their opportunity to let loose.

With the male-female ratio so heavily in our favour, Bonnie and I each got our fair share of attention but no one swept us off our feet, at least not emotionally. Of course, that's not to say we didn't get up to plenty of shenanigans. I even had two fellows fighting over me and a third standing in the wings ready to defeat the tired victor.

The main point of the weekend were the races on Saturday. Proper racehorses had been imported for the occasion. Crowds gathered around the track and cheered on the jockeys. Not even the clouds of dust kicked up by galloping hooves could diminish the enthusiasm.

Of course, betting was at least as important as the race itself. Two experienced gamblers/race-goers, George Pegg and John Rose, took me under their wings. The problem was they had different views on which horse would win. When I listened to George, John's choice won, and vice versa. The consistency with which I lost clearly implied I shouldn't bet on horses.

"If you would just stick with me, you'd at least win fifty percent of the time," John said persuasively.

I had a feeling he was talking about more than betting.

Saturday night was the prize-giving and ball in Laura. 'Ball' in this environment was an inflated description of just another big bash. When that ended around 12:30 am, there was a rowdy, follow-on party at the Kalpowar campsite that went on until breakfast.

After all the intense carousing, Sunday was relatively subdued.

Most people headed back to the city. That night the remaining small group of diehards got together for a champagne party in the back of the Laura pub. Afterwards, we retired to the campsite for a final get-together and singsong. It had been a wild weekend and nearly everyone was partied out.

Early Monday morning we packed up camp and headed back to Cairns. John Smith, one of my weekend admirers, offered us a lift. His car didn't have the height and shock absorber advantages of a large truck but it was a less pungent, more comfortable and slightly quicker ride. About halfway between Laura and Cookstown, we stopped at a station near Butcher's Hill where John had some business. It was a welcome break, especially when the owners gave us a good lunch.

We arrived in Cairns that evening in the midst of a torrential downpour.

"Where are you girls staying?" John asked above the noise of flapping windscreen wipers.

"The Young Australia League hostel's been recommended," Bonnie said.

"Good choice," John said. He peered out the window trying to read the street signs through the curtain of rain. Finally he signalled and turned onto Martyn St where the YAL was located.

He dropped us at the door. We hastily thanked him and promised to catch up in the next couple of days and then dashed into the shelter of the hostel.

Bonnie and I were grubby from the dusty drive but we were too tired to do anything except fall into our beds. Before going to sleep, I shared a poem I had written about our few days in Laura.

> 'Twas the Laura race meeting, an annual two-day event
> When all the peninsulaites gathered and spent
> Their hard-earned dollars on horses and beer.
> Who could blame these poor souls? It was but once a year!
> The populace rose from a mere forty (at best)
> To over four hundred (who could have guessed?),
> But the pub was prepared to face the increase
> With ninety pounds average of liquor apiece.

My audience of one had dozed off.

CHAPTER 20

The comeback is always stronger than the setback.
Anonymous

After a good night's sleep and a decent breakfast, we felt ready to tackle the world. We headed straight to the local employment agency. The baby-faced clerk on duty quickly squelched our optimism about getting a job.

"Sorry, girls. We don't have anything on our books that would suit you," he told us. "Casual jobs for transients are almost impossible to find. I'd go so far as to say they're as rare as a tropical snowfall." He polished his spectacles and chuckled at his perceived humour.

We left the office feeling less buoyant but not totally disheartened.

"We made some good contacts in Laura," I reminded Bonnie. "Now's the time to use them."

We thumbed through the short list of potential employers. George Pegg, one of my racetrack buddies, owned a meat-packing factory.

"I'd love to help you girls," George told us, "but I can't magic up jobs." He paused, probably feeling sorry for us. "I'm not making any promises for long-term employment. Might be a day, might be a week. Go along to the factory tomorrow morning."

"What's the job?" I asked, concerned that carving up large beasts might be a requirement.

"It'll vary. You can fill in for absentees. The money's better than average," he added.

"Sounds good, George. Thanks," Bonnie said. "We'll be there."

"Right-o," the foreman said when we showed up for work the next morning, "we have you on pre-packing today. That means weighing meat in five-pound lots and packing it in plastic bags. The girls inside will show you the ropes."

'Inside' meant going from the steamy hot Cairns climate into a work environment where the temperature doesn't go higher than forty-nine degrees Fahrenheit. I only had a light cardigan to keep me warm. My hands quickly went numb. I was reminded that there's a reason why some jobs pay more than others.

"You get used to it," one of the girls assured me.

"Not something I intend to do," my frigid face responded.

Colleagues chatted amiably about men, soap operas and beauty secrets and quizzed me about how a Canadian had ended up in an Aussie meat factory. By now, I wondered the same thing but I restricted myself to inoffensive responses. Their friendly gossip helped to distract me from my concerns about frostbite.

At tea break—taken outside the packing room—everyone used their powers of persuasion to get me back into the 'freezer'.

"It's just a couple of hours before the lunch break. Another couple of hours and then afternoon tea break. Before you know it, it'll be five o'clock. You can do it," the women insisted.

Thinking only of the good money to be earned, I returned to the frozen hell. As I readjusted to the Arctic-like conditions and diligently stuffed chunks of meat into bags, I noticed women at another work table trimming meat parts and throwing the waste into a large bin.

"Do you feed that to animals?" I asked.

"Lord, no," came the shocked reply. "That's what's used to make snags."

I tilted my head and shrugged.

"You know, for the barbie."

"I think you call them hotdogs," another woman volunteered. "For cooking on the barbecue."

I never had been a fan of hotdogs but, as I viewed the collection of fat, gristle and other unappetising scraps, I vowed never to eat them again.

None too soon, the work day ended. What a relief to step into the warm, humid outdoors. A further boost to my spirits was the contents of the brown envelopes we received. I counted the cash and was almost tempted to think the suffering might be worth it.

The following morning when we showed up for work, we were told there was nothing available.

"Except for the loss of good income, I can't say I'm sorry," I said to Bonnie as we made our way back to the hostel. "Still, it's a bit of a knock to be fired for something as basic as packing meat."

"Laid off, Kath, not fired. Remember we were only filling in for absentees," Bonnie reasoned.

"You don't think my I-passionately-hate-this-job vibes reached the foreman's subconscious?"

"No. But I do think we need to find another job. This little windfall won't last for long."

Once again, George Pegg came to the rescue.

"I can get you onto a prawning vessel, if you like," he offered.

Bonnie and I exchanged glances.

"Can we check it out before committing?" I asked.

"Of course. Go down to the docks tomorrow morning. I'll let the captain know you're coming."

The compact boat looked too small to be at sea for indefinite periods of time. What really convinced us that this wasn't the job for us was the rheumy-eyed, red-nosed captain.

"I'm not great at sea on a boat without stabilisers," I said with feigned regret.

"You get more of a ride this way," the captain said with a leer.

Bonnie and I made our escape, giggling as we scampered along the dock.

That evening we were commiserating with Laura friends about our unemployment when a stranger joined our table. He claimed he was the manager of Ron Ricco, Australia's most famous hypnotist. A demonstration of his own hypnotic skills persuaded Bonnie he could get her to stop smoking and me that I could lose some pounds.

When the restaurant was about to close, he suggested we sit in his car for a full hypnosis. My usually trusting nature did an about-face and shouted a warning but Bonnie wasn't getting the same message. I couldn't let her go off by herself.

"The atmosphere will be good at the cemetery," our friendly hypnotist said as he started driving.

"Absolutely no way," I said firmly.

We compromised by going to nearby woods. *This is an absolutely crazy idea*, my instinct screamed. Against my better judgment, I decided to let the scene play out. And what a scene! One this smooth operator obviously had used on other occasions. The reclining car seat and pillow were for better relaxation, he explained. I have to say, the guy was good. He took me back to my third birthday and my first day at school. Then, for a bit of fun, he told me I was a chicken. When I tried to speak, to my astonishment only clucks and squawks emerged. Before I could panic, he released me from poultry purgatory. His success with Bonnie was limited. He couldn't put her under but he did convince her that her cigarette tasted horrible.

Fortunately, he wasn't as sleazy as I suspected. He returned us to the hostel safe and sound. That night, I silently thanked the overworked angel who watches over us for another lucky escape. I promised myself to be more wary in future and to make sure Bonnie and I were reading from the same page as far as risk-taking was concerned.

When we woke the next morning, it was to the harsh reality that we had no job and a shrinking reservoir of cash.

"The Coloureds have an expression for this situation," Bonnie said. In an Afrikaans accent, she quoted Cape Coloured humour: *It's not a disgrace to be poor, jest a bleddy inconvenience.*

Inconvenience was an understatement. With no other source of income, I sold my guitar to the manager at the YAL. This put twenty dollars in my pocket but left a hole in my heart.

"It's like a third party is missing," Bonnie said.

"It's one less thing to carry," I said with a weak smile.

Bonnie nodded, tactful enough not to dwell on the subject. Some day I would have another guitar but for now it was more important to have money for food and transportation.

***

Darwin, Australia's northernmost city, was next on the itinerary. We couldn't say we had been around Australia if we did't make it to this tropical outpost. We had arranged a ride with Alan Bartley, a friend of a friend. At the last minute his wife called to say he didn't have room to take us.

"He didn't have room, or his wife is jealous?" Bonnie asked.

"Does it matter? Either way, we're stranded."

Because there was no direct route from Cairns to Darwin, it meant going south to Townsville before heading west and north. Hitchhiking might take days and would be exhausting in this heat and humidity. The train was the only practical option.

"We're spending a fair bit of time going in the wrong direction," I said, worried at having to squander time and money for this diversion. "We won't be able to afford to stay in a hotel."

"No problem," Bonnie said. "We can spend the night in the waiting room at the station. It worked for us once, it should work again."

Grudgingly, I paid for the ticket that would take me on this roundabout route.

When we got to Townsville that evening, we headed straight to the station waiting room. Bonnie turned the handle but the door remained closed. We looked at each other in dismay.

"I thought waiting rooms were supposed to stay open," Bonnie said. "Now what do we do?"

As though in answer to her question, a railway employee appeared on the platform. He looked us over and gave a slow shake of his head.

"Looking for a place to spend the night are you?"

We nodded.

"I'm not allowed to unlock the room until tomorrow but maybe you can stay at my place. Let me phone home and check."

A few minutes later he reported that his wife wouldn't be home for much of the evening, so that option was no longer on the table.

"Tell you what, I can let you sleep in my station wagon, if you like. You'll have to skedaddle when I get off duty at 6:00 am, though. Is that all right?"

It certainly was better than spending the night on a park bench. If Townsville had parks. If it had benches.

After securing our luggage in the station office, we settled in as comfortably as possible. Youth and the familiarity of dossing down in strange places made it relatively easy to fall asleep quickly.

Too soon, a tap on the car window told us it was time to vacate our shelter. We thanked our good Samaritan and drowsily made our way to a nearby cafe. After breakfast, we got in touch with John Smith, another Laura contact. He had come to our transport rescue once; maybe he could do it again. Within the hour, he was able to get us a ride with John Gilfoil, a rep from Elders, a large agribusiness. He was able to take us to Charters Towers, eighty-three miles south-west of Townsville, where we had an invitation from Tom and Kent Farmer.

"Stay as long as you like," Tom said when we arrived, "but stay at your own risk. We have five rambunctious boys."

It was certainly nonstop noisier than we were used to but we appreciated having a bed. It also was a great opportunity to get laundry done and fill up on home-cooked meals.

As we headed out the next morning, Kent handed us a brown paper bag.

"A picnic for the journey," she said. "I've given you sandwiches, oranges, biscuits and a big bar of chocolate. That should keep you going for a bit."

We thanked the Farmers for their kindnesses. Starting a trip well rested, with a full stomach, clean laundry *and* a bag of food was no small gift.

To our surprise, we had no luck finding a ride—to anywhere! The few cars that passed didn't even slow down. After waiting nearly three hours, we accepted defeat.

"Let's just take the train to Mt Isa," Bonnie said. "Otherwise we'll be stuck here forever."

I had been feeling rich with ten dollars in my pocket. Now it was evaporating. I tried not to show concern.

The only good news was that the Mt Isa train was due shortly.

It looked like we had done all the waiting we were going to do for one day. We bought out tickets and made our way to the platform.

Once the train left the station, we tucked in to the feast Kent had provided. Satiated and sleepy, we crunched into position in our upright seats.

"A comfortable bed with clean sheets would be the icing on the cake, wouldn't it?" I was becoming obsessed with the notion of sleeping horizontally and having proper linen.

"At least we're moving," Bonnie replied with a yawn. "It could be worse."

I wondered about that.

***

We arrived at Mt Isa at 11:30 am feeling stiff, hungry and apprehensive about the town's rough reputation. According to what we had read, the mine of the same name was 'the world's largest single producer of copper, silver, lead and zinc'. Would a mining town in a remote location be lawless?

We left our bags at the train station and walked into town, stopping at an employment office we passed along the way.

"Sorry, girls, the job market's not good at the moment," the woman told us. "I don't have anything to offer you."

"Do you know if the situation's any better in Darwin?" I asked.

"Worse. It's just not a good time. Check back again tomorrow. Something might turn up," she said, throwing us a crumb of hope.

Bonnie and I were so discouraged that we found a travel agent and looked into going home. We wrote down times, dates and prices of sailings and flights and then went for a coffee to decide our next course of action. Every alternative was debated in detail before being dismissed or tabled for further discussion. No matter how long we danced around the issue, one choice kept shouting to be heard.

"It's not time to go home, is it Bonnie," I said finally.

"It doesn't seem so. I say we listen to our instincts."

With that, I pulled out my address book and retrieved the name of a local contact. We had met Dick Lyman at the Laura races. Dick sounded pleasantly surprised to hear from us.

"Let me ask around and see if I can find you a ride to Darwin," he said. "I'll pick you up at the train station in an hour."

This reaction was promising.

"We'd better head back to the employment office to tell them to take us off their list," I said to Bonnie.

"I'm glad you dropped in," the lady said as we walked through the door. "Two barmaid jobs at the Barkly Hotel have just come up. Are you interested?"

"Absolutely," Bonnie said before I had a chance to disagree.

Doesn't anyone need a secretary in this country? I wondered.

"You'll have to work shifts," the woman explained. She wrote down the address of the hotel and the name of our contact. "You can go for an interview right away. Good luck."

"Beggars can't be choosers," Bon reminded me once we were out on the sidewalk.

"True, but barmaids? I don't know the first thing about mixing drinks."

"That's the beaut thing about being a barmaid in the outback: you don't have to mix drinks; you just have to be able to pull pints. We'll learn fast enough. Anyway, first we have to land the job."

Despite our lack of qualifications, we were hired on the spot and asked to start the following day.

After updating Dick Lyman on the situation, we began our search for accommodation. A man from whom I asked directions turned out to be a godsend. Wally took us around town in a taxi looking for a decent and affordable place to stay. The taxi driver even broadcast our plight on the car radio. Eventually he suggested a Shell service station on the Barkly highway.

"A Kiwi mate of mine manages the place. Maybe he'll let you stay in a back room."

Evidently we passed the manager's cleanliness and respectability standards.

"I have a caravan out back. You can stay there tonight."

"Gudonya, mate," the taxi driver said, giving his buddy a slap on the back.

"Thank you so much," Bonnie and I chimed in.

"Now that you have shelter, what about I take you girls out for a bonza meal?" Wally suggested.

"We can't let you do that, Wally," I insisted, despite the argument to the contrary from my empty stomach. "You've already been generous with your time."

"I can understand you not wanting to go out with a codger like me," Wally said, a smile breaking through the creases of his road-map face, "but it would give me great pleasure."

"In that case, we'd love to accept your offer, Wally," Bonnie said, giving me a subtle kick. "Lead the way."

Once again, the kindness of strangers humbled me. Without looking for anything in return, good people did good deeds, often at their inconvenience. We had been fortunate to witness many instances on this journey.

We spent an enjoyable evening with Wally. There was no nefarious ulterior motive on his part, just the honest desire to contribute to our well-being—and, probably, a craving for female company. Wally didn't act lonely or needy but, from what we knew of outback blokes, most lacked frequent interaction with unmarried women.

Before we returned to the caravan, he insisted on stopping at a local shop and treating us to a few snacks.

"Choose some magazines for yourselves, too," Wally said.

I stared at the racks of mostly unfamiliar titles, mesmerised. On my budget, magazines were a luxury. I hadn't indulged in their purchase since before I left home. I selected a modest mix of fashion and cooking publications.

"Good luck, girls. It'll all come right," Wally assured us as we said goodbye.

Our good fortune continued as word of our accommodation plight spread. The next day we met a Maori named Simon. The only thing I knew about this race was that Maoris were the indigenous people of New Zealand. Like most of the male population in Mt Isa, Simon worked in the mines. His Sumo-wrestler build contradicted his respectful, gentle nature and his sharp wit. During our lengthy chat, the three of us developed a rapport.

"My mate Toko can put you up in his flat until you get settled," Simon offered.

Bonnie and I agreed to meet Toko.

The apartment was simply furnished but clean and tidy. Toko had the same beefy look as Simon but in more moderate proportions. He assured us it would be no bother to put us up.

"There's a spare bedroom," Toko said, showing us a small room with two single beds separated by a bedside table. "Help yourselves to anything you find in the kitchen."

By the end of the day we had met Toko's and Simon's Maori buddies, the curiously named Re and Butterfly. Stockiness, it seemed, was prevalent in this race.

During the week we spent with them, they taught us much about Maori culture, food, music and humour.

On Saturday, Toko offered to prepare a traditional Maori meal. He was a good cook. We all sat in a circle on the floor and helped ourselves to the aromatic dishes placed in the centre.

"At home we eat a lot of fish, herbs and vegetables. It's not easy to get fish here, so we use pork or chicken," Toko explained.

"And plenty of root vegetables," Re said, helping himself to a generous portion of kumara, what I knew as sweet potato.

"When there are a lot of people, we cook in a *hangi*," Butterfly said. "We dig a pit and heat stones on a fire. In the old days, we wrapped slightly moistened food in leaves, put it on top of the white-hot stones and covered everything with earth to trap the heat. Now we might use aluminium foil or wire baskets. The end result is the same, though. After a couple of hours the meal is ready to eat."

"That sounds like a Hawaiian luau," I said.

"Same idea," Butterfly confirmed. "Maoris originally came from Polynesia, so it makes sense there would be similar customs."

"We're going to New Zealand in September," I told them. "We've heard it's a spectacular country."

"The best," Toko assured us. "The scenery's magnificent and the people are beut. You'll have a great time."

Although our living conditions were satisfactory, we couldn't say the same about work. Getting used to the new job wasn't easy. The fact that neither of us ever had been on the serving side of a bar was only part of the problem.

"Crumbs, Kath, how am I going to add up bills? I hate maths! It was my worst subject in school."

"How am I going to remember what everyone orders? I still can't cope with lists," I moaned.

"Right," Bon said, "looks like we both have a handicap. Let's see how we go."

The bar area was immense—suitably sized to cope with the large influx of miners. Long counters lined two sides of the room. Bonnie worked one side and I had the other. It would have been smart for the management to give us some pre-shift instruction on how to pull beer. Instead, we had to learn on the job. My first glasses were all foam.

"Ice cream sold here!" the men shouted good-naturedly.

Another issue was speed. I could only pull two pints at a time, well below the typical nine-pint orders. Fortunately my customers were patient. And that was the third and most serious problem. The other girls didn't like the fact that their regulars were now gathering at my end of the bar. The reason for my popularity with the men, I suspect, was that I was always polite and, whenever possible, I listened to them. This was in sharp contrast to the hardened bar-maids who had speed but little tolerance for their rough customers. They showed their displeasure by refusing to speak to me unless absolutely necessary, offering no training assistance, and 'acciden-tally' spilling pints of lager on me as they passed by.

"Oops, sorry, dearie," I heard on more than one occasion during my shifts.

Not only did the customers stick up for me, they made a show of bringing me boxes of chocolates and other treats. Groups of them squired Bonnie and me around the town after work. All this favour disrupted the normal flow. After the shift on my third day, I was called into the manager's office.

"Sorry, but I'm hearing reports that there's too much spillage. I'm going to have to let you go. I'll give you a week's wages to compensate."

This generosity made me guess he knew the real story, but that didn't stop me from having a small cry when I was alone. Part of it was because I had lost a good source of much-needed income. The main reason, though, was that I realised how much I would miss the rag-tag bag of men who appreciated—and needed—a willing listener.

Bonnie was sympathetic and philosophical.

"It's just a job, Kath. There'll be others. In the meantime, look on the bright side: you're solvent. And remember what some wise person once said: *behind every difficulty there's an opportunity.*"

"By that standard, I should have some great opportunities coming my way," I replied, not yet ready to be jollied out of my morose mood.

For the next four days, we hung out in Mt Isa, partying at night —we had more invitations than we knew what to do with—and job-hunting during the day. The local mine interviewed us but we were honest enough to tell them our desire for short-term employment. That earned us another rejection.

"It's time to move on, Bon. Let's head for Darwin and see if we fare better there."

We planted ourselves at the Shell service station hoping to get a ride.

"Not a good day," our station manager friend told us. "The trucks travel on Tuesdays and Sundays. Otherwise, there's not a lot of traffic."

This was Thursday. Rather than hang around, we bought tickets on the Pioneer coach going to Threeways, a fuel-stop where the roads for Darwin, Mt Isa and Alice Springs meet. This cost me my last twelve dollars.

I was glad I had swallowed my pride earlier in the day and wired home for two hundred dollars. I couldn't even afford the word 'please' in the telegram. The past month has been non-stop hard going, a draining and demoralising endurance test. I prayed for a light at the end of the tunnel.

We arrived at the roadhouse in Threeways just after midnight.

At 4:00 am, after sitting in the café drinking numerous cups of coffee, a kind soul offered us the use of his car until 7:00 am, when he had to go to work. It was a cold, uncomfortable night.

After too little sleep, we cleaned ourselves up as best we could and went into the roadhouse to have a coffee for breakfast. When a Mini pulled in for petrol, we persuaded the two young men to take us to Darwin. After twenty minutes of rearranging suitcases, we crammed into the vehicle. The incessant, loud droning of the engine and the intense heat were too much for my throbbing head. I slept most of the way. Only rare stops at roadside pubs for a reviving beer interrupted the journey.

After fifteen hours driving more than six hundred miles, all four of us heaved a sigh of relief to see the welcoming lights of Darwin.

CHAPTER 21

Every day may not be good but there's good in every day.
Anonymous

We unfolded ourselves from the tight confines of the Mini, retrieved our luggage and thanked our obliging drivers. The long journey had been unnecessarily cramped as a result of rescuing us. We were grateful to them for enduring this discomfort. As they drove off to their own destination, we were left in the centre of town with no contacts and not enough money for a hotel.

"Let's try the CWA," Bonnie suggested.

"Is that like a Y?"

"Sort of. Country Women's Association is an Australian organisation that helps women and children, especially in rural areas. We're women in a sort of rural area who need assistance."

"We're not Australian," I pointed out, "nor are we members of their organisation. I suspect coming to the rescue of unemployed travellers isn't what they have in mind."

"True, but it's worth a try."

Bonnie's instincts were correct. The woman on duty immediately gave us water and then brought us hot chocolate and biscuits. It wasn't dinner but it filled the yawning void in our stomachs. Then, bless her, she bent the rules and gave us a room. The simple accommodation was as good as a night at the Ritz.

The next morning we set out to explore the Northern Territory's capital. This outpost on the Timor Sea not only feels remote, it is remote: Darwin is closer to Jakarta than to Canberra.

Low, uninspired buildings and flat landscape predominated. I might have been tempted to label Darwin as unremarkable but there was something about the town that appealed. Perhaps it was the perception that the place was untamed by bureaucracy and the rule of law. For example, stop signs and traffic lights didn't exist on the uncrowded roads. Nor was there any hint of pretentiousness, simply an easygoing, live-and-let-live attitude.

There was no talk of summer and winter, just wet and dry. We had arrived in late July, the middle of the dry season when every day is warm and blue-skied. Darwin ranks as the second-sunniest city after Perth—up to ten hours each day. In sharp contrast, tropical cyclones, fierce and frequent lightning strikes, thunderstorms and monsoon rains characterise the wet, from December to March.

"During the build-up to the wet, people can go troppo. Their moods might change. Often it's just an unfamiliar tension but some become aggressive. A few are suicidal," a local told us. "The water tank's a favourite jumping spot."

I glanced towards the tallest structure in the town and shuddered, glad we would be long gone before the wet arrived.

When we enquired about things to see and do, everyone recommended that we visit the Darwin Show, an agricultural exhibition.

"It doesn't say much for the place if an agricultural show is top of the Darwin's Must See list," Bonnie said.

"It might be OK. In Canada, they're a big deal. They have lots of things besides best-bull-in-show and best-strawberry-jam contests. I vote we give it a go."

We headed out to the fair grounds. There we bumped into Tony, the manager from the youth hostel in Cairns.

"Well look who's here!" Tony's pleased surprise matched our own. "What are you girls up to?"

"Job hunting, as usual," I said.

"Maybe I can help. I know a couple of people here. Let me ask around."

We agreed to get together the following day.

"The fair wasn't that great but at least we made a contact," I remarked as we made our way back to town.

"What were the chances of meeting someone we know?"

"Especially someone who might help us get a job!"

"In case we have to start work soon, let's go to the beach,"

Bonnie said.

There hadn't been a lot of tanning opportunities lately. Bonnie and I were keen to recover lost colour. Darwin had many miles of unspoiled beaches from which to choose.

When we met up with Tony the next afternoon at a local bar, he proudly announced he had found us a job.

"Doing what?" I asked, scarcely able to believe our good fortune.

"Selling Party Fare. It's a company that makes party accessories. Kind of like your Tupperware concept. You earn money on commission. What do you think?"

"That's a non-starter," I said firmly.

"Why?" His shoulders slumped.

"We have nowhere to show the stuff and we don't know anyone to invite. It won't work for us."

Tony nodded.

"Sorry about that. It's the best I could do."

"Thanks for trying, Tony," we said.

My situation was desperate. Money still had not arrived from Canada.

"Time to hit the employment bureau," I said.

To our pleasant surprise, Bonnie and I were offered jobs immediately.

"The Koala Holiday Inn is looking for waitresses," we were told.

"Another job for which we have no experience and little interest," I complained to Bonnie as we walked to the Koala.

"Beggars can't be choosers," Bonnie reminded me.

"You're right," I admitted.

Rolf, the hotel dining room manager, interviewed us. He gave me the creeps with his leering stare but I gritted my teeth and answered all his questions. Despite my blatant lack of qualifications, he appointed me hostess and head waitress. Bonnie was a regular waitress.

"I guess I'm your boss," I said with a shake of the head after we left Rolf's office. Or lair.

"Something tells me that lizard thinks hostess and mistress

mean the same thing," Bonnie said with a shudder. "Watch yourself."

We began work at six that evening. It was stressful enough starting a new job, especially one where I didn't have a clue what I was doing, but to have my sleazy boss lurking around and finding excuses to brush against me really was too much. I quickly became adept at avoiding Rolf in private and evading him in public.

In sharp contrast to the boss, my colleagues were friendly and helpful. No one seemed resentful of my appointment as hostess. Perhaps they were happy not to have the extra contact with Rolf the job entailed.

Through word of mouth, Bonnie and I found a place to live. The rent was so affordable that cockroaches lived there as well. I've never seen so many. And the size of them! They looked like armoured mice!

"It's the climate," Bon explained, shrugging off the plague of prehistoric creatures.

"I understand them liking the heat and humidity, but why on earth are we finding them in the fridge? It's disgusting," I said, sweeping bodies off the butter.

"You get what you pay for."

On the plus side, we met two crazy Canadian girls, Diana and Melva. When they heard our cockroach stories, they offered to have us share their apartment. For digs that were cleaner, roomier and minus bug infestations, we paid almost the same amount as in the previous apartment.

With accommodation and employment sorted, we could devote out attention to having a good time. Available men far outnumbered single women, so we were never short of invitations. The selection was varied: ship's officers, a journalist and a radio DJ, to name a few.

The beach was a favourite escape. Gangs of us would gather for afternoons of swimming and evenings of barbecues. The sunsets were stunning: a large orange ball would hang above the horizon and then quickly disappear into the ocean. There were no clouds to absorb the colour. The sun was simply there one minute and gone the next.

One of our favourite beaches was Casuarina whose four-mile-long stretch of pristine, uncrowded white sand was bordered by sandstone cliffs. It was only a short walk into the sea to get to a swimmable depth.

"God, this water's amazing," I said, floating on my back in the warm, clear water. "Let me know if you see any crocs."

I wasn't joking. We had heard that the occasional freshwater crocodile invaded Darwin's harbour and swimming areas. The other danger was box jellyfish, or 'stingers', whose toxins can be deadly. These are most prevalent during the October to May period.

Although the sea was our preferred swimming destination due to proximity, friends introduced us to the nature reserve at Howard Springs, eighteen miles southeast of Darwin. It was the first time I had swum in freshwater since leaving Canada. The scenery was beautiful and the atmosphere peaceful. From the main pool, a narrow waterway meandered through the monsoon forest and swamps. We didn't see any wildlife but we were told there were plenty of turtles, barramundi, waterfowl and snakes.

Another swimming option was a place everyone called The Quarry. High cliffs surrounded this fjord-like swimming hole. I gathered the courage to jump off a twenty-four-foot ledge. It was an exhilarating experience but once was enough.

Going to a performance by the South Australia Symphony Orchestra perfectly illustrated Darwin's casual lifestyle: everyone brought lounge chairs or rugs to lie on and a beer-filled cooler—or Eskie, short for Eskimo, the brand of cooler. The stage was set up in the dip of a gently declining grassy hill surrounded by tropical vegetation. The magical atmosphere more than compensated for the less than ideal acoustics.

The calibre of my escorts varied from upper-crust to crusty, from erudite to less learned. Each had a story to tell. It seemed I was as intriguing to them as they were to me. One bloke shyly told me, "Gosh, yer the first foreign sheila I've been out with." On another occasion, a writer at the radio station who had been making eyes at me blurted out, "You're the first woman who has ever appealed to me. I usually prefer men."

Ian Simpson was a tall, slender aristocratic Englishman who piloted helicopters. His devotion could be smothering but his thoughtful, entertaining company made me tolerate this shortfall. I fitted him into my schedule whenever he was in town.

One evening Ian invited me to dinner at Mica beach. This was a popular destination, partly because of the means of getting there. The forty-five minute ferry ride to the beach was only the beginning. Then we transferred to a beast of a machine called the Water Buffalo. This was an amphibious, ex-army tank on top of which had been created open-air passenger seating. The vehicle chugged through swampy areas and along the beach until it arrived at the Mica Beach Restaurant.

The rustic restaurant had a marine theme: fishing nets, shells, chairs with fish names and the like. The seafood was fresh but its preparation and presentation were unexceptional. The owners added entertainment in the form of two musicians playing the guitar and accordion—off key—that encouraged sing-songs, also off-key, from the well-oiled guests. It certainly was a different type of dinner invitation.

There wasn't a lot of entertainment variety in Darwin, so fellows had to be creative if they wanted to impress a date. Bob, a ship's officer, invited me to join him for a 'dinki-di Aussie experience'. Once again I was on a ferry, this time to Mandorah, a town further down the coast from Darwin on the west side of the harbour. The twenty-minute water journey would have taken two hours by road and would have required a 4WD.

After swimming and sunbathing for a while, we made our way to the site of the main purpose of the excursion: a corroboree.

There are more Aborigines in the Northern Territory than in other parts of Australia but there was no effort—on either side, it seemed—to integrate. I was fascinated by ancient peoples who retained traditions that had been handed down through countless generations. My adventurous and culturally-interested side would have jumped at the opportunity to spend time with a local band learning about their myths and rituals and acquiring skills such as tracking, finding food and water where there appeared to be none and making fire. Those opportunities weren't available. I had to make do with this staged sample of the rich Aboriginal culture.

The eight male performers, dressed in nothing more than red, yellow, blue or green loin cloths, sang and danced to the rhythm of thigh-slapping and hand- and stick-clapping. The formidable instrument I knew to be the legendary didgeridoo served as the musical accompaniment.

"That's the first didgeridoo I've heard. The sound is quite haunting. Sometimes it's almost bird-like and other times it's quite ... animal-like?"

"Well spotted," Bob said. "The instruments traditionally are made from trees hollowed out by termites. They range from three feet to nearly nine feet. Length determines the scope of the musical scale. As you probably know, Abos have a special relationship with nature. The vigorous arm, body and foot movements of the dancers are meant to imitate birds and animals," he explained. "Many of the dances have religious significance but there are also war dances and social ones like this. The variations relate to myths going back to creation."

"I've heard corroborees sometimes can last for several days," I said.

"Bloody oath!" Bob exclaimed. "They can last weeks or months, depending on the size of the gathering and the occasion."

The performance was impressive.

"So, waddaya reckon? Worth the effort?" Bob enquired at the end of the show.

"Bonza," I replied in my best Aussie slang.

The only thing to diminish the success of the outing was the sighting from the ferry on the way home of a long, thick black-ringed sea snake. It slithered along the surface of the sea as comfortably as if it were on land. I stared in frightened fascination.

"How do they stay afloat?" I wondered aloud.

"Their tails are flat, like paddles," Bob explained. "Small valves over the nose close when the snake wants to go under water. They hang out around shallow water and swim on the seabed because they use lungs to breathe, not gills. These guys are venomous but not aggressive. Still, you need to keep an eye out for them."

No fear of that! Swimming in Darwin's sea would no longer hold the same attraction for me.

***

It had been a week of ups and downs, the most devastating of which was losing my wallet. I was in the hotel kitchen pilfering bread for my roommates, laid the wallet on the counter and forgot to take it with me. This episode, coming on the heels of my unpleasant work environment, left me feeling like I had been kicked when I was down. As well as losing forty-five precious dollars, it also contained my Australian driving license, insurance papers and the maple leaf pin given to me by Dad. The pin was symbolic, meant to guide me home. I wondered if that plan was off the table now.

Then, on my fifth day of working at the Koala, I got a call from the employment agency to say they had a temporary secretarial job for me at Dalgety's. This was the transport/stock and station agent whose grumpy manager in Sydney had refused to help us get a ride to northern Queensland! Fortunately the Darwin branch manager was friendlier.

"You've got a good CV," Mr Currington said. "We'd love to have you work for us. Hours are nine to five, five-and-a-half days a week. The pay is eighty-six dollars a fortnight. Does that suit you?"

I nearly kissed the man. At last! A job for which I had qualifications, albeit rusty ones.

It gave me immense pleasure to hand in my resignation to Rolf. He begged me to stay beyond the three days' notice. When I declined, he refused to pay me what was owed. This was a situation I hadn't anticipated and couldn't afford.

"Pay up, Rolf, or I'll go to the Arbitration Board," I threatened.

When he didn't relent, I was forced to act on the ultimatum. The wishy-washy Board official was more interested in avoiding conflict than in resolving my dispute.

"Get your pay first and we'll try to settle things later," the annoying man advised.

"I've tried and failed. That's why I'm here," I fumed.

"Try again. You might find he's come to his senses."

Left with no other option, I went back to see Rolf. My exaggeration about the reaction of the Arbitration Board persuaded him to relent, minus the overtime that had been agreed. He was dishonourable as well as being a sleaze. I was glad to see the back of the dreadful man.

Now that I wasn't working at the Koala, there were no more free meals or easy access to the kitchen but that was less of a hardship than expected. Eddy, the hotel chef, sent care packages of cooked chicken legs and vegetables on the nights I wasn't invited out for dinner. John Kidney—yes, that's his real name—the friendly corner butcher, and one of our drinking buddies, sold us 'scraps'. One day it might be four large steaks for eighty cents, another day it could be six thick chops for forty cents. A generous bakery foreman at Quong's Bakery custom-baked loaves of cinnamon bread heavily laden with raisins and decoratively braided on top. Delicious!

"Come at midnight," he told us. "That's when the bread comes out of the ovens."

We did as instructed. It was worth the trip for the aroma alone. The air was full of satisfying smells that spoke to the soul, making all seem right in the world.

"Wait until the bread cools, otherwise it's too doughy. Not good for your digestion," he warned. "Sits like a lump in your gut."

Good advice but I seldom resisted the temptation to sneak a few torn pieces. My young gut was healthy enough to tolerate the abuse. Nor was my budget badly affected: when he charged at all, it was minimal, as little as twenty cents for a couple of large, ingredient-packed loafs.

***

Despite the attention of many men, I had eyes only for one: Maury Simpson, the assistant manager at the Koala. Maury had a sturdy build of medium height. I fell for his charming personality, soft New Zealand accent and twinkling blue eyes. Of course, I wasn't the only female to be attracted to him. Finally, though, I beat out the competition. And so did he.

"You're like an exotic flower with all the honey bees gathering around you. I had to figure out how to edge everyone else out of the way," he told me when we finally went out for a quiet dinner.

Seriously? Could he not see that this exotic flower was ready to be plucked by him? Instinct told me he was an experienced player who knew the words that would make my knees weak but I didn't care. Maury wasn't the man I wanted to marry. He wasn't even the man for whom I would consider delaying my travels. In this time, this place he made me happy. Period. We became an item.

Maury's job made it difficult to schedule time together. We might plan an evening out and then a crisis in the hotel would pull him away. Sometimes he would be gone only half an hour, other times he would send a message telling me we would try again the next day. My infatuation carried me through these disappointments.

Life was good in Darwin. Bonnie and I had decently paid work, a place to live, plenty of friends and romance. We had spent nearly six weeks here, longer than any of our other stops in Australia but now it was time to move on. We would leave in a few days. Was this why I felt so strange? So uncharacteristically on edge? Unable to conceal my disquiet, I consulted Maury.

"You've been in the tropics too long without a break, not to mention the fact that the wet's coming" Maury explained. "You're going troppo."

Bonnie and I had been warned about this malady when we first arrived.

"You don't want to be with anyone but you're afraid to be alone," Maury continued.

He had nailed my symptoms on the head. I was glad that if I had to be affected, it was so late in our stay. Now that I knew what was wrong with me, I could cope. I *would* cope.

CHAPTER 22

You don't grow when you're comfortable.
Anonymous

As usual, getting from one destination to the next was not straightforward. My helicopter-flying friend Ian Simpson already had left for Sydney but that didn't prevent him offering assistance.

"I've got you a ride south," Ian said by phone. He sounded pleased.

"That's fantastic news. Where do we go and who do we contact?" I asked.

Ian gave all the details but added a small proviso.

"It's a cargo plane, so you won't be travelling in the lap of luxury."

"As long as the pilot's licensed and the plane is flight worthy, we can manage a few hours of discomfort," I responded cheerily.

When we contacted the pilot, we learned that the plane wasn't flight worthy.

"No problem coming along with us," the pilot said, "but I can't tell you when we'll be taking off. Could be a day, could be two weeks. She's got engine problems. We have to wait for parts to arrive."

I thanked him and said we would make other arrangements.

"Other arrangements?" Bonnie said, rolling her eyes. "You mean hitchhiking?"

At the last minute, Fred and Walt, Canadian friends of Bonnie, offered us a lift as far as Alice Springs. It was hitchhiking without having to wait by the side of the road and stick our thumbs out.

We agreed they would pick us up at 8:00 am on Saturday morning.

Friday 5 September was my last day working at Dalgety's. Although my replacement had arrived nearly two weeks earlier, the manager offered to keep me on until my departure. Not only was my final pay packet correct but Mr Currington paid me for the unworked Saturday as well. What a pleasant change from working for Rolf at the Koala!

"Just a little thank you," he said. "Enjoy the rest of your trip."

I would, thanks to the infusion of cash. When I calculated the amount of time I had been paid since the beginning of the year, the total came to sixteen weeks and four days. No wonder I was skint all the time!

Friday night, Bonnie and I made our rounds of goodbyes. We would miss the many characters who formed our close, supportive group. And they, no doubt, would miss us. Our absence would disrupt the male-female ratio even further!

Most of all, I would miss Maury. The sex and the pillow talk during our last night together were tender and prolonged. I woke the following morning still held tightly in Maury's arms. I gave a contented stretch and glanced at my watch.

"Oh my god," I said frantically jumping out of bed and throwing on my clothes, "I've got to get back. We're being picked up in less than half an hour."

Maury drove me to the apartment and gave me a final fond kiss.

"Keep in touch if you have the time, my exotic flower," he said.

"You know I will," I replied, looking into his roguish blue eyes one last time.

As I rushed to the door, I heard my name called. Bonnie, too, had overslept—in someone else's bed. We hurried into the apartment to shower and pack. Departure was delayed by twenty minutes.

Our mode of transportation was a Volkswagen van outfitted with a small kitchen. The table and bench seats converted into sleeping space—for three, at a pinch. We had become expert at cramming suitcases and ourselves into small areas. This journey would be no exception.

We took a last look at Darwin and were on our way, relieved

to escape the cloying humidity and atmospheric pressure that was becoming more intense each day.

The journey to Alice was long and tiring: nearly one thousand miles of narrow bitumen and, for the most part, monotonous tropical savannah or monotonous desert. At least, that's how it looked from the window of the van as we whizzed past. A couple of interesting stops reminded me there was plenty to see for anyone who took the time to look.

The first break was to check out a small 'city' of termite mounds. I had seen impressive ant hills in South Africa but the Aussie constructions were skyscrapers in comparison. The mounds built by magnetic termites average six feet but those of the aptly-named cathedral termites soar to more than twice that height.

"It's easy to identify a magnetic termite mound," Walt said. He pointed to a series of jagged-edged, mud-built structures with broad fronts and backs and narrow edges. "The wide sides are always in a north-south orientation so they get minimum exposure to the extreme heat of the sun."

"Automatic temperature control," Bonnie said. "Clever."

"The underground foraging done by the termites creates channels in the earth," the well-informed Walt explained. "This makes it easier for the deluges of water in the wet to be absorbed. When the millions of young, winged termites appear, they're food for birds and lizards."

I marvelled at nature's creativity and efficiency.

It wasn't until Robin Falls, one hundred miles south of Darwin, that we enjoyed a break from the red/beige landscape.

"What do you say we stretch our legs?" Fred suggested.

Everyone welcomed the opportunity. We walked alongside a wooded stream until we came to a small, three-tiered waterfall. The scene brought back favourite memories of Canada. Although Canadian water features tended to be on a grander scale, for me it was a particular joy to find a hidden woodland stream whose clear waters gurgled over rocks, sometimes forming a miniature cascade. I took a deep breath of the scented air and felt more invigorated than I had for a long time. The refreshing water cleansed my sweaty, dusty face and revived my spirit. It would have been nice to linger but our schedule didn't permit such indulgence.

At dusk we made camp. Fred and Walt had travelled around Australia in this van and were adept at rustling up good meals with little cooking space or equipment. Rustling up comfortable sleeping accommodation for four adult bodies was another matter.

"The temperature's good. I'll sleep outside," Fred volunteered.

I was relegated to the narrow front seat of the van. It wasn't the best sleep I'd ever had but neither was it the worst.

After a breakfast of toast and coffee, we were on our way by 7:20 am. Darwin was twenty-three hours and three hundred seventy miles behind us. We still had a long way to go.

We expected to find a rest stop that had shower facilities but no such premises materialised. If we had known, we would have done a better job of bathing back at Robin Falls. We carried on, each tolerating without comment the heat-induced build-up of stale body odours.

The only point of interest on this leg of the journey were strange formations called Devil's Marbles, reddish granite rocks that lie scattered across a shallow valley on either side of the Stuart Highway. These geological products of millions of years of erosion vary in size from large rocks to boulders twenty feet across. Adding to the surreal vista, some stones balance precariously on top of others. The ancient site is sacred to the Aboriginals.

That evening we made camp about thirty miles from Barrow Creek, a fuel and rest stop whose claim to fame is an operational telegraph repeater station installed in the late 1800s.

After not eating all day, our simple supper of beans and toast tasted delicious. Bonnie and I washed dishes and tidied and then we all sat around the small fire for a nightcap.

"I'll sleep outside tonight," Walt offered.

"It's getting too chilly for that, don't you think?" I asked.

"I'm Canadian. I'm built for the cold," he joked bravely.

Bonnie, Fred and I, donning extra layers of clothing, crowded into the back of the van.

In the early hours of the morning, the van door slid open and built-for-the-cold Walt stumbled inside, frozen. We squeezed together like sardines. Body heat was more important than movability.

Hot toast and hotter coffee went down well at breakfast. If we had been prepared with proper warm clothes, we might have seen the dramatic temperature change as invigorating. Instead, we were miserable.

"This definitely puts me off returning to Canada," Fred announced, digging in his bag for another pair of socks.

I had similar thoughts but I was committed to sail home from New Zealand in two months. Nevertheless, I didn't discount the possibility that the lure of New Zealand might be stronger than the lure of a Canadian winter.

On the final leg of the journey we passed Mount Stuart on our right. The red sandstone peak rose out of the desert a couple of miles away. Its significance wasn't its height—or lack of impressive loftiness—but its location at the geographical centre of Australia.

The other major event of the day was crossing the Tropic of Capricorn, indicated by a roadside sign. I now had passed through three of the earth's five circles of latitude: Cancer, the equator and Capricorn. I had no immediate plans to visit the remaining circles: Arctic and Antarctic.

At 1:00 pm we arrived in Alice Springs. Alice wasn't a beauty but she wasn't without merit. The Todd River, which runs through the town, could be considered a feature except that the waterway is usually dry and wasn't wide, even in full flood. Far away, the flat-topped, bald peaks of the MacDonnell Ranges run east and west of the town.

The most popular attraction in the area was Ayers Rock, an egg-shaped, sandstone monolith rising to an elevation of nearly one thousand feet. To give an idea of just how big a monolith can be, the distance around the base is six miles. From pictures we had seen, Ayers Rock looked like a large, isolated island emerging from the calm desert sea surrounding it. Uluru, as the rock is called by the Aboriginals, features prominently in their creation myths and is one of their sacred sites.

We would love to have explored the famous landmark and witness the rock's dramatic change of colour to ochre red at dawn and sunset but the two hundred eighty-mile journey to the site took five hours one way. We couldn't afford the unnecessary two-day delay. The wet was fast approaching and Bonnie and I had to get to Sydney to catch the boat to New Zealand.

Our first order of business was to locate a place that offered free showers. This mission failed. Instead, we had to pay for the privilege at the Wintersun Caravan Park, a mile north of the city. After luxuriating in hot showers, we went back into Alice to explore and get some chow for a barbecue.

The town had a strong Aboriginal influence. Interesting shops sold the distinctive native artwork as well as books, instruments, carvings and other collectibles. Between a bulging suitcase and a slim wallet, I wasn't able to give in to the temptation to buy souvenirs.

After a simple but delicious supper cooked by Walt and Fred on the barbie, we headed back into town to see what was going on. For a small place smack dab in the middle of nowhere, it had a good spark of life. Not surprisingly, the bars were crowded. If outback Aussies can do nothing else, they can consume alcohol. Tired from our long journey, we decided after one drink to head back to the campsite.

That night I once again was relegated to the front seat of the van. Bonnie had secured a permanent spot in the back because Walt and Fred were her contacts ... and she had been dating Fred. I borrowed clothes from Fred and, at first, was toasty warm. I woke at 4:15, chilled to the bone. The campsite's toilet block was less chilly than the van, so I spent the rest of the night in there.

"That'll be seventy cents, missy," the caretaker told me the next morning.

"For sleeping in the toilets?" I asked, incredulous at his mercenary attitude.

"For using the facilities. How you use them is your business. Seventy cents!"

The insensitive man refused to consider my arguments and

pleas. With no other option, I relinquished the precious coins.

After breakfast, we headed into town. Bonnie and I made our way to the Dalgety office. I explained to the manager that I had worked for the company in Darwin. Friendly Mr Hall arranged for a ride the following day.

"The first driver will take you to Port Augusta and then he'll transfer you to a driver going to Adelaide," Mr Hall told us.

"Fantastic," I said, relieved to have this burden lifted. "Thank you so much."

"You're timing's good. Alice is one of the most difficult places to hitch from. With the wet expected in a few days, there are even fewer vehicles. I'm glad we could help."

Pleased with our transportation success, we met up with Walt and Fred at the tourist office and gave them our news.

"Well done," Walt said. "That means we have to make the most of today. We're going to be tourists."

"What do you have planned?" Bon and I asked.

"Since Ayer's Rock is out of the question, we'll go to Standley Chasm and Simpson's Gap. The chasm is only thirty miles from Alice and the gap's nearby."

We piled into the VW and went on our excursion. A few miles from the chasm, we came across a group of Aboriginals and their camels. We hopped out of the van and asked if we could take photos. The old chief introduced himself as Mick. He and his men obligingly posed and chatted. Then, as we thanked them and said good-bye, Mick put a damper on things.

"That'll be forty cents, please."

We stared at each other, astonished. The amiable elder had morphed into a crafty businessman. Each of us forked out ten cents.

"We walked right into that tourist trap," Bonnie muttered on the way back to the van.

"True, but we got some unique pictures." I figured this expenditure was better value than the unexpected accommodation cost I had paid that morning.

A twenty-minute creekside walk through lush terrain led us to a series of dramatically cleft rocks. The sheer, two hundred forty-foot walls of Standley Chasm were impressive. We arrived just before midday, the best time to view the chasm. The sun lit the alleyways between the rocks, at last allowing us to see the famous changes of rock colour.

I had fallen in love with the landscape around Alice.

"The peace and beauty remind me of the Karoo," I told Bonnie.

"Except there's more colour here."

"But no less wildlife, presumably."

We had seen snakes, lizards, and a variety of birds, but we knew the area was rich with reptiles, insects and mammals, including dingoes, bats, emu and possum.

Simpson's Gap, another sacred site, wasn't as imposing as Standley Chasm, but the gorge cut into the MacDonnell Range and its waterhole had a special allure. We didn't see any of the famous black-footed rock wallabies that live in the area.

Before returning to Alice, only an hour's drive, we visited the stone-faced block where the ashes of John Flynn, the Presbyterian minister who founded what would become the Royal Flying Doctor Service, are interred. Flynn's experience of the rigours of outback life and the absence of medical assistance in remote areas, prompted him to campaign for a solution. The inaugural 'air ambulance' took off in 1928. That first year of service, the pilot/doctor team flew twenty thousand miles and treated two hundred twenty-five patients. The Aerial Medical Service, as it was called, was declared a success. I admired the setting on a rise overlooking a dry river with the MacDonnell Ranges as a backdrop, the centre of the vast territory Flynn's flying doctors look after.

Once we got back to town, our Canadian friends dropped our luggage at the police station where we had been told we could leave it temporarily. Then it was time to say goodbye.

"You're sure you girls are going to be OK?" Walt asked.

"No worries. We'll be on our way south tomorrow," Bonnie said.

"We'll miss you guys. Drive safely to Cairns," I added. "Don't drown in the wet."

When the van had disappeared over the horizon, Bonnie pulled out her address book. It had produced contacts in unlikely places; Alice Springs was no exception. Bonnie made the shmooz call and arranged for us to meet Tim Egan for drinks just after lunch. We hoped to get an invitation to dinner and, if luck really smiled on us, be asked to spend the night with them. The possibility looked good until the austere Mrs Egan joined us. No hint of benevolence emanated from her, let alone an invitation of any description. We got the message she didn't approve of itinerant females.

Left with no alternative, we booked into a church hostel. It was the last night they were taking guests. Most tourists had left Alice in advance of the wet, so we had the dorm to ourselves. I piled the blankets from all the empty beds onto my own bed. After the previous night's experience, I never wanted to be cold again!

In the early evening we had an appointment to meet with Des, our designated driver. As we greeted each other in the bar of a hotel, a description my dad might have used came to mind: he was built like a brick shit house. Des was thick in body and thick in mind with slim-to-none social skills. Bonnie and I did our best to carry on a conversation but his monologue answers made it difficult. Suddenly he threw out a question, accompanied by a probing stare.

"So, do you girls play?"

"I do," I responded enthusiastically, welcoming the communications breakthrough. Had we at last hit on a topic that interested him? "I play guitar. Do you play?"

Without explanation, Des swallowed the last of his beer and said he had to go home. Bonnie and I found his behaviour strange but we were relieved to be rid of him.

"It's going to be a long journey with that man. I am *not* going to be solely responsible for conversation," Bonnie warned. She paused before asking, "Do you think he was talking about musical instruments when he asked if we played?"

I frowned. What else could he mean? Then I got it.

"Really? You think he was expecting ... a ride for a ride?"

She shrugged. "We need to stay alert."

The next morning we showed up at Dalgety's.

"Sorry, girls, Des won't be leaving until tomorrow." Mr Hall seemed embarrassed by the pronouncement. "Can you hang on for another day?"

"Sure," I said, knowing we had little choice.

Once again, Bonnie got out her address book and found the name of Alice-based friends of friends of friends.

"It's worth a shot," I agreed, "but you have to make the call."

We walked out of town to the Calders' home. They offered us a cup of tea but nothing more. Like Mrs Egan, the Calders had no surplus of goodwill towards us. I wondered if we had developed a patina of impropriety.

"I heard about a church-related place called Griffiths House," Bonnie said during our walk back to town. "Maybe they'll put us up."

Neither of us was religious but, as Bonnie liked to say, any port in a storm. The kindly man in charge guided us to the room used for Sunday school. We expected to camp on the floor but moments later he appeared with two brand new fold-up cots and some blankets.

"There's a bathroom down the hall," he said as he gave us a key. "You'll be on your own but it's safe." He looked uncomfortable for a moment and then blurted out, "Please don't bring anyone back with you."

We assured him we wouldn't abuse the hospitality.

After depositing our bags, we headed to the Alice Springs Hotel, a good place to meet people. The first person to latch onto us was an obnoxious filmmaker in town to make a movie. This, his attitude signalled, gave him a special cachet that made him irresistibly appealing. Wrong. Two solidly built men saved us from his unwanted attention.

"Is this yobbo bothering you?" the larger of the two asked us.

"I'm just leaving," the filmmaker said quickly. "I've spotted another table where the company looks like it could be more congenial."

We invited our rescuers to join us. It turned out they were off-duty policemen. After about half an hour of enjoyable conversation, one of them excused himself. When he reappeared, he was followed by a waiter bringing a feast of food.

"I thought you ladies might like some decent tucker," John said.

This was the first proper meal we had had in two days.

They wanted us to go on a pub crawl with them but we were too tired.

"If you like, I'll drive you back to the hostel," Bill said. "On the way we can go to Anzac Hill."

"Is it far?" I asked before Bonnie had a chance to agree. I needed a rest from driving, especially since we had a long journey ahead of us tomorrow.

"It's just outside town," Bill assured us.

The lump of a hill served as an ideal lookout over Alice to the MacDonnell Ranges which could be seen gracefully sweeping into the valley. The vista was a study of limited green vegetation and ample red desert, like a nature painting in progress. At the top of the lookout, the ANZAC (Australia and New Zealand Army Corps) war memorial commemorates all Australian and New Zealand lives lost in conflict since World War I. We paid our respects and returned to the car.

"Sure I can't persuade you to come out drinking?" Bill asked one more time.

"Thanks, but we have an early start tomorrow," Bonnie said.

"I'm sorry you have to leave, but now's a good time. The road will be closing soon. Mind how ya go," he said as he dropped us off.

***

When we showed up at Dalgety's, Mr Hall had bad news.

"I'm really sorry but Des Turner was rerouted to Darwin."

Bonnie and I stared at Mr Hall and then at each other, shock and worry written on our faces. We had counted on this ride. By delaying our departure we reduced our chances of getting alternate transportation. How would we make it to Sydney in time to catch the boat?

"My best suggestion would be to go to a service station and hope to catch a car going south. I really am sorry," he repeated.

We left the office, dismayed at the sudden unwelcome turn in our fortunes.

"Rerouted, my foot," Bonnie muttered as we lugged our bags along the street. "Bloody Des wanted 'playing' company and wasn't going to put up with anyone who didn't meet that benchmark!"

"At least Mr Hall had the good grace to look embarrassed," I said.

Twenty minutes later we had set ourselves up at the last service station on the south side of town.

"You've missed all the trucks," the manager told us. "Most of them went in the last few days to beat the wet. The ones that were left, took off early this morning. There's floods further south. Five buses and thirty cars are bogged down so far. I'd say you'll be hard-pushed to get a ride at this stage."

Just as we were absorbing this grim prediction, a car with a Victoria number plate pulled into the forecourt. I rushed over to the driver and asked if he could squeeze in two passengers. He didn't refuse but he didn't welcome us into his vehicle.

"Please," I implored. "You're probably our last hope."

He still didn't offer a ride but I suspected his resolve to travel alone was weakening.

"You'll have to get rid of the two heaviest cases," he said. "I can't fit you and them into the car. I'm already cramped for space."

"We can't just dump our luggage," I sputtered.

"I'm not suggesting that," the driver said in an eye-rolling tone of voice. "I'm saying you'll have to send them with a shipping company. Wridgeways can take care of it for you."

"Give me a minute. I need to discuss this with my friend."

Bonnie and I quickly weighed the pros and cons. Quickly, because there were no worthwhile cons. This might be our last chance to get out of here.

"Besides," I added, "it'll be two less suitcases to worry about."

"You're OK travelling with this guy?" Bon asked.

We glanced in the direction of our potential lift. The driver was not much older than us. He looked unkempt but so did we. Travelling through desert does that to a person. We decided to risk it.

We exchanged introductions and agreed to meet Ron at the Alice Springs Hotel in an hour.

"I'll be having lunch. I suggest you grab a bite yourselves. It's a long way to the next hot meal."

Bonnie and I hurried off to ship the suitcases directly to Sydney. It cost us ten dollars for the service but it was worth it.

By 3:20 pm we were on our way. As we drove out of Alice, a large sign warned motorists to carry extra petrol and water as it was one hundred sixty-eight miles before the next fuelling station. We prayed we wouldn't get caught in any flooding. Or worse. Unwelcome words from my sometimes dramatically pessimistic mother sounded in my brain: *desert area, no traffic ... a perfect spot to commit a murder and get rid of the body.* I shuddered. Ron seemed decent enough but I hadn't knowingly encountered murderers, so I had no yardstick by which to judge them. I decided not to share my concern with Bonnie but promised myself to remain vigilant.

CHAPTER 23

Into the wild I go: losing my way, finding my soul.
Kapten & Son

The six hundred twenty-mile road from Alice to Port Augusta, South Australia was 'unsealed', as the Aussies say. In other words, it had no hard surface. As a result, any disturbance to the two-lane track kicked up clouds of fine dust that penetrated everything and contaminated breathing. Had there been traffic in front of us, visibility would have been nil.

It was bad enough enduring the tedium of the journey as a passenger in these hot, grubby conditions but it was worse for the person driving. Ron constantly had to focus on the road, carefully guiding the car over rough spots and negotiating the detours that temporarily led us into sandy desert. As we snaked along the difficult route, I remembered how I used to complain about the final thirty-mile stretch of dirt road we had to travel to get to our summer cottage three hours north of Montreal. "It could be worse," my father would say to downgrade the discomfort. He was right. This was worse. Much worse.

At midnight, after more than eight hours of non-stop concentration, Ron pulled to the side of the road.

"That's it," he said, letting his hands slide off the steering wheel and onto his lap. "I can't go any farther."

"You've done a great job, Ron," Bonnie said. "We'll all feel better after a proper rest."

It suddenly occurred to me that I hadn't thought about sleeping arrangements. I certainly wasn't going to volunteer to spend the night on the sand.

"The car seats fold down to make a double bed," Ron said as though he read my mind. He pulled a lever and pushed the back of the driver's seat until it lay flat, then repeated the exercise on the passenger side. It was a nice set-up for two people but less appealing when it had to accommodate three adults.

Ron dug out an extra blanket and we all donned multiple layers of clothing. Despite having no wiggle room, we managed to get a few hours' sleep.

At 6:30 am, I woke to the sour smell of socks that had long passed their freshness date. Bonnie and I were diligent about seeking out laundries whenever possible, so that left Ron as the offender. He magnified his olfactory affront with an almost silent but excessively deadly fart. I quickly exited the car, breathed in the crisp air and examined my surroundings: flat, sand-coloured nowhere that stretched as far as the eye could see.

Bonnie emerged after me, her face twisted into a grimace inspired by the foul odours. Ron soon joined us, offering a mumbled 'good morning' and disappearing behind a scraggly bush for a pee.

It was in this desolate setting that the car decided to get temperamental. Despite repeated attempts, there wasn't so much as a cough from the motor to show signs of life. *I told you so,* my mother's voice whispered. *It's the old problem-with-the-engine trick.*

I wished I had paid closer attention to Jerry Foxton's frequent tutorials because Ron evidently didn't have a knack for mechanics.

"I'm hoping it's nothing more serious than being out of petrol," Ron said.

"You make it sound like being out of petrol in the middle of the desert isn't a problem," I said to Ron's back. He had disappeared to the rear of the car.

"Not for the moment." He grunted as he dislodged two heavy containers from the trunk. "I've got reserve tanks. They should get us to Coober Pedy."

'Should' sounded uncertain. I preferred 'will'. Ron siphoned fuel into the tank and we loaded ourselves back into the car.

"Here goes nothing," Ron said.

When he turned the ignition, the engine, thirsty no more, gave an encouraging response: first a bit of a squeak, then a wheeze, and then a rumbling purr. We were on our way.

By the time we got to Coober Pedy several hours later, the need for a shower was even more urgent than the need for petrol. We headed to the town's hotel, hoping they could help us out.

"Sorry, folks, water restrictions until the rains come," the receptionist said.

There didn't seem to be much option but to continue on in our smelly, dishevelled state. I had got used to wearing dirty clothes but it was more difficult to adjust to having a perpetually unclean body. I wiggled my toes to dislodge caked sand and restrained the inclination to touch my dust-crusted hair.

"If you girls wouldn't mind staying with the car, I'll go see what I can find out about road conditions," Ron said.

While Ron was gone, I observed our surroundings. The only thing I knew about Coober Pedy was that it was the world's largest opal mining area and the principle provider of gem-quality stones. It sits about halfway between Alice Springs and Adelaide and is the main hub of civilisation along this stretch of the Stuart Highway. This makes it an important provisioning point. Yet there was little sign of homes and retail outlets. Where did everyone live? Socialise? Shop? Despite the paucity of buildings, instinct told me this could be a rough and dangerous place. Even Mt Isa hadn't had such a sinister air. I shuddered, anxious for us to be on our way.

When Ron returned, he was followed by another man.

"Meet Robbie Hamilton," Ron said. "We got chatting in the pub. He's offered to let us go to his place for a shower."

Bonnie and I introduced ourselves and shook hands with this tall, ruggedly handsome individual who was prepared to share his precious water supply with strangers. I didn't know who he was or what he did, but desperation made me willing to follow this man wherever he led if it meant having a shower.

"My house is number 105," Robbie said, pointing to the left. "Give me ten minutes to get things set up and then come on over whenever you're ready."

While we disciplined ourselves to wait the required time, I imagined the sound of fresh water pouring onto my head, washing away sweat and soil, leaving me with clean hair and body and a refreshed soul. What luxury! Better than a hot meal!

When we arrived at the designated destination, three structures, all addressed '105', awaited us.

"This is odd," Bonnie said. "These are nothing but shacks. How can anyone live in a place like this, let alone have shower facilities?"

"My guess is that this narrow building in the middle is an outdoor bathroom," I said.

We were about to knock on the door of the largest of the three sheds when the 'bathroom' door opened.

"Welcome," Robbie said. "No trouble finding the place? Come on in."

I wondered how all four of us could possibly fit into such a small space—and why he would expect us to do so. Suddenly Robbie disappeared. Where had he gone? Then Bonnie entered and she, too, disappeared. It was like we had found Alice in Wonderland's rabbit hole. Reluctantly, I entered. Mystery solved: descending stairs. When I reached the bottom, I found myself in a marvellous underground flat. There were no windows, of course, but the artificial lighting was perfectly adequate. Robbie had decorated with taste and succeeded in giving this grotto in the ground both style and comfort.

"Most homes in the area are built like this," Robbie explained.

"Underground accommodation gives a whole new meaning to the word 'sub-urb'."

My remark was met with groans.

"We live like this or in caves bored into the hillsides, what we call dugouts, in order to escape the scorching summer temperatures. Neither of these options requires air conditioning. We've even got a church in town," our host said. "The only underground church in the world."

"Physically speaking," I said. "There are probably a few underground religious organisations, in the sense of clandestine."

Another groan.

"Let's get you people cleaned up," Robbie said, perhaps hoping to avoid more Canadian humour.

Bonnie and I insisted that Ron deserved to go first. When he exited the bathroom a short while later it was evident he had a new lease on life. I have to say, he cleaned up pretty good. When it was my turn, I stepped into the cubicle with expectations of a similar reincarnation.

The shower looked normal except for the shallow tin of burning oil under the open end of a metal pipe. This was the not terribly effective water heater! Worse, the water came out in dribbles rather than cascades. I reminded myself to thank heaven for small mercies and refused to let the set-up diminish my pleasure. Hoping the weak water supply would at least remain constant, I sudsed my hair, revelling in the sensation. A short while later I emerged feeling like a new person.

"Do you have time for a drink?" Robbie asked once we had showered.

"A quick one, maybe," Ron replied. "We've still got a long way to go."

"You might want to think twice about hurrying off. We've had reports that rains further south have delayed plenty of travellers. They've let up for the moment but the forecast isn't good."

Ron didn't have any pressing urgency to get to his destination. Bonnie and I, on the other hand, had a boat to catch. Nevertheless, we didn't want to push Ron to take unnecessary risks.

At first, Ron made no comment. He just stared into his glass, as though seeking inspiration.

"I'm going to chance it," he said finally. "You girls can stay here if you feel more comfortable. Otherwise, I'd welcome the company."

"Let's get moving," Bonnie said, swigging back the remains of her drink.

We thanked Robbie profusely and then headed into uncertainty. It was nearly five hundred miles to Adelaide.

Driving conditions were miserable. A large emu suddenly appearing in the middle of the road added to the dangers. The rain shower we drove into made bad circumstances dreadful. When the predicted heavy downpour came that evening we already had got past the worst flooding areas. We pulled to the side of the road, grateful to have made it this far without serious incident. The weather was cold, the car was crowded and all of us were uncomfortable. No one complained. Whinging might have angered Fortune.

***

We pulled in to Port Augusta around 11:00 am. Heavy vehicular and pedestrian traffic made it clear we had hit civilisation again. I wasn't sure I liked it. We refuelled the car and ourselves and stretched our legs before continuing the journey. No one wanted to linger.

By mid afternoon the Adelaide skyline appeared. Bonnie persuaded Ron to stop at Liz Chapman's house so we could say hello. The meeting was abbreviated: Ron didn't want to turn off the ignition in case the car wouldn't start again!

"Do you remember meeting Cynthia Higgins in Wentworth at the polo matches?" Liz asked.

"Yes, of course," we said.

"She lives in Melbourne. I'll give you her address. She might be able to help."

We bade Liz a final farewell and were on our way. The road from Adelaide to Melbourne was bordered by hilly countryside with lots of sheep grazing on verdant pastures. What a change from the arid scenery along the Stuart highway. Yet, I couldn't help but feel nostalgic for the slow pace of life and the open spaces of the Northern Territory. The desert's quiet mystery and lack of distraction made it easier to hear thoughts and see solutions. The desert cleansed, restored. Now I was back in the land of stimulations.

Not far from Melbourne, Ron took a wrong turn, prolonging the agony of the trip by three hundred miles. We stayed in Ballarat for the night. Again, we nearly froze. My teeth were chattering when I woke to a drizzly, cold, positively miserable morning. We finally reached Melbourne at 8:30 on Sunday morning, sixty-nine hours after leaving Alice.

Ron dropped us off at Toorak, an inner suburb of Melbourne. We took a cab to Cynthia Higgins's flat, located in a beautiful converted mansion.

"Come in," she said, surprised to see us on her doorstep. "This is turning into a bit of a reunion. Mike Keenan arrived a couple of days ago."

Mike had been our host in Wentworth. This was the second time we had crossed paths since then.

"We have to stop meeting like this," Mike joked as he gave us both a hug.

"What are you doing here?" I asked, pleased to see him.

"Cynthia and I are engaged. I spend rather a lot of time here."

"Congratulations," Bonnie and I said in chorus.

"Thanks, Kathy and Bonnie," Cynthia said. She and Mike exchanged lovey-dovey glances.

"What are you girls doing in Melbourne?" Mike asked. "When we met in Canberra a few months ago you were headed up north."

We gave a quick update of our activities and then confessed to looking for a bed.

"I'm afraid I have bad news and good news. We're in the process of moving out of the flat but you can certainly have a nice bath and then we'll fill you up with a hearty breakfast."

Cynthia was right. It was bad news and good news but the good balanced the bad.

Cynthia and her sister Mary were wonderfully hospitable, despite the early hour and the fact that Bon and I were like two waifs off the street—dirty, smelly and tired. We bathed and washed our hair and then had a scrumptious hot breakfast, the first proper meal we had had in days.

"Any suggestions on budget accommodation and where we can do laundry?" I asked over yet another cup of strong coffee.

"The Traveller's Aid hostel isn't far away and there's also a laundrette nearby," Cynthia said. "I'm so sorry we can't help out."

"Not to worry," Bonnie insisted. "You've been more than generous. We appreciate it."

As we got ready to leave, Mike handed us a bulging bag of

oranges.

"Here's a little souvenir from Wentworth," he said.

"We'll enjoy these. Thanks," I said. "I must admit, my muscles still twitch when I see oranges."

"Picking is tough work," Mike said with a laugh, "but I hear you girls did well."

"We'd better let you people get back to packing," Bonnie said, signalling our departure. "Thanks again for everything."

The rest of the day was spent getting a room and then washing virtually everything we owned.

"Now I know why they say *cleanliness is next to godliness*," I remarked, folding my share of the laundry. "It will be positive heaven to wear clean clothes again."

The next day we set out early to explore the city. The damp, bleak weather was only in the forties or fifties Fahrenheit. We weren't in the tropics anymore! Nor was the city's ambience endearing. Big buildings, crowds of people, traffic and noise were overwhelming.

The vast selection of shops took getting used to. For eight months we had lived in remote areas whose retail outlets leaned more towards necessities than luxuries. Now we gawked at the enticing, professional window displays of Meyer's, Melbourne's famous department store.

"Let's go in and have a look," I said to Bonnie, admiring the stylish mannequins.

Bonnie needed no convincing.

"Things are a lot cheaper here than up north," Bonnie said as she held up a pretty cotton shirt.

"Cheaper but still out of budget," I said with regret.

We managed to get through the entire store without succumbing to temptation—until we came to the perfume department. When I was sixteen, I persuaded a teacher to escort a group of classmates from Montreal to New York during the Easter break. The trip included numerous cultural activities and, of course, shopping. My big expenditure was a small bottle of *Casaque* perfume that cost twenty-five dollars, no small amount for a schoolgirl in the 1960s. My girlfriends came home with suitcases full of trendy clothes for that amount of money.

I couldn't afford such indulgences these days but I could at least spray on a sample of something nice. When the saleslady asked if she could help, I pretended to be looking for a gift for my mother. This, I thought, made me seem like a serious buyer.

"Let's see if we can match a scent to her personality," the woman said. "What sorts of things does she like?"

I hadn't expect an interrogation but the idea of a customised scent appealed. I played along.

"She's good at sports," I lied, "but she's also creative. And sophisticated," I added for good measure. Maybe there was a brand I could grow into.

The saleslady thought for a moment.

"Try this one," she said finally.

She squirted a wonderful haze of floral notes onto my wrist. I sniffed. I smiled. The fragrance was divine.

"This is amazing. I don't need to try any others. I'm sure she'd love this one."

"You have good taste," the woman said, pleased with my response. "*Joy* is the most expensive perfume in the world."

"Of course it is," I said with a sigh. Grannie Daley frequently reproached me for having champagne taste on a beer income. This supported her argument. "I'll have to think about it."

The saleslady nodded—and gave me a generous going-away spritz. Someday, I vowed, when solvency was less fleeting, *Joy* would be my trademark scent.

By late afternoon we headed back to our hostel. We stopped at an almost grotty, almost nice café, the only eating spot we had come to in this almost grotty, almost nice street. We entered the fluorescent-lit space and sat on stools at the formica-topped counter. A paunchy server with a grease-flecked apron and a friendly smile handed us menus. Low funds didn't allow much more than a pick-me-up cup of coffee but we nevertheless scanned the list of offerings.

"Look," I said excitedly. "There's homemade tomato soup for

the same price as coffee, only fifteen cents."

"Great choice," Bonnie agreed. "Much healthier."

The thick, surprisingly delicious soup and accompanying slice of bread kept us going until the next morning. Our tummies grumbled but didn't growl.

The following day, we went to the Victoria Tourist Office with the intention of doing some sightseeing. According to all the brochures, the city had plenty to offer but suddenly it was all too much. We couldn't work up the enthusiasm to be tourists. Perhaps it was the dreary weather or perhaps our batteries were simply running low. In the end, we shopped for final bits and pieces and prepared for our departure to Sydney.

We caught the 7:30 am train to Fawkner, a suburb on the Hume highway eight miles outside Melbourne. This would be an easier start for hitchhiking. Someone stopped almost immediately.

"I've toured the world. I know how difficult it can be to get a ride," the young man said.

For the next couple of hours, we exchanged travel tales. It was a shame this companionable driver wasn't going all the way to Sydney.

After this lucky pick-up, we got a ride in an army truck, another car and then a transporter. We caught a final ride with a couple of truckies. They were travelling in tandem, so Bonnie and I split up. When we stopped at a diner, my driver insisted on buying me a trucker-sized meal.

"Steak and eggs'll stick to yer ribs," he said tucking into his own mega portion.

Because I hadn't eaten that much food for a couple of days, I felt a little ill and a lot tired afterwards.

"Sorry, but I just can't stay awake," I apologised when we had gone only a short distance. "I feel like a bear that has to hibernate."

"Don't worry," he said, "Curl up on the seat and have a snooze."

At 5:00 am, the truckies dropped us in Liverpool, eighteen miles from Sydney. We had been travelling for nearly twenty-four hours since we left Melbourne.

"There's a train station here," my driver said. "It'll be easy enough for you to get into the city."

A commuter train arrived soon after we got to the platform. We jumped on board. When the conductor asked where we had got on, we couldn't remember the name of the station. He looked at Bonnie, then at me, perhaps wondering if we were trying to scam him. After taking our rough state, foreign accents and the early hour of the morning into account, he believed us.

"Ten cents will do just fine," he said.

It was too early when we got to Sydney to make begging phone calls. After killing time until a respectable hour, Bonnie got in touch with our previous hosts, Jack and Janice Mitchell.

"No go," Bonnie reported after she hung up. "They're expecting other guests."

"Or maybe she just doesn't want to receive another strange house gift from us," I said, remembering the tin of smoked octopus I had thought was such a good idea at the time.

I then phoned Frank Tennant, a fellow our Melbourne friends had recommended.

"I'm flying out of town within the hour," Frank told us, "If you can get here before I leave, you're welcome to stay in the flat. I've got three roommates, if that doesn't bother you."

He gave us directions to Paddington. This, we found out, was the most 'in' residential area in Sydney. It used to be the red light district until many of the brothels were converted into trendy, expensive homes. I smiled at the thought that we would be staying in a former bordello.

Frank's whitewashed two-storey house had charming Victorian gingerbread ironwork on the rooftop and on the small upstairs balconies. Inside, it was spacious but sparsely furnished. A bit of decorating finesse would have turned the place into a showpiece.

"Sorry I have to dash," Frank said after he had greeted us. "My flatmates come and go but James is in town for the next few days. He'll see you get settled in."

If the other flatmates were as good looking as these two, staying here wouldn't be a hardship. Or so I thought. Frank had neglected to warn us about a fifth lodger whom I met unexpectedly.

Catching movement out of the corner of my eye, I turned to see a large and long snake slithering lethargically in my direction. The words 'boa constrictor' sprang to mind.

"Sorry about that," James said when he responded to my glass-shattering scream. "That's Adolf. He's a bit of a cheeky bugga and likes to sneak up on house guests. He's absolutely harmless, though."

"I have a bit of a phobia about snakes," I explained in a shaky voice. My nerves were vibrating at an alarming frequency.

"That's not good," James said. "We'll keep him locked away while you're here."

I didn't see Adolf again but I was never completely at ease, worried that the 'cheeky bugga' might find a way to get back at me for his temporary confinement.

We went the next day, Friday, to pick up our boat tickets from Shaw-Saville. The agent frowned as he examined Bonnie's passport.

"We can't release your ticket until you have a valid visa for New Zealand."

"Crumbs," Bonnie said as we made our way to the New Zealand consulate, "I didn't even think about a visa. I hope it doesn't in-volve some long-winded palaver."

"I sometimes forget how convenient it is to be a Canadian. It's lucky we've allowed extra days."

At the consulate, we explained the urgency of the situation.

"It's no problem issuing a visa quickly but you have to show us that you have a ticket leaving the country," the clerk explained.

This was a dilemma we hadn't expected.

"Looks like you're going to have to make up your mind about what you'll do after New Zealand," I said.

Bonnie had been toying with the idea of going with me to Can-ada but family ties tugged. Now push had come to shove. Bonnie would have to make up her mind, never an easy task for my friend.

"I'll be back on Monday with the required ticket," she said to the official.

In the meantime, we explored Sydney. My enthusiasm for the

city hadn't changed from the previous visit. As much as I loved Montreal, it felt like yesterday, whereas Sydney felt like tomorrow. In Sydney there was excitement in the air, a desire to be different, to make a mark. Montreal was stylish and sophisticated, but comparatively conservative. It had become apparent to me that I wasn't a conservative person.

A trip to the post office resulted in a welcome trove of letters. As well, there was a telegram. I thought it might be from Maury or John Clark wishing me bon voyage. Then I saw it was from home. Why would anyone send a telegram from Canada except to convey bad news? Had my entire family been wiped out in a freak accident? I forced myself to read the message: *Impossible to airmail sleeping bag. Letter and funds waiting in Auckland. Mom.*

I nearly cried with relief. This wasn't just good news, it was great news. Hopefully there would be money left over from buying a sleeping bag, a necessity, we had been told, for hiking around New Zealand.

After discussing and reflecting on various options over the course of the weekend, Bonnie decided she would go home. Monday morning we returned to the New Zealand consulate, ticket in hand. The visa process went smoothly. Shaw-Saville released our boat tickets.

On our final trip to the *poste restante* on Wednesday, the day before our departure, I had a premonition. This was an experience I had rarely but knew not to ignore. The last one had been about my impending car accident. This one, too, felt ominous.

"There's something wrong with my grandmother," I said to Bonnie as we walked through the stately Victorian entrance. I stood stalk still, feeling a chill go through me and a certainty I couldn't dislodge.

"What are you talking about?"

"Grannie Scott has died or she's dying."

"Why would you say that?" Bonnie asked. She knew how close I was to my maternal grandmother. "No letters have mentioned a decline in her health."

"That's true. But I feel a change, like she's not able to be with me anymore," I insisted.

"Let's collect our post. Maybe there's a letter for you."

I had a number of letters but nothing from family.

"No news is good news," Bonnie said trying to assure me.

I remained unconvinced but the common sense of her words made me feel less apprehensive. After all, if my mother could send a telegram about a sleeping bag, surely she would use the same means to alert me if something was seriously wrong with Grannie.

CHAPTER 24

No rain, no flowers.
Anonymous

The suitcases we shipped from Alice Springs nearly two weeks earlier still hadn't arrived.

"Sorry," the Wridgeways rep told us. "They got held up in Adelaide. We're doing our best to get them to Sydney as quickly as possible."

"We leave tomorrow! What if they don't make it in time?" I heard my voice rise an octave. "Can you forward them to us in New Zealand?"

"We can, but it would take at least four weeks to get shipping space," he said. "Look, luv, there's still a day before you leave. Don't give up yet."

What choice did we have? We couldn't influence the outcome, I reminded myself, so there was no point wasting more energy fretting about it.

To add to our last-minute distractions, Melva, one of our Canadian roommates from Darwin, arrived in Sydney on our last day.

"I made it! Can I drop by the house?" her cheery voice asked through the phone wires. "It would be great to spend a bit of quality time with you guys before the final sendoff this evening."

Melva was on her way back to Canada and had timed her arrival in Sydney to coincide with our departure. I couldn't refuse her request.

"Now there's dedication for you," Bonnie said with a wink. "Are you going to invite her to visit you in Montreal?"

"Not bloody likely. It seems I can't *dis*courage her but I definitely won't *en*courage her."

Melva had a crush on me. Unfamiliar and uneasy with this sort of female regard, I tried to keep her at a distance without hurting her feelings.

Despite my misgivings, we enjoyed Melva's visit. She brought all the latest Darwin news. We laughed at the accounts of friends' mischief and gasped at the scandals. Then, after nearly two hours of catching up, we had to show her the door.

"Sorry, Melva," I said, "but we've got a ton of things to do."

"I understand," easygoing Melva said. "I'll see you this evening."

No sooner had Melva left than the doorbell rang once again.

"I have a delivery for Misses Daley and Southey," a man said.

"That's us," we replied.

"Give me a minute."

He went to the back of his truck and retrieved … our two suitcases!

"Better late than never," I breathed, closing my eyes and saying a silent prayer of thanks.

While we were repacking, the phone rang. It was Ian Simpson, my besotted helicopter pilot.

"I wasn't sure you'd get here in time," I said. It surprised me I was so pleased to hear from him.

"It was touch and go at times, and I might have broken a few rules, but I was determined," Ian said. "My mates and I would like to take you girls out for a fancy dinner and a few drinks before you disappear."

"That sounds fantastic. It'll be great to see you again."

I said these words with sincerity. More often than not, I enjoyed being with Ian. He was an intelligent gentleman who treated me with respect. But. He adored me! I wasn't comfortable with blind devotion, especially in steady doses. Despite my affection for Ian, it was a relief that I soon would be out of easy range of his attentions.

I gave Ian our address and suggested a pick-up time.

In the meantime, Bonnie and I repacked suitcases and got ready to leave.

"Thank you so much for putting us up," Bonnie said to James.

"And for putting up with us," I added. "Thank Adolf for his patience," I said, giving James a hug. "But wait until we're off the property until you let him out!"

Ian and his friends arrived on schedule. Somehow they managed to fit us and all our gear into the car. We went for a superb dinner in a classy restaurant. I suspected Ian wished we were alone in this romantic atmosphere of low lighting, soft music and attentive waiters. I squeezed his hand under the table to signal that I appreciated the gesture of trying to make my last night in Australia special.

After dinner, Ian insisted on a grand tour of the best watering holes in Sydney. We were having such fun that the reality of our imminent departure faded into the background. Amid the noise of laughter, conversation and music, Ian leaned into me and whispered, "I'm going to miss you, Kath."

The sentiment suddenly unclouded my brain. We had a boat to catch! I checked my watch.

"My God, we've got to leave. Embarkation was between 8:30 and 9:30 pm. It's 9:40!"

"Don't worry, they won't sail without you," Ian assured us.

"Let's not take the chance," I said, already heading for the door.

When we arrived at the docks at 10:10 pm, Melva rushed through the crowd to reach us.

"They've already taken up the gangway!" she announced.

Sure enough, the passenger access had been removed but, in our inebriated state this didn't seem particularly grave. After all, the boat was still tied to the dock. We hadn't missed it; we simply couldn't embark. Presumably someone would solve the problem. In the meantime, we waved to all and sundry, covered in stockings, streamers and lengths of toilet paper. Frank Partridge got carried away with his comic act and threw Bonnie's ticket over the railing. Ian did the noble thing and chased after it, catching it just before it blew into the water.

One of the crew must have recognised us from our previous sailing because suddenly an official rushed up to us.

"We've been paging you," he remonstrated, relief written on his face. "Please follow me to the Purser's office so we can get you checked in."

It would have been gracious to give Ian and our friends a dignified farewell but there just wasn't time.

"Keep in touch," I heard Ian call.

The crowds cheered as we were poured aboard through a crew entrance.

Bonnie added to the drama by being unable to locate her rescued ticket.

"It's here somewhere," she said, digging into the black hole of her handbag.

Out came an odd and extensive assortment of treasures but no ticket. Finally, she remembered she had put it down the front of her dress 'for safe keeping'. We made our way to the deck to wave and throw kisses to the friends who had helped make our departure memorable.

Sailing from Sydney at night is an impressive sight. The illuminated skyscrapers, opera house and harbour bridge present a glittering panorama, like jewels displayed on black velvet. Bonnie and I leaned on the deck railing, each of us saying our own goodbyes to a land that, for us, had been full of unique experiences. Our eight months working our way around Australia had had ups and downs. We had been cold, hungry and financially stressed but we also had loved well, laughed often and benefitted from the unreserved kindness of the many people we met along the way. Doubtful about coming here, I now was sad to leave.

Before we were even out of the harbour, officer friends from the Cape Town-Fremantle sailing invited us to join them for drinks. We certainly didn't need to indulge more, but the night was still young and we looked forward to the reunion.

"Well, you girls certainly have become more ... muscular ... since we last saw you," Mac said as he placed a bloody Mary in front of me.

I took a deep sip and observed Mac over the rim of the glass. These weren't the words a woman wanted to hear from a lover but I refused to take offence at this tactful attempt to avoid blurting out surprise at my weight gain. Mac, on the other hand, hadn't changed at all. He was still the shy man whose appeal lay in his decency.

"Serious partying over the next couple of days will get you back in shape," one of the officers said.

He turned up the volume of the music and we all started shaking off calories.

As well as hard dancing, there was hard drinking. It impressed these diehard sailors that I was able to down half a bottle of vodka in a short time and still remain conscious. Bonnie's constitution was less strong. She had found herself a place to lie down and was semi-asleep.

"Time for me to go back to the cabin," she said drowsily after a while.

"I'll help you," I offered.

Only when we tried to get up did it become apparent how tiddly we were. I stood at the top of the stairs on the officers' deck wondering how to descend gracefully. The next thing I knew, the two of us sat in a heap on the bottom step. Bonnie bravely continued to the lower decks but I was catatonic. Officers weren't allowed on the passenger decks at this hour of the morning, so they had to carry me back to their quarters. I was woken at dawn and managed to get to my cabin before the steward brought tea.

Our morning-after misery wasn't helped by the fact that the Tasman Sea crossing is one of the worst in the world. The first day at sea was exceptionally rough. Poor Bonnie was deathly ill. Only strong determination saved me from being sick. As long as I remained horizontal, I was marginally fine.

By the second evening, calmer seas prevailed. I teamed up with a couple of fellows with guitars to entertain the passengers. It felt good to sing and play again.

The four-night sailing got us to Auckland on Monday, 29 September 1970. As the MV *Akaroa* followed the tug boats into the harbour, I looked at this country at the bottom of the world. New Zealand was said to be exceptionally beautiful. In this grey, early morning light I saw nothing to distinguish it from any other place I had been. But, then, Australia had created a similar impression, I reminded myself, and look at the adventures we had had there!

***

Bonnie and I had a whopping great breakfast before disembarking.

"Who knows when we'll get another good meal?" Bonnie said, as she spread a thick layer of jam onto her third piece of toast.

We left our luggage on board while we went into Auckland to the post office. The premonition I had had in Sydney still bothered me so I didn't know whether to be pleased or concerned when the clerk handed me a stack of letters. I quickly checked stamps and return addresses. Sure enough, there was a letter from home. I opened it nervously. An enclosed money order allayed immediate financial concerns. Now there would be enough money to get the gear we needed for hiking around New Zealand. I devoured the news in my mother's chatty missive. No mention of Grannie, thank goodness, but my great-uncle Eric had died. Was this the death I had foreseen? No, it couldn't be. The feeling of loss was for Grannie Scott, not some uncle to whom I wasn't particularly close. I placed the letter back in the envelope, still unable to dispel the nagging sense of foreboding.

Another letter was from Mary, a cousin of Grandpa Daley. She and cousin Maura were nuns who had emigrated to New Zealand from Ireland after the second world war. I had made contact with them soon after getting to Australia. Now Mary was confirming an invitation to Bonnie and me to stay with her. The letter included contact details. I phoned her right away.

"Welcome to New Zealand," Mary's melodious voice said.

We spent a while chatting pleasantly before she hit me with a bombshell.

"I'm so sorry to have to give you this news, Kathy, but I received a cable from your mother. She asked me to let you know that your Grannie Scott has died."

A hot, searing pain in my heart was followed by cold numbness. I broke down and cried. *Oh, Grannie. Couldn't you have waited until I got home? There was so much I wanted to share with you. And so much you still had to teach me.* Grannie had been a guiding rudder in my life. How would I navigate without her?

Mary let me weep, eventually offering soothing sympathy.

"When?" I asked when I regained control of my emotions. "When did she die?"

"The message said Friday the twenty-fifth. Of cancer," Mary added.

Why hadn't my mother given any indication of Grannie being sick or dying? Sydney is sixteen hours ahead of Montreal. This means that although I had the premonition on Wednesday, it was only Tuesday in Montreal. I explained the inexplicable to myself as Grannie thinking of me before she died.

"Let's head back to the ship," I said to Bonnie. "I'd like to say goodbye to everyone. Also, I could do with a stiff drink."

The stiff drink evolved into a serious intake of vodka and, for good measure, a cigarette, my first. I got no pleasure from either activity but they dulled the heartache. Bonnie and Mac kept me company, observing my distress with concern.

"I hate to rush you on your way," Mac said, breaking the spell of misery, "but the Customs hall will be closing soon."

We looked at our watches, astonished that it was now late after-noon. We rushed to our cabin to collect our belongings. By the time we got to Customs, the officials were getting ready to go home. They didn't bother to look in our cases but, instead, helped us carry them to a taxi.

Our destination was The People's Palace, a Salvation Army hos-tel. It was clean, affordable and served nourishing meals.

"Do you suppose it's appropriate we're staying in a place that has a reputation for giving shelter to wayward women?" Bonnie asked.

"I'm sure Grannie Daley would think so."

I tossed and turned all night, unable to come to terms with Grannie Scott's death. I knew virtually nothing about cancer except that it was a fatal disease too dreadful to discuss in front of chil-dren. I imagined Grannie being stoical in the face of death as she had been throughout her life. I also realised she must have been adamant about not wanting me to know of her illness. Grannie knew how much this trip meant to me. She chose to spare me the sacrifice of returning early to be with her before she died. It was considerate of Mom to have Mary break the news instead of having me receive the shock via an abrupt telegram but my heart felt raw nevertheless. I cried myself to sleep.

The next day I felt slightly better. I had come to terms with Grannie's escape from a consuming disease.

Bonnie and I walked to Queen Street, the heart of the city. I expected Auckland to have charm, perhaps even quaintness, but it fell flat on this score. There seemed to be no spirit or energy to the place. We heard that all businesses closed down tighter than a drum on Sundays but this was only Tuesday. I hoped the rest of the country would be less disappointing.

One thing Auckland did have was a great outdoor equipment shop called Wright-Stephenson. The place was a treasure trove of the latest and best camping/hiking/fishing gear, suitable for everyone from weekend enthusiast to Antarctic explorer. We restricted our purchases to good backpacks and sleeping bags as well as a couple of impossible-to-resist accessories, including a handy knife/fork/spoon set.

This left me with only forty dollars. It would be a tight squeeze to get around New Zealand on this amount but with my experience of penury I had faith in making it through yet another financial trial.

The following day, we reorganised and repacked, squeezing what we needed for the next six weeks into our packs. We checked our suitcases at the railway station's Left Luggage.

"That'll be fifteen cents for a month," the agent said.

Bonnie and I looked at each other in surprise, grateful to have such a bargain.

"We'll pay for two months," I said without worrying about cost for a change.

The brief train journey to Papakura took us out of the city. We struck up a conversation with Patty, a friendly fellow traveller.

"Where are you off to?" I asked.

"Out of Auckland," she said vaguely. Then she shrugged. "Actually, I'm trying to create distance between me and the police. They seem to think I was involved in a couple of car thefts."

"And were you?" I asked naively, fascinated I might be associating with a felon.

Patty gave another shrug, smiled and changed the subject.

"Is this the first time you guys have hiked?"

"Yes," Bonnie answered. "Does it show?"

"It looks like you're carrying a fair bit of weight." She pointed at our packs. "Adjusting the straps will help with the distribution. Put them on and I'll help you."

While Patty fiddled with the straps, she entertained us with stories of her life on the run but also suggested places to see and places to miss. By the time the train pulled into our station, we had good tips and more comfortable packs.

"Thanks, Patty," I said as we made our way to the door. "Good luck with …" With what? 'Escaping the police' didn't seem like an appropriate farewell. "… everything," I finished weakly.

She gave us a smile and a wave. "You, too."

***

The journey to *Kinross Stud*, halfway between Auckland and Hamilton, was forty miles.

"What a treat not to have to travel huge distances like in Australia," Bonnie said as we set off.

Despite the weight of our backpacks, we were enjoying ambling through pleasant landscape in mild spring weather that had a whiff of green pastures in the air. I inhaled deeply, imagining I could feel the benefits of the clean smells course through my body.

When we eventually decided to thumb a ride, lifts came easily. No wonder New Zealand had the reputation of being a hitchhiker's paradise.

In no time at all, we had arrived at our destination. As John Malcolm, *Kinross's* owner, welcomed us into his home, I studied our slender, lofty host. Grey hair belied John's young-at-heart attitude; intelligent eyes suggested he deserved his reputation as a respected breeder and trainer. We immediately understood why Bonnie's brother Geoff spoke so highly of his former employer and why he had insisted that we stop to see him.

"Are you able to stay until Saturday?" John asked. "I'd like to take you to the Ellerslie races."

Saturday was three days away. We didn't want to outstay our welcome but we weren't on a tight schedule. John seemed genuine about having us as guests, so we accepted the invitation.

Once we had settled in, John took us on a tour of the stud. White-fenced paddocks dotted the pretty, rolling landscape. Nearer the house and multiple barns was a smaller circular paddock for showing horses. John ran a professional, high-quality operation.

The following day, John drove us to Rotorua, an area in the north-east of the island famous for its geothermal activity.

"What's that awful odour?" I exclaimed when we got out of the car. "It smells like rotten eggs."

"Or Ron's socks," Bonnie said. She told John the story of our hitchhiking adventure.

"Locals call Rotorua 'sulphur city'," John said. "The smell's from hydrogen sulphide emissions. The health advantages of mud baths and natural springs compensate for the bad odour."

I had read about benefits that included relief of inflammation and skin conditions but I would have to be pretty sick to endure the nauseating sulphur smell for any period of time. Nevertheless, it was fascinating to see the bubbling mud pools, steaming springs and shooting geysers.

We wandered over to watch a Maori woman using the hot springs to boil food. She demonstrated the technique by dipping a basket of vegetables into a conveniently shaped hole in the rocks. I wondered if the food had a sulphur flavour.

We returned home via Lake Taupo, in the centre of the island.

"Now this is what I call a lake," I said admiring the massive body of water.

"It's New Zealand's largest lake. The perimeter is one hundred twenty miles, nearly as big as Singapore. That's pretty impressive, even by Canadian standards, but more so for our little country. In fact, I'm pretty sure it's the largest lake in all of Australasia."

John explained that a volcanic eruption had formed the lake nearly two thousand years earlier.

"Geothermal currents warm the water at some of the beaches," he added, "but the area is most famous for what's probably the best trout fishing in the world."

I liked the lakeside town of Taupo and its pleasant holiday atmosphere. Considering it was such a beauty spot, I was surprised it remained unbothered by an influx of tourists.

Our final stop was the beach town of Mount Maunganui or The Mount, as locals call it. It sits on a sandy peninsula that juts out from Pilot Bay, the harbour at Tauranga, on the east coast. The ocean side of the peninsula has New Zealand's best beach, a draw for swimmers and surfers. We explored the endless stretch of white sand, collecting shells and wading in the lapping water of the South Pacific.

"That's Mauao," John said, pointing to a peak at the end of the peninsula. "It's an extinct volcano. A Maori legend tells of a nameless mountain wanting to escape the misery of hopeless love. He appealed to the *patupaiarehe*, the people of the night, to make a magical rope and drag him into the sea to drown. They had got as far as the end of the peninsula when the sun started to rise. Before abandoning the forlorn mountain and fleeing back to the dark safety of the forest, the *patupaiarehe* named the mountain Mauao, meaning 'caught by the morning sun'."

The Maoris had a story to explain every occurrence in nature.

"The geography of all the countries in Europe is represented in New Zealand," John said proudly. "We have alps, glaciers, geysers, surfing beaches, lakes, lush fields, the works. You name it, it's here."

John was right. Nature had blessed these compact islands with beauty and geographic diversity. Moreover, the people seemed to be good stewards. From what we had seen and read, there had been no commercial rape of the land, no wilful destruction of flora and fauna. The harmony between the people of New Zealand and nature was almost tangible.

The following day, Bruce, one of the stud hands, took us to the

Waitomo caves on the west coast.

"'Wai' is Maori for water and 'tomo' means hole," Bruce explained. "There's an amazing labyrinth of sinkholes, rivers and more than two hundred caves under these hills."

The extensive guided tour took us through two levels of caves with names like the catacombs, the banquet chamber, the pipe organ and the cathedral, an area with a ceiling of sixty-five feet and excellent acoustics.

"I can never remember which are stalactites and which are stalagmites," I said, admiring the limestone deposits.

"Stalagmites form from the floor upward and stalactites form from the ceiling downward. It takes them about a hundred years to grow just one cubic centimetre," Bruce said.

"I'm guessing these are several million years old?" I said, eyeballing the tall shapes.

"Close enough," Bruce agreed.

The guide drew our attention to an unusual cluster.

"When stalagmites and stalactites join together," he said, "they're called pillars or columns. Occasionally they'll twist around each other. Those formations are called helicti."

The highlight of the visit was a boat trip on the underground Waitomo river to see the famous New Zealand-specific species of glowworms. The sparkle of these tiny creatures on the cave ceiling create an impression of a night sky with millions of stars. They provide the only light in the chamber.

On the way home we stopped in a pub in Hamilton and sampled New Zealand beer.

"It's weaker than the Aussie stuff but it's still pretty damn good," Bruce said.

Bonnie and I agreed. The lower alcohol content certainly wouldn't hurt us.

On Saturday, John took us to Ellerslie, one of the world's finest thoroughbred racecourses.

"In 1874, when the track opened, Ellerslie was several hours by coach outside Auckland. To increase the popularity of horse racing, the owners put a lot of effort into making the destination appealing. No other course dedicates so much space to landscape attractions."

We walked around the grounds, admiring ponds, a variety of trees and wonderful flower beds. Then we gave our full attention to the purpose of the visit: the races. John introduced us to trainers and owners and pointed out features that make a horse a potential winner.

I had learned not to get my hopes up about a win at the races. Today was no exception. Although I was with one of New Zealand's premier breeders—John's stallion Summertime was an Australasian champion— that didn't help my run of luck. After a couple of exciting wins, I eventually came out with a minus balance of nearly two dollars. Not a large amount by betting standards but the limit of what I could afford to lose.

"Now that you've seen the main tourist sights, I'd like to show you the island's best studs before you head off," John said.

Neither Bonnie nor I had any special interest in such a tour but Bonnie had to pretend enthusiasm since her family was in the business. In fact, we both enjoyed ourselves. This was horse breeding at the highest level. We visited the properties of the biggest names in New Zealand's equestrian world.

At one home, we attended a cocktail party to celebrate a major win. A blown-up photo of the full-length body of the stallion flying across the finish line with no other horses in sight was meant to convey an impressive victory. The guests oohed and ahed, congratulating the proud owner and the pleased trainer on the remarkable achievement.

I studied the picture closely.

"There aren't any other horses in the picture," I remarked.

"That's the whole point," the owner said, taking a puff on his cigar. "He was more than a length ahead of his nearest follower."

I looked again and shook my head.

"But how do we know he's not coming in last?"

Stunned silence met my innocent observation. It was like the air had been sucked out of the room. Everyone stared at the photo with renewed interest. Then there were chuckles and animated conversation.

"You might want to use a different photo of the win," one of the guests suggested to the scowling owner.

CHAPTER 25

Difficult roads often lead to beautiful destinations.
Anonymous

"It's been great having you girls here," John said as we got ready to leave. "Stop in at the end of your trip, if you have time."

We had spent a cushy few days at *Kinross Stud*. Now it was time to hit the road. Unlike our travels in Australia, we wouldn't stop anywhere for long. This was a tour, not a search for jobs. It would have been great to have some income, of course, but our priority was to see the entire country in the six weeks before I sailed home.

Today's destination was Hawera in the west of North Island. This was where my cousin Mary worked as a nursing nun.

The route's magnificent scenery took us on roads that went from wide and flat to steep, narrow and twisty. The landscape evolved from farmed plains to rocky mountains, from populated to wild. Nothing was bland, everything was beautiful, a feast for the eyes and a balm for the soul.

At Stratford, I phoned Mary to give her a heads up about our arrival.

"Goodness me," she exclaimed, "you're hardly any distance at all. You'll be here in no time."

The driver of our final ride insisted on taking us right to the door. In an unladylike manner, we slid out of the high Frosty Cola truck, landing with a thump on the pavement. When we presented ourselves at reception, we learned we were at the wrong hospital. We had to walk a mile and a half, arriving later than the anticipated 'no time'.

Mary gave us a warm welcome and settled Bonnie and me into a cosy cottage on the grounds.

"She seems like a sweet old lady," Bonnie said.

"She does," I agreed, "but a bit suffocating. And talkative! She barely pauses for breath."

"Maybe she's just excited to see a relative. That probably doesn't happen too often, if ever."

After getting cleaned up, we had tea with Mary. She quizzed me intently, wanting to know every detail about our travels but especially about the family. Once I had answered all Mary's questions, I asked about her life and what she knew about my grandfather, who died when I was thirteen. I remembered Grandpa Daley as a dapper gentleman of medium height with twinkling eyes and smoothly combed silver hair.

"Records were destroyed in a fire in the early 1800s but I have information about your grandfather's side of the family back to that point," Mary said.

She excused herself to get a stack of paperwork. When she returned, she went through the names and stories of ancestors.

"Who is this Dobbins you keep referring to?" I asked.

"Why, your grandfather, of course." Mary looked surprised that I would have to ask.

"But my father's and grandfather's name is Daley."

"True ... up to a point. Your grandfather's family was Dobbins, from County Cork, Ireland. During the first world war, your grandfather joined the British Army. They put him in intelligence work. Eventually, your grandfather decided he would prefer combat to clandestine activities. Because of his seniority and access to privileged information, his superiors refused permission. Your grandfather didn't accept this verdict. He used his undercover contacts to create a new identity for himself: passport, birth certificate and any other necessary papers and props. He kept his original initials because of monogrammed things he owned."

"But wouldn't someone recognise him? Wouldn't his fellow spies go looking for him if he suddenly didn't show up for work one day?"

"Remember, it was wartime. There was lots of confusion. Perhaps he faked his death. I don't know the full story, just the few sketchy details he provided."

The dramatic disclosure flabbergasted me. The most shocking aspect was that I wasn't a real Daley. I felt like I had been deprived of an identity, that I wasn't who I thought I was.

"No one told me. I can understand my grandfather wanting to keep it secret at the time but he's been dead for years. Why didn't someone reveal this important piece of family history?"

"I'm sure your questions will be answered when you return home," Mary said gently. "In the meantime, I'll give you everything I have."

This was something, at least. Mary proved to be a font of knowledge. I enjoyed getting to know my grandfather from a different perspective. Instead of the kindly but somewhat remote scholarly gentleman with whom I was familiar, I now saw someone determined and daring. Perhaps this was where my craving for adventure came from.

Bonnie and I stayed with Maura for a couple of days. It was good to rest and refuel but we weren't sorry to escape her incessant chatter.

"*Hirrah*, but that woman can talk for Africa," Bonnie said as we made our way to the main road early in the morning.

"That's an understatement! But I sure got some astounding revelations from her. I'm still reeling!"

"Do you think your dad knew about this and didn't tell you?"

"I have no idea, but I'm certainly going to find out."

A car pulled up beside us, interrupting the conversation and getting my mind off the skeleton that had come out of the closet.

"Where are you headed?" the driver asked.

"Wellington," we answered.

"I can take you a good part of the way. Hop in."

We were going to visit the Bradshaws, another entry in Bonnie's address book of strangers. They lived just outside Wellington, North Island's southernmost city. Mid morning, a local bus from Wellington dropped us near the entrance to their property. We walked up a steep driveway to get to their house, no easy task with heavy packs, even for our level of fitness.

The Bradshaws were lovely people, very much the outdoor type. We left our packs at the house and then Mrs Bradshaw took us to Mount Victoria for a view of Wellington harbour. We had a perfect day to admire the sheltered turquoise inlet: hot, sunny and no wind.

After lunch, their family and friends took us on an energetic excursion to the southern tip of North Island. We scampered down deep hills that reminded me of a Scottish landscape. At the sea-shore, we discovered a bounty of paua shells, a species of sea urchin called spiny sea eggs, and a rope-covered glass buoy from a fishing trawler.

By late afternoon, we were at the Wellington docks, ready to board the inter-island ferry going to Christchurch.

"Look!" I said to Bonnie. "The *Akaroa*'s in port. Let's pay the guys a surprise visit."

We talked our way on board and made our way to Mac's cabin. I knocked and opened the door. The surprise was on me. Mac had a female visitor! Talk about a girl in every port! After we both re-covered from the embarrassment, we were able to laugh.

"Do you have time for a drink?" Mac asked.

We all went to the officer's bar. It was nice to say hello/goodbye to everyone a final time.

***

The Cook Straight crossing was brief but bad. The boat pitched and rolled, making it difficult to do anything except get knocked about. My watch strap broke when I was thrown against the cabin wall. Our 7:00 am arrival in Christchurch didn't come soon enough.

As it was too early to book into the Youth Hostel, we killed time by exploring this largest city in South Island. It was built to a plan that has Cathedral Square at its heart and four smaller surrounding squares with parkland in between. The result is an urban centre of considerable charm.

After leaving our gear at the hostel and having breakfast, we hitched to contacts who lived at *Mill Farm,* near Annat, thirty-seven miles northwest of Christchurch. Because of the good weather, we preferred to walk as much as possible. Our ambling took us past fertile agricultural and grazing lands and across glorious, undulating countryside with the snow-capped foothills of the Southern Alps in front of us.

We arrived at our destination in time for lunch and spent a lovely afternoon. In the evening, our hosts drove us back to Christchurch, took us to dinner and then dropped us at the Youth Hostel. It had been a perfect day: pleasant walking, enjoyable company and three full meals.

The next day we met up with Dave Clarkson, someone with whom John Malcolm put us in touch. Dave was New Zealand's foremost sports commentator. Due to his busy schedule, the meeting was brief.

"I'm not free today but I'll pick you up first thing tomorrow and we'll find something interesting to do," he promised.

I felt guilty that we would be responsible for him spending his precious time looking after a couple of young women who had no serious interest in the sporting world. Still, no one was twisting his arm, and the idea of 'something interesting' definitely appealed.

We headed back to the YHA, arriving a few minutes too late. They had closed for the afternoon. I sat on the front steps contemplating our predicament: if we couldn't get our bathing suits, we couldn't go swimming. Then I heard Bonnie's voice calling me— from above!

Bonnie gave a triumphant wave from a second-storey window.

"How did you get up there?"

"I employed a little lock picking trick I acquired on my travels," she said with a grin. "Go around to the back door. It's open now."

We made our way to the dorm, put our bathing suits on under our clothes and took a bus to Sumner, a nearby seaside suburb. Rocky, volcanic outcrops feature prominently on the fine-sand beach. When swells are high, this is a popular spot for surfers. Today, however, the sea was calm and the weather balmy.

The next morning, Dave Clarkson picked us up at 9:00.

"My schedule's crazy again today," he said as we drove into town. "I'm going to put you into the capable hands of my assistant

Geoff Brunns."

Dave's idea of finding something interesting to do, alas, was instructing Geoff to take us on a tour of important studs, lunch and then the races at Riccarton. Bonnie and I resigned ourselves to our horsey fate. Admittedly, the studs were interesting and the prize stallions splendid but Riccarton fell far short of the impressive Ellerslie track in Auckland.

"The unique thing about this course," Geoff said, "is that, unlike tracks in Australia and the rest of New Zealand, races here run counterclockwise."

"Doesn't that confuse the horses?" I asked, fascinated by this piece of information.

"Not really," Geoff said with a laugh. "They train on the track before the race, so they're used to the direction."

"What's the reason?" Bonnie asked.

"I don't rightly know," he admitted. "All the tracks in North America run counterclockwise; it's just an oddity here."

It seemed the change of direction gave us better luck with betting. Bon won nearly twenty dollars. I won only a dollar and twenty-five cents but was grateful to be in the black.

The next day, Dave had another assistant, Tim Mailing, drive us fifty miles to Ashburton, about a quarter of the way to Palmerston, our next destination. We phoned the Cassells.

"I'll collect you," Judy Cassells said.

Ten minutes later, a car pulled up and a personable, middle-aged woman stepped out.

"How lovely to meet you," she said graciously before loading our gear and us into the car.

In no time at all, we arrived at *Bushy Park Stud.*

"This is one of the most historical properties in New Zealand," Judy explained. "My husband Dave used to be married to the granddaughter of JG Johnson, a chairman of the board of the stock and station agents Wright-Stephenson. As well as being a famous stock-stud breeding centre for Corriedale sheep, this was his week-end and summer home. Now it's our permanent residence."

The sprawling one-storey homestead was magnificent. Two

bay-windowed wings flanked a long central portion. As we sat having drinks in the living room, Dave identified the many species of birds that could be seen winging past the window, perching in the trees or hopping across the lawn searching for worms. Only the robin was familiar to me. The others had exotic names such as saddleback, stitchbirds, tui and kereru.

On the second day of our stay, Dave took us on a tour of the property that included forest and wetland as well as extensive grazing lands. The beauty of the place penetrated the curtain of drizzle.

"It must be breathtaking when the sun shines," I said admiring the view.

"Yes," Dave said with pride. "This is a corner of paradise. We count our blessings to live here."

Judy had prepared a lunch of a New Zealand specialty called whitebait fritters.

"I've never heard of whitebait," I said, eyeing the wormlike food suspiciously.

"Whitebait are juvenile fish, up to two inches long," Dave said. "They're tricky to catch but delicious to eat. The New Zealand variety is the best in the world, a real delicacy. European whitebait are small herrings, not nearly as tasty."

"Because of the delicate flavour, we traditionally cook them as fritters," Judy added. "It's basically a light omelet. Some people use only egg whites to make the batter. Do try some."

Like Dave said, they were delicious. I added whitebait fritters to my list of culinary discoveries.

Our departure the next day coincided with Mel Dickson, the Cassells' accountant, completing work on the stud budget.

"I can give you a ride into Dunedin," Mel offered.

From there we took the train forty-eight miles northwest to Middlemarch. This small town in the Otago region lies at the foot of the long, flat-topped Rock and Pillar range. The Taieri river surrounds the gentle hill-and-valley scenery.

Bonnie had reestablished contact with Jessica, a woman she and her brother Dave had met in Scotland. I marvelled at the diverse and sometimes distant friendships created by travel, and at the bond that encourages travellers to help each other. Kind strangers, unstinting in their generosity, had taught me a lot. I hoped some day to emulate such unsparing hospitality.

Jessica and her dad picked us up and took us to *Gladbrook Station*, an historic sheep farm her great-grandfather had settled in 1872. I immediately fell in love with the handsome two-storey home set within an exuberant garden. The pretty dormers and multi-paned windows added to the charm of the old house. An expansive veranda offered wonderful views over the countryside.

The family could not have been more welcoming. The following morning, Jessica brought us breakfast in bed! I hadn't had a treat like that since Cape Town.

"You need to wipe that this-is-what-I-deserve look off your face," Bonnie said with a chuckle after Jessica left the room.

"It's that obvious?" I replied with feigned innocence.

Jessica also made sure all our laundry got done. While the clothes were drying, we took a walk over some of the property. What an idyllic location. Contented sheep grazed in many of the lush fields. It reminded me of vistas I had seen in Ireland.

After a delicious outdoor lunch in the sun, we went riding. I had Smokey, a big grey mare. Unlike many Aussie horses I had ridden, she was well-behaved, making the outing the most enjoyable thing I had done for ages. It felt invigorating to canter across the fields and over the hills.

The only downside of our otherwise perfect visit was my discovery of a set of bathroom scales, the first I had seen on my travels. I couldn't resist the temptation to know how far I had strayed from my once ideal weight. Gingerly, I stepped onto the scale, fearing bad news but not anticipating the disaster the numbers revealed. To my horror, I had gained fourteen pounds since leaving home! In British terms, this is a stone, which is what I felt like I had tied around my waist. The Aussie phrase 'bag of donuts' came to mind.

"Muscle weighs more than fat," Bonnie consoled, herself a victim of unwanted but not unwarranted weight gain.

I looked at my strong arms and powerful thighs and was almost convinced. My belly was still pretty flat but a pinch of the skin indicated the warning sign of flab. My hips seemed fuller, too. I sighed. Getting back in shape would have to wait until I had a more regulated lifestyle.

After two really delightful days and a filling lunch, we left *Gladbrook*. In keeping with her exemplary thoughtfulness, Jessica drove us thirty miles to the main road. It was such a beautiful day that we relaxed for a while by a bridge and stream. Bonnie rolled a cigarette and I stretched out on the grassy bank. When we eventually decided to make a move, a truck took us ten miles to the Bypass road to Alexandra. There our good luck came to a screeching halt.

"It's been three hours. If someone doesn't come along soon, we'll have to go to that farmhouse and ask if they can put us up for the night," I said, pointing to a building in the near distance.

Just as we were about to go begging, a motorist took us all the way to Queenstown.

The town sits on Queenstown Bay, an inlet on the shore of Lake Wakatipu, a glacier-moulded body of crystal clear water. The land area of the Queenstown-Lakes District comprises four thousand square miles of craggy peaks, wide and winding waterways, nature trails and generally exceptional scenery. This region in the southwest of South Island is the picturesque jewel of New Zealand and a main resort centre.

We weren't expected at the Smiths until the following day so we spent the night at a motor camp where we had our own cabin.

First thing the next morning, we loaded our packs on our backs and took advantage of the fine weather, choosing to walk part of the seven-mile distance to *Closeburn Station*, a high-country sheep and cattle farm bordered by three lakes.

When the Smiths asked if we would like to stay for lunch, we realised that would be the extent of their hospitality. If we had known, we would have left our heavy packs behind. At least Mrs Smith was good enough to give us a ride back to Queenstown.

On our way to the motor camp, we bumped into Chris Bleckett, a fellow we had met in Christchurch.

"Fancy seeing you girls again," Chris said with a broad grin. "What are you up to?"

"We got here yesterday and are planning to explore the area," I said. "What about you?"

"Just arrived. I have a car. Are you interested in joining forces?"

Bonnie and I jumped at the opportunity. It would be nice not to have to lug our backpacks or worry about getting rides for a couple of days. Chris, we anticipated, would be an agreeable travel companion.

Bright and early the next morning we drove to Coronet Peak, a ski centre. Although we were coming into the summer season and there was no sign of snow, I recognised that this roller coaster terrain would provide a remarkable downhill experience. In Canada, I had been an avid skier, escaping after work on Fridays to the Laurentian mountains near Montreal and returning to the city tired and windburned on Sunday evenings. Coronet Peak reminded me there was a positive side to the long Canadian winters.

From the ski resort we went to Arrowtown, a century-old gold mining centre that sits on the Arrow River, once famous for its alluvial gold finds. More than sixty of the original buildings had been restored and preserved. A small museum displayed examples of Maori and pioneer life in the mid to late 1800s when the gold rush was at its peak.

In the afternoon, the three of us took a minibus tour of Skipper's Canyon, a dramatic, thirteen-mile gorge forged by the Shotover river. The route was little more than a track. Sometimes we didn't think the bus's axles would handle the hairpin bends. An encounter with a large truck on one of these curves made my life flash before my eyes. I looked out the window at the unprotected edge of the road. It wouldn't take much to send a vehicle rolling hundreds of feet until it came to rest in the river. Fear of imminent disaster aside, the magnificent surroundings left us in awe.

We were grateful to have a ride with Chris through the Haast Pass. The weather was bleak and there were few cars. This was not a good place to be marooned.

"The drive must be glorious on a sunny day," Bonnie said.

"True," I agreed, "but the recent rainfall makes the waterfalls more prominent. I suppose each type of weather brings its own drama and beauty."

We stopped to see Fox Glacier, a mountain of ice that falls nearly eight thousand feet as it travels eight miles from the Southern Alps to the west coast. Apart from being unusually accessible, Fox has the distinction of ending its journey in a rainforest less than nine hundred feet above sea level.

We were headed to Franz Joseph Glacier, only a few miles away and one of three temperate glaciers in the area. It had been our intention to do a hike on the glacier but the miserable weather spoiled that plan.

I never had seen a glacier. Coming from a country buried under snow and ice for several months of the year, they didn't interest me until I saw them through Bonnie's and Chris's eyes: marvels of nature whose advance or retreat depends on the difference between snowfall at altitude and meltwater near the base. Once again, this trip had taught me to open my mind as well as my eyes. When I allowed myself to expand my viewpoint and see things as other people saw them, I invariably came out wiser—and more humble —from the experience.

After checking into the Franz Joseph Youth Hostel, we drove around and then went to the pub for a couple of hours.

"There's not much to do here," Bonnie said, after ordering a round of drinks. "It's actually kind of desolate."

"This is one of the more remote areas of New Zealand," Chris confirmed. "It's beautiful, though. The world is sure to discover it some day."

"I'm glad we got here first," I said, grateful to have witnessed this pristine show of nature.

***

Greymouth, the largest town on the west coast of South Island, was the home of my cousin Maura, aka Sister Thomas, a teaching nun. She had emigrated from Ireland with Mary. Like Mary, she was anxious to meet me. She insisted I come to see her immediately

"We're kind of unkempt," I protested.

"Not a bother," Maura said firmly. "I don't want to waste a moment of seeing you. Please come as soon as you can, exactly as you are."

Bonnie and Chris dropped me off.

"It's better you get to know each other without adding us to the mix," Bonnie said.

"Is that thoughtfulness," I teased, "or are you afraid she'll be a non-stop talker like Mary?"

"There's that, too," Bonnie said impishly as she waved good-bye.

Maura and I hit it off immediately. It was as though we had known each other forever. I sensed in her calm, wisdom and intuitiveness, a talent she displayed after we had chatted for a bit.

"Let me draw you a nice hot bath," she offered.

Had she read my mind ... or had she simply noticed my discomfort in presenting myself to her in an unwashed state!

What luxury to soak in scented water and then give my hair a good wash. Afterwards, I had afternoon tea with the rest of the teaching nuns, all of whom were as eager to meet me as Maura had been. Evidently they didn't get to see many young women hitchhiking around the world! I was an object of fascination. At first I felt awkward under the microscope of their scrutiny, feeling they attributed more to my escapades than they deserved. Their sincere interest, however, soon persuaded me to enjoy telling my stories as much as they seemed to enjoy hearing them.

When Bonnie and Chris came to pick me up, all of us were invited to have dinner at the convent. It was a lovely evening and a delicious meal—the first hot food we had had in days. It felt great to be clean, well fed and warm—all at once.

The evening's conversation was lively—and animated. In the course of waving my hand as I described something, the diamonds and sapphires in my ring caught Maura's eye.

"Where did you get that ring?" she asked suddenly.

It seemed like a strange question. Why would a nun be interested in jewellery?

"Grannie Daley gave it to me on my sixteenth birthday," I replied.

"May I see it?"

I removed the ring and handed it to her. Maura examined it and gave a sad smile.

"This was my mother's engagement ring."

The news astonished me. What were the chances that the Canadian recipient of her mother's ring would visit her in New Zealand?

"When I became a nun in Ireland, I gave all my jewellery to your grandfather. How do you come to have it?"

"Ever since I was a girl, Grannie let me wear an antique ring with a large solitaire diamond when I visited her. She said she would give it to me when I turned sixteen. On the day of my birthday, a package arrived. I was so excited. And then I was shocked. Instead of the diamond ring, she had sent this one. It's beautiful but, to me, it represented a broken promise. Now it has a happier association. Thank you."

"It sounds like your grandmother made use of a good opportunity to offload a reminder of what she considered to be a threatening relationship."

I looked at Maura enquiringly.

"Your grandfather and I were cousins. We grew up together in County Cork. As well as being inseparable, he and I had a telepathic connection. After the first world war, he married and ended up in Canada. I already had emigrated to New Zealand. Your grandmother was jealous of our strong bond." Maura smiled as she returned the ring. "How lovely that through you I would have the chance to see the ring again. It brings back happy memories of my mother and your grandfather."

"And it gives me another aspect of family history. I'm certainly picking up a lot on this trip!"

"Mary probably has given you plenty of information. She's always loved genealogy."

When I told Maura about the discovery of Grandpa Daley's real name, she was surprised this was a family secret.

"I suspect your grandmother won't be pleased the cat's out of the bag, especially if she's the only one who knows about it in her immediate family."

"It'll be another black mark against me. I have quite a collection of them."

Maura and I chuckled. This was something we had in common.

With much reluctance, Maura and I said our goodbyes.

"Promise to keep in touch," Maura said, brushing her hand down my cheek.

"I have a feeling we'll be in touch, with or without letters," I said.

"Like grandfather, like granddaughter," Maura said with a smile.

CHAPTER 26

Every exit is an entry somewhere else.
Tom Stoppard

After four days travelling with Chris, our journeys now took us in different directions.

"We'll miss your company—not to mention the convenience of having a personal chauffeur," Bonnie said, giving Chris a hug.

"I'll miss you girls as well. It's been fun."

Chris dropped us on the main road to Nelson, a seven-mile detour for him. It should have given us a good start. It didn't. Car after car passed. No one even slowed down.

"You'd think *someone* would stop," I grunted. As we laboured up the steep incline, I looked at the threatening sky. "I sure hope we don't get caught in a downpour."

"Not a good place to be stranded—or soaked," Bonnie muttered into her chest, head bowed against the climb.

Travelling with Chris had given my aching feet a rest. Now that we were back on the road with our heavy gear, my right foot telegraphed its objections, first as steady throbs, then as insistent pain. This type of terrain didn't help matters.

We walked three miles before getting a ride in an ambulance that took us quickly and smoothly as far as Dobson. We had a bite to eat and then started walking through the three thousand-foot Lewis Pass, one of only three main routes through the Southern Alps. The low volume of traffic gave us particular cause for concern. Then our luck changed.

"You look like you could use a lift," a driver said through his open window. "Where are you headed?"

"Nelson," we responded.

"Nelson?" The driver's face showed surprise. "I hate to tell you, but you're travelling in the wrong direction."

Bonnie and I looked at each other in dismay. This wasn't the place to make directional errors.

"The best solution is to let me drive you out of the pass. You might have better luck getting a ride on the back-country roads."

After all the time and energy we had expended, we didn't like the idea of backtracking but we agreed it was the best option. Eventually the driver dropped us at a crossroad.

"Make sure you stay on that side of the cross," the driver said, perhaps not trusting we wouldn't get lost again. "There's not a lot of traffic but something should come along. Good luck."

Soon enough a pickup truck stopped.

"Sorry, there's no room inside the vehicle. I'm happy to give you a lift, though, if you're willing to ride in the back."

We hopped into the open back, snuggled into our sleeping bags, leaned against the cab and enjoyed the spectacular scenery and the agreeable weather. By late evening, we had arrived at the youth hostel in Nelson.

The next morning we phoned Arthur Newth, another of those mystery contacts that filled our address books. Like nearly everyone else we had approached on our journey, he made time for us.

"I can show you the sights of Nelson, if you like," he offered.

We readily accepted the invitation. We always read as much as possible about the places on our itinerary but it was more interesting to have a local guide.

"Nelson's been a city for more than one hundred years," Arthur said as we walked the streets. "It's the oldest in New Zealand. And South Street, where we are now, is the country's oldest preserved street."

This northernmost city of South Island on the eastern shore of Tasman Bay had plenty of appeal. I particularly enjoyed Queens Gardens, a beautiful Victorian garden created to commemorate Queen Victoria's jubilee in 1892. Water features, bridges and sculptures intermingled with the vast collection of plants and a pleasing and plentiful variety of bird life.

"I'm taking the family to the beach tomorrow," Arthur said when he dropped us back at the hostel. "Would you like to join us?"

"We're always up for a trip to the beach. Thanks." Bonnie answered for both of us.

"Is it too early for you between 8:30 and 9:00?"

"Not at all," I replied, hoping I wasn't telling a lie. "We'll be ready."

"Sorry I can't be more precise. With kids, it's a bit like herding cats!"

Later in the afternoon, Bon and I climbed the meandering trail up Botanical Hill, on the eastern perimeter of Nelson. At the summit, a monument told us we had arrived at the geographical centre of New Zealand, point zero-zero. Here is where the first trigonometrical surveys were taken in the 1870s. The lookout platform allowed excellent views over Tasman Bay, Nelson and the surrounding area.

In the evening, we went to the Nelson Hotel, drinking, reminiscing and planning. Despite the fact that I already had booked passage to Florida, Bonnie never gave up trying to lure me in the opposite direction, back to South Africa.

"It's tempting," I admitted, "but I just feel it's not the right time. I need to go home. To my Canadian home. If all goes well, some day I'll return to my South African home."

Bonnie continued to make attempts to change my mind but I held firm. I was on a homeward trajectory and I couldn't imagine anything that would deter me at this stage.

"Anyway," I said, turning a deaf ear to yet another of Bonnie's compelling arguments, "it's your turn to visit me."

"You're right. Like you, I need to go home first but then I'll make plans to go to Canada."

With our immediate futures decided, we returned to the hostel.

"I'm on my way to a party," the warden said as we walked in the door. "Care to join me?"

Who can resist a party? It was 4:00 am before we got to our beds.

Arthur showed up less than five hours later. We wiped the sleep from our eyes and went through the motions of showing enthusiasm for an early outing with noisy kids.

We drove to Kaiteriteri, a golden beach across the bay from Nelson. After our late night, it was nice to do nothing more strenuous than stretch out on the sand and snooze. Friends of the Newths staying at the local caravan park joined us for a picnic lunch. It was a surprisingly pleasant day.

That evening the Newths invited us to accompany them to dinner at the home of their friends the Parkers. We feasted on mussel and pipi fritters and curried mussels. Pipis, I learned, are a local type of clam.

"You're lucky," Arthur said as he scooped another helping onto his plate. "The June-to-October spawning season has just finished. We've had to do without these little beauties for a while."

After supper, Richard Parker and I had a good singsong and harmony session. I missed having my own instrument but I had hooked up with enough guitar players along the way to compensate.

After nearly a month exploring the spectacular beauty of South Island, it was time to catch the ferry back to Wellington.

"I'm taking the family on a day trip tomorrow. We could drive you halfway to the ferry terminal at Picton," Arthur offered.

Unexpected rainfall the next day proved to be a boon for us.

"The picnic's spoiled but the family's still up for an outing. We can take you all the way to Picton. I don't know the sailing schedule but there should be a few ferries throughout the day."

"That would be fantastic," I said gratefully. "We don't know the schedule either but we don't mind hanging out."

When we got to the dock at Picton, no ferry was in sight.

"You'll be right?" Arthur asked as we unloaded our gear.

"We'll be fine," Bonnie assured him. "Thank you both again for your many kindnesses."

We made our way to the ticket booth.

"You need a reservation," the agent told us. "There's no availability until ten this evening."

This was more 'hanging out' than we had anticipated. Perhaps our forlorn expressions softened his attitude.

"Wait on the side," he instructed. "There definitely aren't any seats on the afternoon ferry, but I'll try to squeeze you on."

True to his word, he got us on the earlier sailing. It seems he helped a number of young people in this way because the ferry was crowded with passengers who sat on the floor or stood.

Thankfully the seas weren't too rough—relatively speaking. Several people with guitars got a rousing singsong going to liven up the three-hour crossing.

We spent the night at a hostel outside Wellington. Early the next morning we headed to Auckland, three hundred ninety-five miles north. We had errands in the capital. Our first stop was the Canadian consulate. Bonnie wanted to enquire about visa requirements.

It was my first contact with anything Canadian in nearly one and a half years. I stared at the Canadian flag and felt a surge of pride. I never thought of myself as patriotic but there was no denying that the long absence from my country made me see it in a new light. On my travels, many people had shared their admiration for Canada. From them, I learned much about my homeland's discreet but exemplary performance on the world stage, its contributions to science and medicine and its policy of good governance. Until now, I had been sensitive to American teasing about Canadians being boringly 'wholesome'. I now realised this wasn't a bad thing.

While waiting for Bonnie to collect the visa application forms, I read a few Montreal newspapers. It dismayed me to see that the situation between French-speaking and English-speaking Canadians had deteriorated to a point of riots. What was happening to my beautiful city, my once united country? It seemed Canadian governance might not be ideal.

When Bonnie reappeared, she looked triumphant and waved a thick brown envelope.

"Step one accomplished," I said. "Now you just have to worry about whether or not the Canadian government will consider you a suitable applicant."

"Oh, Kath, you're always so practical. Sometimes it's more fun to see how things unravel rather than planning."

"The problem with your schemes, my friend, is that too often they do unravel."

"It'll all work out. You'll see."

Bonnie was right, of course. Things always worked out ... just not always as anticipated. I stuck to my more organised tendencies.

We had ten days before I had to board the *Southern Cross* in Auckland. Since we had seen most of what we wanted to see in North Island, we planned to revisit a couple of friends. Typical of our sometime erratic itineraries, we retraced our steps and headed back to Wellington at the southern tip of the island and where we had just come from! The Bradshaws had invited us for a return visit. It was nice to reconnect and sit down to a hot dinner.

The next day we hitched north and west to Hawera. After a few rides in vans and trucks, we arrived at Calvary Hospital. Cousin Mary was thrilled to see us. Suddenly she noticed my injured foot. Slipping into her nursing mode, she examined it closely.

"How did it get so swollen?"

"Too much walking with forty pounds on my back," I said grimacing at the touch of her prodding fingers.

"Let me draw you a nice hot bath to ease the muscles. First thing tomorrow I'll make an appointment with Mr Morris, the physiotherapist. He's very good."

This sounded like an excellent idea. I could hardly walk.

"You have a bad case of strained muscles," Mr Morris diagnosed. "An hour of heat and electric current will help but the injury will take time to heal completely. I'll give you another treatment before you leave."

Mary also arranged for Bonnie to have a wart removed from her finger. When I saw Bonnie after the procedure, she was seething.

"The bloody doctor was bloody rude about me being South African. Like apartheid is my fault!" she said, fists clenched. "The Hippocratic oath says *do no harm*. He should know that words hurt!"

The experience was disturbing. This was the first time in our travels that we had encountered targeted malice. I tried to comfort Bonnie but she broke down and cried. I had been brought up to show tolerance, so it upset me when I saw a lack of it, especially when my friend was a victim. Fortunately, Bonnie bounced back quickly. Perhaps her resilience was due to the fact that she saw ethnic bias regularly. We kept the incident to ourselves.

At Mary's urging, we stayed until Saturday. It was in this period of resting and healing that Bonnie announced she would travel to Canada with me.

"That's great news, Bon," I sputtered, "but, at the risk of being overly practical, have you considered what this impulsive decision might involve?"

"Like what?" she asked innocently.

"Like getting a Canadian visa, which takes time. Like a berth on the ship. Like disappointing your family."

Bonnie looked sheepish for only a moment.

"It'll work out, Kath, you'll see," she replied flashing a pearly smile.

I still wasn't immune to getting sucked into Bonnie's crazy, spur-of-the-moment ideas. The chances of everything falling into place in only seven days were slim but the challenge appealed to both of us.

Finally it was time to be on our way. My foot had improved noticeably and once again could cope with the rigours of hiking. To my surprise, I became teary-eyed when saying goodbye to Mary. Although her ceaseless chatter was irritating, her affection was sincere—and reciprocated. I would miss her fussing attention.

The last of Mary's many kindnesses was to arrange for Father Begley to take us as far as Waitara, a distance of forty-five miles. This was about a quarter of the way to our next stop at Te Kauwhata where John Malcolm had *Kinross Stud*.

Along the way, Father Begley entertained us with tidbits of local history.

"That's Mount Egmont in all her glory. Also known as Mount Taranaki." He pointed to a distant snow-capped peak. "It's the most symmetrical volcanic cone in the world. Pretty impressive for something that's more than six thousand feet high. I'll stop so you can take pictures."

"That's a volcano?" I asked.

"It is, but don't worry, she's dormant. It's been more than three hundred years since the last major eruption." Father Begley smiled, anticipating my next question. "Scientists tell us it will probably be another two hundred years before the next one. We're safe for now."

At Waitara we thanked Father Begley for the ride—and for all his stories. By the time we arrived at *Kinross Stud* it was early afternoon.

"You're just in time for lunch," John Malcolm said as he greeted us.

Mention of food was always welcome.

"So, tell me about your adventures," he said, pouring us glasses of a nice Beaujolais.

Once we had updated him, he gave us some news of his own.

"We've got a mare due to foal sometime tonight," John said. "Are you interested in sitting it out with the vet?"

Bonnie passed. She had witnessed the birth of foals. A good night's sleep held more appeal. For me, though, it was a rare opportunity.

For the first part of the evening, the vet and I stationed ourselves in an observation room above the stable floor. A single bed provided a place for the vet to rest in case a birth was delayed.

When the mare went into labour, we went to her stall. I stood to the side, not wanting to get in the way. Things seemed to be proceeding normally—at least I assumed so since the vet didn't indicate otherwise. After twenty minutes, however, she became anxious.

"The mare's in distress," she said going to the sink to wash her hands.

I had assumed the rolling and snorting were part of the process but the vet recognised something wasn't right. With calm professionalism, she inserted both arms into the birth canal. I watched in fascination as her elbows disappeared. After a moment, she seemed to have found the problem.

"I'm going to try to turn the foal. Then I'll need your help. Wash your hands."

Help? What was I supposed to do? I was nothing more than an interested but untrained bystander.

"Quick as you can, please!" she urged.

When I returned she had her next set of instructions.

"Now I want you to put your hands in, feel for the legs and pull."

I gave her a horrified look. The mare, and therefore the foal, were worth small fortunes. I couldn't afford to reimburse John if something I did resulted in disaster.

"Hurry!" she said urgently.

With a loud exhalation, I approached the rear of the whinnying mare. While the vet made sure the foal was in the correct position, I pulled. Soon a bag containing a wet, furry creature emerged. The vet cut the umbilical chord and then tended to the mare.

After shaking its head and looking around at its new surroundings, the foal unfolded its spindly legs and made a tenuous effort to stand. It fell and rolled over. Undaunted, it tried again. The second attempt was successful. Its legs remained splayed for a couple of minutes while it made sure of its balance and figured out what to do next. The mare, now standing, gave her newborn a nuzzle and a gentle push. After a shake and a wobble, it headed to his mother's belly for a nourishing drink.

"Well done," the vet said as she cleaned up. "That complication was unexpected. I'm glad you were here. Thanks."

Still astonished at my role in the night's events, all I could do was give her a silly grin. Of the many first-time experiences I had had, this was the most remarkable. I felt awed to have participated in the miracle of birth. I gave the foal a fond pat before returning to the main house and my own bed. It was a perfect ending to a perfect trip.

***

As soon as we arrived back in Auckland on Wednesday 3 November, we made contact with the Kings, friends of cousin Mary. They owned the DB Tavern.

"Please come for lunch," Mr King said. "I'm sorry we can't offer you a room. We're fully booked at the moment."

It was good news and bad news but we capitalised on the good news and eagerly accepted the invitation for a meal. We had become neurotic about filling up whenever possible.

The only remaining name in our Auckland contact list was Pam and Joe Bleakens, friends of my Darwin beau Maury Simpson. I mentally crossed my fingers as I dialled their number.

"Maury said you might call. He told us to look after you. Come on over and stay as long as you like," Pam said warmly.

She gave me directions and said they would expect us whenever we arrived. I gave Bon the thumbs up.

"Whew," I said when I got off the phone. "That was an easy one. Thank you, Maury!"

"What's she like?"

"She sounds really nice. Maury said they're a great couple."

As we headed towards the bus stop that would take us to the Bleakens' home, I reflected on the many people in Australia and New Zealand who had taken us in.

"As grateful as I am for all the generous hospitality we've received, I won't miss having to be pleasant to and conversant with all these strangers. It isn't easy being 'on' all the time. It would be nice to let lose and be grumpy once in a while. I've almost forgotten how."

"The emphasis is on 'almost'," Bonnie said with a mischievous grin.

We both felt relief at not having to spend money on accommodation for the five days before my sailing. I was down to the equivalent of thirty US dollars. I pushed aside the concern that this wouldn't be enough to last for three weeks on the ship and then get me from Fort Lauderdale to Montreal. As Bonnie said, things always work out. At least I didn't have to worry about getting as far as Florida. I had paid the two hundred eighty-eight dollar passage a couple of months earlier.

In these final days, there were a number of tedious but necessary last-minute things to attend to: resoling riding boots, washing and mending clothes, packing and, of course, writing letters to inform everyone about this latest—and final—stage of my adventure.

The most difficult letter to write was to John Clark, the man I had loved and left in New South Wales. In the stack of mail we had collected in Auckland, there was a letter from John telling me he was getting married in December! I was shocked. There had been no hint in previous correspondence that he even had a girlfriend, let alone a fiancée. It's not that I begrudged his happiness, it was the fact that he was the first person I had gone out with who was going to get married—and not to me! Feeling rejected made no sense at all. I know I made the right decision to leave him but that didn't mean I wasn't sorry for this fact. Nor did it mean I couldn't feel dejected.

The sensation of loss for John might have been less underscored if I also weren't suffering the anticipation of separation from Bonnie. After seven months in South Africa, eight months in Australia, six weeks in New Zealand and more than a month sailing together, my days with Bonnie were nearly at an end. We had spent so much time in each other's company that I almost couldn't remember what it was like without her. She was my second self. How could I go anywhere without her? There hadn't been enough time for her to get a Canadian visa. Tomorrow, after one-and-a-half years, we each would be on our own. Judging by her less bouncy demeanour and the absence of pranks and crazy ideas, I suspected Bonnie felt like I did: sick and sad.

The imminent absence of my close friend was bad enough, but I also had to contend with the reality of going back to where I began. I had left Canada because I wanted adventure, new experiences. On that score, my mission had been accomplished. Now I almost felt like a traveller venturing to an unfamiliar land. I had witnessed the sights, sounds and smells of foreign countries, and absorbed the knowledge of foreign cultures. These experiences had altered my perspectives. Perhaps I would view my old life differently, with less satisfaction. I hoped my family and friends could accept who I had become and that I could adjust to who they still were.

CHAPTER 27

Have faith in your journey. Everything had to happen
exactly as it did to get you where you're going next.
Mandy Hale

It was an exciting time, it was a sad time. I was setting off on a three-week journey that would take me through the South Pacific and the Panama Canal but I was also saying goodbye to my dear friend.

"We'll be together soon," Bonnie promised. "I want my coat back!"

Because I had no clothing suitable for a Canadian winter, Bonnie had lent me her duffle coat. I counted on her coming to Montreal to reclaim it. In the meantime, I frittered about, trying to delay the departure that would result in our indefinite separation.

"The bags are in the car, girls. We should be off," Joe Bleakens said.

The Bleakens tried to cheer us up on the drive to the docks. They had been unstinting hosts and deserved a better show of appreciation but we felt too glum.

"Let's get these things put into the cabin," I suggested after we thanked the Bleakens and said goodbye.

"You're on A Deck," Bonnie said reading the ticket.

"Since I got the cheapest ticket, I expected to be in the bowels of the ship."

Bonnie studied the sheet showing the ship's layout.

"There's only one accommodation deck below you, so A Deck kind of qualifies as bowels. Four of the six upper decks have cabins."

We descended via a staircase that got narrower the lower we went. Finally we came to the appropriate door.

"It's not the SA *Vaal*, that's for sure," Bonnie said observing the pokey space.

I looked around the windowless cabin with four berths, a chest of drawers and a cupboard.

"It looks like I'm the first to arrive, so I get to choose where I sleep." I threw a bag onto the bottom bunk near the door and laid claim to the top drawer of the dresser. "At least for the next three weeks I won't have to worry about having a comfortable bed and a good meal."

"Every cloud has a silver lining," Bonnie mumbled.

"I'll unpack later. Let's check out the ship."

The British vessel *Southern Cross* had been innovative at the time of its launch in 1954, featuring air-conditioning throughout and an engine room and funnel aft instead of midship. This allowed space for passenger facilities in the section least affected by rough weather. The one thousand one hundred-passenger, one-class vessel had been a popular transport for people emigrating from Britain to Australia and New Zealand. Now, air travel had become more popular. The ship would be revamped as a cruise liner within a few months.

Long past its heyday, the *Southern Cross*'s reputation for mediocrity preceded it, thus the nickname Suffering Cross. Still, a library, smoking room, a two-deck cinema/dancing venue, bar, three swimming pools, two large lounges, two restaurants and extensive wood panelling were evidence that the vessel once had been something special.

The blaring of the ship's horn indicated imminent departure. Bonnie and I hugged tightly, each of us holding back tears.

"Look after yourself, Kath. Try not to be too practical."

"You look after yourself, too, Bon. Try to be a little more practical."

We smiled at each other. I would miss Bonnie's frequent lapses of common sense.

"I'll be in Canada before you know it."

"Is that a promise or a threat?" I teased.

When we walked to the point of disembarkation, we were astonished to see that the gangway had been removed.

"Bloody hell! We missed the announcements. Maybe I'll be sailing with you after all!"

We explained the problem to a passing steward who led us to the crew gangway. This mode of embarkation/disembarkation was becoming a habit!

With a final hug, Bonnie left to take up a position on the dock. The ship slipped its moorings and was towed to open water. I waved until my friend was no more than a distant speck. Overwhelming loneliness made me feel ill. I told myself that the pain would fade and the memories would not, but it wasn't much of a salve.

When I returned to my cabin, two girls my age were unpacking. They introduced themselves. Jenny was blond and petite. Diana, more solidly structured, had a row of piano-key teeth that gave her a horsey look. Both were English; both seemed agreeable. I was grateful not to have to share the small space with intolerant matrons.

Low spirits made me consider staying in the cabin for the evening but I forced myself to go to dinner. The forward dining room seated three hundred ninety passengers. I smiled at the four older women already at my assigned table but inwardly I cursed my bad luck. It seemed I had been relegated to dining purgatory. Could the staff not have thrown one or two charming and witty males into the mix? Or were there none on board? Dear God, this might be a tedious trip. We introduced ourselves. Two of the women were full-chested, outspoken Americans whose vocal vigour left the two comparatively reserved Englishwomen in the shade. Not one of them looked like *joie de vivre* was in her repertoire but that might have been because these women, too, would have preferred a more age-appropriate companion.

The anticipation of enjoying three hot meals a day was dashed with the disappointing dinner. Quality and imagination had not found a place on the menu. The upside was that a disinclination to eat might allow me to lose weight.

The service wasn't a lot better than the food. Our waiter made a decent effort but he had the annoying habit of always saying 'yes', drawing out the word and emphasising the 's'. I expected a reptilian forked tongue to come out of his mouth.

I had planned on going to bed immediately after dinner but instead went to The Tavern to have a whiskey for Bon. I missed her. Life seemed so quiet, so routine without her. If she had been here, she would have come up with one of her hare-brained schemes to liven things up.

Before I had a chance to get maudlin, the British couple at the next table introduced me into their conversation. We discovered a number of common interests, not least of which was a determination to enjoy the voyage. This is what Bonnie would have expected from me.

Initially, I spent much of my time reading in a deck chair or sunbathing by the pool. Windy weather for the first couple of days caused the ship to pitch and roll but stabilisers minimised the negative effects. Soon we were sailing through calm waters. When the Portuguese sailor Vasco de Balboa discovered this enormous body of water in 1521, he named it *mar pacifico*, peaceful sea.

Three days after leaving Auckland, we arrived at Suva, the capital of Viti-Levu, one of the three hundred thirty-two islands of the one hundred twenty-four thousand-square mile Fiji archipelago. Tales of south seas adventure and intrigue came alive in Fiji. This nation once was famed for its fierce, cannibalistic warriors, a reputation which kept European settlement at bay until the 19th century. The ship's information sheet told us that a ritual greeting between commoners and tribal chiefs was "Eat me!". Today's native population shows visitors a friendlier face.

Suva had an old-fashioned look to it, as though there had been a spurt of building energy long ago that quickly exhausted itself and had not been reinvigorated. Horns honked, bicycle bells rang and people called out to one another, creating an appealing atmosphere of relaxed busyness.

After a wander through the town, my cabin mate Diana and I headed for the celebrated market. This hive of open-air commerce sold an impressive range of goods that included poultry and pigs, beads and bangles, fabrics and furnishings. The maze of stalls was a feast for the senses. Women attired in colourful shifts brushed past us, their hips swaying under the weight of woven baskets carried on their heads. The thwack of kanga knives cutting off fish heads or slicing pineapples rang out above the din of vendors promoting their wares. Powerful aromas of spices and unfamiliar foods floated in the air.

Despite the fact that everything already was dirt cheap, we had been advised by the ship's crew to barter, a ploy with which I had no experience. After a few hesitant efforts, I got the hang of it and enthusiastically adopted the technique. For a cost of only five dollars, I purchased sandals, sarongs, rain tree seed necklaces and other gifts to bring home. An old man sitting on a table skinning and cutting pineapple sold us pieces of the delicious fresh fruit every time we passed his stall.

"Let's get a couple of pineapples for the midnight feast," I suggested to Diana.

Because the dining room was open only at meal times, we had started bringing food back to the cabin to eat later in the evening. Jenny's newly acquired boyfriend was a French passenger on his way home. As well as being a charming romantic, he was a professional chef who put his talents to good use preparing tasty creations from the contributions we laid out on the top of the dresser. One of our favourite dishes was a tropical fruit salad.

That evening the ship began its easterly migration from Melanesia to Polynesia. The stopover in Fiji had brought about a change in the passengers. Everyone was more sociable. Apart from Jenny who already was in the throes of a romance, commitments were loose in the group of people with whom I hung out. Frank O'Neill, a likeable fellow from the Falls Road area of Belfast, singled me out for his attention. He fascinated me with stories of his war-torn city but I saw him as an interesting friend rather than an amorous attachment.

And then Ron Pugh appeared on my radar. He wasn't a keeper —too tall and big-boned for my taste, not to mention having a background that might not pass muster with my parents—but his impossible-to-ignore sex appeal made him irresistible as a borrower. Ron and I became an item and shipboard life became magical.

***

Two days after leaving Suva, the ship dropped anchor off Rarotonga. The circumference of this capital island of the fourteen Cook Islands is only twenty miles. Coconut palms and sandy beaches fringe an interior with a jungle-clad volcanic peak. No one was allowed to go ashore, the cabin steward told me, because of the temptation for crew to abandon ship. Naively, I believed him until wiser heads informed me that the shallow lagoon couldn't accommodate the ship's draught.

Instead of us going to the island, the island came to us. Flotillas of dug-out canoes brought a group of natives to the ship. Their singing and beating drums could be heard long before they reached us. They secured their boats and then scampered up rope ladders, an invasion of smiling, half-naked men and women. They brought locally-made souvenirs and thousands of flowers in the form of leis and crowns which they hung in layers around passengers' necks and wove into their hair. The ship smelled like a perfumed garden.

After mingling with the passengers, the Rarotongans gave a performance of island song and dance. To everyone's surprise, one of the crew members was welcomed by them, joining in their dance like he had been born to it. It turned out he had jumped ship and spent a couple of years living with the locals. I felt vindicated to know that part of the steward's account was true.

When the natives paddled back to the island, trails of flowers and palm leaves floated behind them like a floral carpet.

Our next port of call was Papeete, the capital of French Polynesia, on the island of Tahiti, nearly four thousand miles north-east of Australia. I had looked forward to this destination more than any other. The Tahiti of my imagination was the stuff of exotic adventure. The reality was less dramatic but didn't disappoint.

The first thing that struck me was the delicious, dizzying fragrance in the air. This came from the colourful glut of tropical flowers that grew in gardens, on walls and along roadsides. Ship-wrecked sailors must have been grateful to wash ashore in Paradise. Until Tahiti, I didn't know geography and climate could be sensuous.

French is Tahiti's official language. My rusty school-girl French got me selected as the group's interpreter. My skill at translation leaned towards effort rather than accuracy. For example when a fresh juice vendor explained that the flavour of the drink we were enjoying included an ingredient called *pamplemousse*, I couldn't remember that this was the word for grapefruit. I explained to my friends that it was a special fruit found in the South Pacific. Everyone bought the story.

Opting out of cultural attractions, four of us headed for Taaone beach, famous for its black volcanic sand. We took a public, open-air bus. The rickety, wooden contraption with its bench seats chugged along the narrow streets, stopping wherever someone flagged it down.

We spent most of the hot, sunny morning swimming in the clear water, spread out on the beach, or drinking from freshly-cut coconuts. It was peaceful and picturesque but not ideal. The sand was coarse rather than fine and the bits of coral in the water could slice the skin. There was also the danger of stonefish whose camouflage resembles a rock. Their venomous sting can be fatal. All of us kept our sandals on in the sea. Despite these potential hazards, we returned to the beach for the afternoon after having lunch on the ship.

Once the sun lost its heat, we packed up. Instead of waiting for the local bus, we decided to hitch back to the ship. The man who picked us up was an officer at the island's French navy base.

"Eef you 'av time, I can take you on a tour of zee island," he offered.

Having declined to take the pricey excursion offered by the ship, we jumped at the opportunity. My favourite stop was the famous *marché*, the vast municipal market. Our new friend Jacques was an adept translator and bargainer. I bought a brightly coloured *pareu*, a typical Tahitian length of fabric that serves a number of functions, from dress to shorts to shawl, depending on how it is tied.

"May I invite you for a night on zee town?" he asked when he dropped us at the dock.

He looked at me but then politely included my three companions in his gaze.

"Absolutely," I answered without consulting the others. It would be interesting to see what a 'night on the town' in Tahiti was like.

He picked us up after dinner and took us to the island's best hotel, designed in Polynesian fashion with a thatched roof and spacious outdoor entertainment areas. A couple of floor shows demonstrated Polynesian dancing featuring beautiful women and virile men clad in little more than grass-skirts and flowers. The rhythmic beating of the drums and the energetic shaking of hips got the pulse racing. Then, to my embarrassed astonishment, one of the male dancers singled me out, gave hands-on-my-hips tuition and, to the delight of the audience, included me in their group. I felt transported to another time, as though I had become part of some ancient, primitive ritual. It was a disappointment when the Polynesians left the stage and a Western band took over. I soon got into this more familiar rhythm and danced under the stars until I was ready to drop from exhaustion. The balmy evening, the sound of the sea lapping on the shore, and the smell of frangipani made me heady with the enchantment and romance of the island. I suspected that if Bonnie were here she would recommend jumping ship ... and perhaps I would have gone along with the notion.

***

For the next week we sailed without seeing land. This allowed everyone to focus on shipboard life. Some passengers preferred to do their own thing but no one could complain about a lack of planned entertainment. Periodically there were special events. The first of these was South Pacific Night. Thanks to market shopping in Fiji and Tahiti, most passengers had suitable attire. I wore a sea green sarong, beads and barefoot sandals. The good music had me dancing the *tamouré* I had learned in Tahiti until I thought my hips would fall off. All this exercise was helping me to trim down. At dawn, I led twenty die-hards around the deck in a bunny hop line. The sailor swabbing the decks gave us a playful splash with the large hose, sending us scattering and, at last, to our beds.

Three nights later the crew organised a Race Meeting. My many losing experiences at the track made me steadfast in refusing to place a bet on the improvised horse races. A late-night supper of fish and chips served in newspaper brought the fun evening to a close.

Then, unexpectedly, life wasn't quite so jolly.

The crew knew most of the comings and goings—proper and improper—of the passengers, but passengers didn't know much about crew members. That's why is was unusual to hear rumblings of the sailors' discontent. Declining levels of service and surly staff confirmed the rumours. Something was amiss.

"The captain's shut off the taps," our steward said in a low voice as he changed the bed sheets.

"What does that even mean?" I asked. "Is the crew not allowed to have showers? That certainly would be cause for complaint in this climate."

The steward frowned and tipped his head at my interpretation of the phrase.

"It means no beer," he explained.

"Why would he do that?"

"Disciplinary action," he answered vaguely. "Even so, the captain can't take away our beer."

"Evidently he can. So, what do you have to do to have the privilege returned?"

"Don't rightly know." Another wooly response. "The trouble started with a few blokes but it's spread and everyone's being punished. There's serious trouble brewing. If the crew mutinies, it'll be dangerous for the passengers. Make sure you have a couple of blokes with you all the time."

This was like a Hollywood movie theme. What were the chances I would be on a ship in the South Pacific where mutiny was being discussed?

Other passengers must have received similar warnings from their stewards. Tension on the ship became palpable.

"Keep this knife under your pillow, and carry it with you whenever you're not with me," Ron insisted.

He handed me a razor-sharp blade of medium length with a bone handle.

"Really?" I said weakly. "I don't do weapons. You know, being Canadian and all that."

"This isn't a joke, Kathy. Unless the captain and the crew come to an agreement, the situation could get ugly."

Fortunately the storm blew over almost as quickly as it had started. The steward wouldn't offer more information than to say, "The taps are back on," with a happy smile.

With the threat of mutiny eliminated, not to mention all the crisis it implies—murder, rape, being set adrift in a small boat—the passengers got back to partying.

The Fancy Dress Ball didn't come close to the show of elaborate costumes that appeared on the SA *Vaal*. Without Bonnie's imaginative talents, I was at a loss to come up with something original. I simply got my Polynesian gear out again and went as a Tahitian princess.

At the equator, the ship organised the traditional line-crossing ceremony. King Neptune dunked initiates in water, thus promoting 'tadpoles' or 'pollywogs' (people who have never crossed the equator) to 'shellbacks'.

The onset of cloudy skies reminded us we were heading into the northern hemisphere's winter. I dreaded having to face the extreme cold of Canada. Perhaps weather would be my excuse to set off on another excursion. I shook my head. I hadn't even arrived home and already I anticipated leaving. Evidently the wanderlust had not waned.

***

On the afternoon of 26 November 1970 we reached Balboa, the Pacific terminus for the twenty-five-mile Panama Canal. This would be our last port of call before Port Everglades, Florida.

I read everything I could get my hands on about the canal. Many aspects of the story of this engineering marvel were immersed in high drama. During the seventeen-year construction, more than twenty-five thousand workers died because of disease, fierce rains, exhausting heat and humidity and extreme terrain that included marshes, jungle and mountains. This was nearly a third of the workforce. Despite great odds, determination brought the ambitious dream to fruition. The canal's successful completion in 1914 shaved nine thousand three hundred miles off the journey between the east and west coasts of the United States.

Balboa, a northern suburb of Panama City was created by the Americans at the beginning of the 20th century when they took over the canal project from the French. I had been looking forward to my first visit to Central America until Ron insisted that I have at least three fellows with me when we went ashore.

"I've been here before. It's a dangerous place. We'll look after you," he assured me. Ron opened his jacket slightly to reveal the knife he recently had lent me.

This canal zone town with its turn-of-the-century architecture had the potential to be interesting but the dirty streets and un-cared-for communities removed any desire to discover redeeming qualities. Perhaps this prejudice was due to the fear Ron had instilled.

"The weather's certainly depressing." I looked at the heavy, grey sky and shuddered.

"A constant cloud formation circles the globe at this latitude," Ron explained. "The result is subdued sunshine, prolonged calms and major thunderstorms. Sailors call it the doldrums."

"Well named," I muttered, already affected by the stagnant air.

With little to attract us in Balboa, we spent most of our time in the bar of the Hotel Panama. I was the only one with a smattering of Spanish so, once again, I acted as translator. Fortunately my limited Berlitz vocabulary was able to cope with the minimal demand of ordering drinks. We returned to the ship in time for dinner. I was too tired and too uninspired by the place to go back on shore for the evening so Ron, John and Kevin headed off without me.

At 5:20 am, I was wakened by pounding on my cabin door. I opened it to my erstwhile companions.

"We went to the rough part of Panama," Ron said with a sloppy grin that was sheepish and proud at the same time.

"And it looks like you've consumed some rough alcohol," I said, not amused.

"One and a half bottles of tequila," John slurred.

"Get dressed," Ron insisted. "You have to see the ship going through the canal."

If it hadn't been for my inebriated friends, I would have missed the start of the event. Jenny and Diana already had left.

A magnificent molten sunrise greeted us. This alone made the early rise worthwhile. The deck was crowded with passengers watching the busy crew's dawn activity of preparing to enter the first locks. We positioned ourselves at a railing and watched the performance.

A pilot came on board to guide the ship the eight miles from Balboa harbour to the approach wall and the Miraflores locks. As we settled into position in the gravity-powered lock, four towing locomotives stationed themselves at the bow and stern on either side of the ship. Chains ensured the vessel stayed centred and travelled at the appropriate speed.

Each lock in the system is one thousand fifty feet long, one hundred ten feet wide and thirty-six feet deep. Pairs of locks allow the simultaneous transit of vessels in either direction. Our ship dwarfed the surrounding structure, including the control tower. We were a giant Gulliver in the land of Lilliput.

By the time we passed through Miraflores' two flooded chambers, the ship had been raised fifty-four feet above sea level. The second lock released us onto the small, open body of water called Miraflores Lake.

Less than two miles further, we arrived at the single-chamber Pedro Miguel lock. A similar procedure raised the ship a further thirty-one feet.

After seven miles, we came to the famous Gaillard Cut. This most challenging aspect of the canal construction excavated a channel through the Continental Divide. At the time, this was a monumental feat of engineering. As we went through the narrow passage, I felt I could reach out and touch the dense growth. A large, ocean-going vessel seemed incongruous in such a setting. Every now and again the screech of birds could be heard. I scanned the foliage for colourful plumage but saw nothing. I wondered who or what watched our stately passage. Jungle lay ahead of us and on either side. It looked as though we would be trapped in a vegetal dead end when suddenly a right-hand turn revealed an exit.

The next major event was Gatún Lake, a two hundred sixty-seven-square mile, man-made body of water that was the largest of its kind when it was completed in 1913. This carried us twenty miles across the isthmus to the Gatún locks, the final in the journey. Here the ship was lowered eighty-five feet to sea level. Limón Bay, seven miles from the locks, marked the end of our amazing six-hour transit through the Panama Canal. The experience was a fitting finale to a remarkable voyage.

CHAPTER 28

If we were meant to stay in one place,
we'd have roots instead of feet.
Rachel Wolchin

Of my four dining companions, the American Mrs Weston was the dominant—and sometimes domineering—personality. She tended to pry, but from concern rather than nosiness. I was a source of worry for her. First she fretted about the seasick cabin mate I had invented. The white lie popped into my head and out my mouth at dinner one evening when Mrs Weston asked why I always left the table with small stockpiles of food. These were contributions to our midnight feasts but I didn't offer this explanation. There was no need for deception so I presume mischief inspired the fiction.

"One of my cabin mates is seasick. The rest of us bring her food."

Eventually Mrs Weston's interest threatened to spoil the hoax.

"She's been ill for too long," Mrs Weston said when we had been at sea for more than a week. "She needs proper medical attention."

"No, she's fine," I assured her. "She says this always happens on boats but she's getting better. In fact, I saw her on deck this afternoon."

Mrs Weston peered at me over her cup of tea. I guessed she had doubts about the story but no further action was taken. At least, none I was aware of. I had a sneaking suspicion she and the Purser had got together to check on the fate of this poor girl—and learned no such person existed.

My sad state of finances also caused Mrs Weston anxiety.

"Fifteen dollars is not nearly enough to get you home," she said when she had ferreted out my exact balance. The other ladies at the table looked suitably alarmed and nodded their agreement. "You can't hitchhike in the States like you could in Australia and New Zealand. It's not safe."

"A solution always appears. It may not be the one I was expecting but it's a solution. Thank you for caring, though," I said with sincerity.

Mrs Weston would not be put off so easily. She took matters into her own hands.

"I've wired my friend Governor Kirk to tell him about your situation," she announced a couple of days later. He's invited you to stay at the Governor's mansion. He'll see you get to Montreal."

A range of emotions came and went. First it surprised me that the Governor of Florida would respond to a request to accommodate an unimportant stranger. Who was Mrs Weston that she wielded such influence? Then I was excited at the prospect of spending a couple of days at the Governor's mansion. That would be another unique experience to add to my long list. Finally I became practical: I wanted to get home without further diversions, no matter how appealing those diversions might be.

"Think about it," Mrs Weston said when I explained why I was declining Governor Kirk's kind offer. "There's still time to change your mind."

Not a lot of time, unfortunately. Final disembarkation loomed but my gang of friends, all of whom were travelling onward, was anxious to keep me on board.

"Continue to Southampton," Ron begged.

"I don't have enough money to get home from Fort Lauderdale. I certainly can't afford the extra fare to England."

There was a moment of silence while everyone considered how to resolve the dilemma. Most of my companions were as broke as I was, so options were minimal.

"You can stow away!" Ron's brother John said, eagerness in his voice. "There are plenty of places to hide until the ship gets underway. The captain can't put you off anywhere because there are no stops until Southampton."

I didn't reject the idea immediately. Nor did anyone else. Such an action was risky to the point of being foolhardy but it held a romantic appeal. There was already one stowaway we knew about. Danny was a lofty, well-upholstered Englishman with an exceptional voice. Most nights he gave impromptu performances that were as good as any singer on the professional circuit. His signature song Delilah always sent the audience wild. It therefore came as a shock to everyone to learn he was travelling illegally. I thought stowaways stowed away, in other words kept out of public view. Danny, however, was larger than life. I guess his strategy was to hide in plain sight. When his misdemeanour came to light, the captain exiled him to the brig for the duration of the voyage. Danny was so popular, however, that passengers lowered bottles of beer and other treats to the barred window of his cell from an upper deck. Presumably petitions for clemency were sent to the captain but I never knew the outcome.

Despite the example of Danny's discovery, I agreed to discuss the possibility of stowing away with our friendly cabin steward.

"Don't even think about it," he admonished. "There's no way you wouldn't get caught sooner or later. I'm assuming you don't want to end up in a British jail."

I could be rebellious and even daring but that didn't equate with desiring a criminal record. Besides, after three weeks of hard partying, I was wrecked! I didn't need the stress of trying to avoid detection. I chose scheduled disembarkation.

***

For the last day of the voyage, every minute counted. I made sure most of them were spent with Ron. Our relationship was no more than a shipboard romance but that didn't make leaving any easier.

That evening there was a party to end all parties. The ship was hopping all night. A number of people would be parting from new friends so, for many, it was an emotional time.

No sooner had I got to bed than I had to get up to go to US Immigration. We had arrived at Port Everglades, the seaport on the southeastern coast of the Florida peninsula. Ron, John, Kevin and I walked around the decks until it was time for me to leave. Then

Kevin and John gave Ron and me our final moments alone.

"I'm sorry you're not sailing to England," Ron said, combing his fingers through my hair. "I don't want to say goodbye."

"It's not what I want either." I buried my face in Ron's chest. "It was wonderful while it lasted. I have that to keep. Thank you."

After a final kiss, I retreated down the gangway before Ron could see my eyes water.

Popping flash bulbs greeted me when I reached the dock.

"Are you Kathy Daley?" a reporter asked.

"Yes."

What on earth was this about? I looked around and saw the indomitable Mrs Weston pass by.

"I thought a bit of publicity might help your cause," she said with a wink. "Safe travels."

She waved and disappeared into the crowd. Her intentions were good but the effects of publicity would take time. I didn't intend to hang around waiting for a good Samaritan to come forward. The reporter was especially curious about how I planned to get home with only fifteen dollars. This, I presumed, would be the hook to the story. I had no answer to that question.

"Can you send me a copy of the article?"

"Sure thing," the reporter said, taking my address.

I made my way to the taxi rank.

"How much to go to the Fort Lauderdale airport?" I asked the first driver in line.

"Eleven dollars."

I bit the bullet. It wasn't as though I nearly had enough for a plane ticket. My few dollars didn't even come close, so even less wouldn't make a difference.

A line of airline counters faced me as I walked in the door of the small terminal building. I headed straight to Air Canada. The large red maple leaf logo felt welcoming.

"I'd like a one-way ticket to Montreal, please," I said to the agent.

He checked fares and schedules and told me it would cost ninety dollars; the next flight would leave the following morning.

"The problem is, I only have four dollars. I don't suppose I could pay after I get to Montreal, could I?"

"Do you have a credit card?" he asked.

"No, just my word."

He looked perplexed. Evidently this wasn't a ploy with which he was familiar.

"I'm sure your word's good but I can't issue a ticket without payment. I'm really sorry."

I had hit a brick wall as far as transportation was concerned. Maybe I would have better luck with accommodation.

"Can you recommend somewhere to stay?"

The agent looked sceptical. If I couldn't pay for an airline ticket, how could I pay for a hotel room? Nevertheless, he pointed towards the reception desk for the upstairs hotel.

"Hi," I said with a bright smile, "I'd like to have a room but I have no money and no credit card. Can you help me out?"

"Do you have luggage?" the receptionist asked, unfazed by my request.

"I do."

"Any plans on how to pay?"

"I'm counting on my folks to come to the rescue."

He gave me a registration form and then he handed me a key. As soon as I got to the room, I phoned home, reversing the charges. My parents were delighted to hear from me. This was only the second time we had talked since I left home. I told them I was at the Fort Lauderdale airport hotel but couldn't pay for either my room or a plane ticket.

"You couldn't have picked a worse time," my father said. "Apart from the fact it's Sunday, it's also Thanksgiving weekend in the US and Grey Cup football weekend in Canada. Everything's closed."

My heart sank. So near and yet so far. I was too tired to get creative about finding a way home. I wondered if the Governor still would be willing to take me in. Then my resourceful father spoke again.

"Let me make a couple of phone calls. Give me your number and I'll get back to you."

Dad often said *It's not what you know, it's who you know.* I prayed he knew someone to get around this impediment.

While waiting for his call, I checked out my room. The bed was larger than I was used to and the TV had a dizzying range of channels filled with unfamiliar programmes. The well-appointed bathroom had a bathtub that I would put to good use later. I mulled over the room service menu that listed American staples, such as hamburgers, steak, apple pie and ice cream.

While deciding what to order for dinner, the phone rang. I didn't answer immediately. I couldn't bear disappointment at this stage. Finally I picked up the receiver.

"OK, everything's taken care of," my father said.

I breathed an audible sigh of relief.

"If you go to the Air Canada desk, they'll give you a ticket and whatever spending money you need."

"Thank you so much. How did you do it?"

"Friends in high places," was all he would say.

***

I hung up and collapsed on the bed. It would have been nice to drift into a deep sleep and let the tension dissolve. Instead, I forced myself to go downstairs.

The ticket agent was expecting me.

"I'm glad things worked out," he said. "All of tomorrow's flights are full but come early and you'll get a standby number. How much cash would you like?"

I did some quick calculations and then asked for twice as much as I thought I would need. The extra was just-in-case money. If I had learned nothing else on this trip, I had learned that 'enough' was never sufficient. This time, if life threw a curve ball, I wanted to be prepared.

From Air Canada I went straight to the hotel reception.

"Thanks for trusting me," I said to the receptionist as I counted off bills to pay for the room.

"I figured it was a pretty safe bet," he said with a smile. "Enjoy your stay."

I went back upstairs and drew a hot, bubbly bath. After a long soak, I ordered room service, watched some TV and had an early night.

Despite getting more than twelve hours' rest, I overslept. I dashed down to Air Canada only to discover I had forgotten my ticket in the room.

"Can you save my standby place?" I asked the agent.

He studied the screen and nodded. Perhaps there was a note of my special circumstances.

"What are my chances for getting on the flight?" I asked when I finally presented my ticket.

"Pretty good. There are always cancellations."

I returned to the room to have a relaxed breakfast.

When I checked in later in the morning, I got a less friendly agent.

"You're overweight," she said. Was she referring to my personal poundage? Then she added, "By more than sixty pounds."

She pointed to the number on the scale. Neither of us said anything for a few seconds. I mentally went through the contents of the cases, wondering what I could jettison. Did I really need those New Zealand paua shells? Could I part with some books?

"You're lucky there's a note on the file to forego charges."

Thank you, Air Canada mystery person who arranged all this.

As predicted, there was a cancellation. I sank into my seat and buckled up for the last major leg of the journey. In just under four hours, I would be back at Dorval airport. The circle would be complete. I was reminded of a verse from Tolkien's *Lord of the Rings*:

The Road goes ever on and on
Out from the door where it began.
Now far ahead the Road has gone.
Let others follow, if they can!
Let them a journey new begin.
But I at last with weary feet
Will turn towards the lighted inn,
My evening-rest and sleep to meet.

Soon the plane banked over the St Lawrence, the mighty river that connects the Great Lakes with the Atlantic and flows around the island of Montreal. I noticed it hadn't been cold enough to freeze the water. There wasn't much snow on the ground but the greyness of November left no doubt winter had begun. Bitingly cold, short days would be an adjustment after eighteen months of warm weather. The smart thing would have been to delay my return until spring but once the heading has been set for home, smart decisions don't always come into the equation.

There hadn't been time to let the folks know if I was on the flight, so no one met me at the airport. For the first time in a long time, I was alone. I found a pay phone and called home.

"Take the train to Rigaud," he told me. "We'll pick you up there."

Getting from the airport to the train station exposed me to nippy, unwelcoming temperatures. I was grateful to have Bonnie's duffle coat but it quickly became apparent I would need better protection against the penetrating cold that would get worse as winter progressed.

The journey to Rigaud took less than an hour. When the train pulled into the station, I immediately spotted my parents and sister standing on the platform. I rushed into their arms, all of us kissing and crying and talking at once.

It took half an hour to drive from Rigaud, in the province of Quebec, to Hawkesbury, in Ontario. Everything about the passing towns and landscape was new to me. I looked forward to exploring this area where my parents had chosen to live.

"I have a horse," Liz said excitedly as we turned into the driveway. She pointed to the weather-worn barn on the right. Evidently it contained a stable. "His name's Joey. You can ride him."

I hoped Canadian horses were more docile that their Australian counterparts.

The car halted in front of a two-storey brick house with gingerbread trim on the roof line.

"It's Victorian, more than a hundred years old," my mother said with pride. She loved old houses. Now she had one of her own.

The back entrance brought us immediately into a large kitchen/ pantry/eating area, a perfect example of a farm kitchen, the heart of the home.

"The previous owners must have been midgets," I said, pointing to the unusually low counter tops and sink.

"It's not long since we moved in," Dad said. "The kitchen's the first job on the list."

"Come on," Mom said, "let's take a tour of the house."

She showed me reception rooms, bedrooms, and spaces that had been converted to a library, an office and a sewing room.

"There's lots of work to be done but the place has plenty of potential, don't you think? It even has poltergeists," Mom said with approval.

"And maybe a couple of ghosts," Liz added.

Finally we arrived at my room. Apart from the usual furnishings of a bedside table, armchair, writing desk, chest of drawers and bookcase, there was the maple bed that had belonged to Grannie and Grandpa Scott. The absence of my beloved grandmother was the only thing that marred my homecoming. I missed her dreadfully.

"We thought you might like to decorate this room yourself," Mom said, breaking into my thoughts.

"That would be great."

Suddenly, exhaustion overwhelmed me. I had run out of steam.

"Do you mind if I have a nap?"

The nap evolved into a week-long recovery sleep. One and a half years on the road had caught up with me.

***

When I felt more settled, Mom and Dad introduced me to their new friends. I thought I had escaped the perpetual need to make nice with people I didn't know but here I was back in the territory of showing interest and engaging in conversations with strangers. At least it had become easier! I finally had learned how to avoid awkward pauses and engage in 'cocktail' chatter.

Another change was my perspective. I began to see Mom and Dad as mere mortals rather than as all-knowing adults on a pedestal. Time spent in the homes of people who grappled with family decisions made me realise my parents went through those same struggles, doing the best they could to arrive at equitable solutions. I now understood that one of their struggles must have been whether or not to let me pursue my dream. I was grateful for the courage of their decision.

There was plenty to keep me busy at the farm. Noodie, the black lab mongrel my parents had acquired, was a constant companion as I chipped old plaster off the kitchen walls, fed the chickens and rabbits, cooked and did other chores to help out. Life in the outback had prepared me well for life at home.

On a couple of occasions, Mom and I drove into Montreal, an hour away. It was great to be back in the city where I had grown up, to walk along familiar streets, browse in fashionable shops and eat in favourite restaurants.

Catching up with former classmates was no less satisfying—eventually. I quickly realised they couldn't imagine the world I had come to know. Nor did they necessarily want to. They were content in their safe, predictable environment. The unknown and the unexpected held little appeal. I also realised it would require an effort to fit back into their world. I wasn't able to discuss the latest fashions, current hit songs, popular movies or best-selling novels. Knowing how to skin a sheep or muster cattle didn't hold much sway here. Marilyn Hawkins greeted me with open arms. Our bond of friendship remained as strong as ever. She hadn't changed, but I could learn to live with that.

Less than a month after my return, Christmas was upon us. The house was gaily decorated and smells of baking hung in the air. As much as I had enjoyed the warm-weather Christmas in South Africa, cold days with the promise of snow created the holiday atmosphere I knew and loved.

On Christmas eve, just before going to bed, Liz came to my room.

"I'm really glad you came home," she said.

I heard emotion in her voice. Had she thought I might not return? That never had been a possibility but evidently my enthusiasm for being abroad had planted doubts. It meant a lot that she had shared her feelings.

Christmas brought out our happy family traditions. Santa came in the night and filled the stockings Liz and I had placed at the ends of our beds. Dad put the coffee on first thing in the morning and Mom poured glasses of rum-laced eggnog. As we gathered around the tree in our dressing gowns, Noodie sniffed out her present and enthusiastically tore off the wrapping. The squeaking carrot kept her entertained while the rest of us opened our gifts. Of the many thoughtful presents I received, the one from Dad was most special: a beautiful guitar. I felt complete.

Grannie Daley never called to welcome me home. Dad told me she was furious that my discoveries about Grandpa forced her to reveal his secret. Of course, it didn't help my cause that I not only had defied her wishes but had succeeded in achieving my rash, ambitious goal: going around the world before I turned twenty-one. I was three months away from that birthday,

It had been an amazing journey, one in which I had crossed oceans and deserts, accomplishments reminiscent of the adventures I had read in books as a child. It was a journey of discovery, both geographic and personal, a coming-of-age of an apprehensive girl who circumnavigated the globe and returned home a confident woman. Every morning of those eighteen months, I woke with a tingle of excitement that pulsated from the tips of my toes right up to my head. No matter how challenging the day might prove to be, these difficulties always were cushioned with gratitude to be on this journey. Every evening, I went to sleep happy, wondering what the next day might bring, convinced it would be unique, stimulating, and that I would view the experience as extra-ordinary, no matter what happened. It was a remarkable state of being.

Of the many lessons learned on the trip, one thing was certain: Grannie Daley had been wrong. Nice girls *do* travel.

AFTERWORD

You always had the power, my dear.
You just had to learn it for yourself.
The Tin Man, The Wizard of Oz

And then what? How did the story continue?

My shipboard romance with Ron Pugh was harder to get over than expected. After pouring my heart out writing pages of (bad) poetry, I wrote to Ron. Soon after, I received a thick envelope showing his return address. I tore it open, eager to read Ron's words. My unopened missive fell out. It was accompanied by a compassionate letter from Ron's mother informing me he was engaged. The news shocked me. This was less than two months after he returned to England—an eerie repeat of the John Clark scenario. What was it about the men I loved having sudden engagements? Mrs Pugh wrote that she knew how much I had meant to Ron and hoped I wouldn't complicate the situation. What could I do? Ron had been a 'borrower', not a 'keeper'. I still have the returned letter. It remains unopened.

In February, I got a job in Montreal. Sixteen months later I had saved enough to go on another trip, destination undecided. Ian Simpson, my devoted admirer from Darwin, tried to persuade me to travel via Fiji, where he then worked. He enticed me with the promise of getting me attached to a scientific expedition exploring the interior of the main island. It was sorely tempting but I knew Ian hoped for a relationship I couldn't give him. I travelled east instead, stopping in Belfast for an eventful week to see Frank O'Neill, my friend from the South Pacific crossing. He and his family were the epitome of hospitality but the ongoing violence between warring Protestant/Catholic-British/Irish factions wasn't something my nerves could tolerate. This was highlighted when a street worker engaged his pneumatic drill just as the bus I was on passed by. A number of passengers (me included!) fell flat on the floor, thinking it was gunfire. It was a relief to escape the daily undercurrent of danger—real or imagined.

I had intended to wander around Europe experiencing 'typical' activities such as studying Spanish guitar in Spain, taking a gourmet cooking course in France and perhaps working in a chocolate factory in Switzerland. Instead, unexpectedly, an influential contact in Geneva got me a job at the United Nations. After ten enjoyable months, during which time I became fluent in French, I left Geneva. The reason? A marriage proposal from my French lover. I declined. Certain I had made the right choice but nevertheless heartbroken, I spent a couple of months touring Europe as far east as Turkey before returning to Montreal to recharge my batteries and replenish the coffers.

After two years working as a legal secretary, I was offered a job as secretary to the Project Manager of a hydro-electric project in northern Labrador. This extreme destination appealed to my sense of adventure. Equally appealing was the excellent salary augmented by hardship pay. This would allow me to quickly earn money to go to South America. With odds of one hundred twenty men for every woman, male attention was inevitable but I had no desire to let romance interfere with my travel objectives. Then I met Sean, an Irish engineer. Sean's decency, intelligence and humour convinced me to change my plans. It was the best decision I ever made. Sean has been an exceptional husband and father who, notwithstanding occasional misgivings, always has allowed me the freedom to be me.

Despite the passage of time and the inconvenience of distance, Bonnie and I have remained friends throughout the decades. As promised, she came to Canada soon after we parted ways in New Zealand. During the months she spent with me in Montreal, she obtained a work visa. Then she headed west to Calgary to visit Diana, our flatmate from Darwin days. From there, she ventured to the Northwest Territories (Norman Wells, Innovic, Hay River and Yellowknife) where she worked for two years. Her time in the

Australian outback was good preparation for this type of remote living.

Like me, Bonnie married an engineer. She met her future husband, a British national, on a flight from London to Rome. After living abroad for a short time, they settled in South Africa. Marriage and motherhood have not dented Bonnie's sense of fun.

Many of the people I met on my Great Adventure became lifelong correspondents. Some of them made the trek to our home in Ireland. Peter Rex, my first employer in Australia, showed up at our door unannounced one summer day. He had with him his handsome, twenty-two-year-old son Rob. This was the adult version of four-year-old Robbie who had stolen my heart. He had grown into a fine young man. Barbara Fraser, of roof-painting fame, came to visit with her sister. Bonnie, her two young children and her widowed mother Val spent a couple of happy weeks with us. I was thrilled when Bonnie and her husband David were posted to Riyadh, Saudi Arabia during the time my family and I lived there. I met the Hahlos and the Duncans in London whenever our itineraries overlapped.

I never made it back to Australia, New Zealand or the South Pacific but I returned to South Africa on two occasions, introducing my husband, son and daughter to the land and people I loved. During each visit, that mysterious, primal energy I first encountered was still evident. I felt like I had come home.

It has been fifty years since I set off from Montreal to travel around the world. I remain grateful to have made much of that journey in the company of a loyal friend whose antics ensured there was never a dull moment. Bonnie's mischievous spirit always took the tarnish off difficult days.

I remember those eighteen-months as one of the best times of my life. The journey infused me with liberating self-confidence and helped form me into the woman I wanted to become. It confirmed that determination is a potent tool. Yet, when I was writing this book, forensically reliving the events, I questioned how I could have thought that period was so wonderful. Yes, I met interesting people, had unusual experiences and visited new places, but often

I was hungry and didn't have a proper bed. Too frequently, I was desperately short of cash. Then I realised that those tribulations had hidden value: they taught me to appreciate life's many small gifts that I might otherwise take for granted.

Adaptability, possibly the most useful skill I acquired, has enabled me to thrive as an expat and to embrace a variety of careers. Among other things, I have been a journalist, a public relations consultant, an author and the founding partner of a company that designed Arabian-themed gifts.

Grannie Scott told me that if I could gather the courage to take the first step, the rest would be relatively easy. This truism has pushed me to go places I might not have gone, do things I might not have done and accomplish more than I ever imagined.

I continue to follow my dreams. I continue to enjoy a rich and fulfilled life.

Printed in Great Britain
by Amazon